The Book of
EXMOUTH

From Fishing Village to Coastal Resort

HARRY PASCOE

HALSGROVE

First published in Great Britain in 2002

Frontispiece photograph: *Coronation Day, 1911,*
being celebrated in the Lifeboat House.

British Library Cataloguing-in-Publication Data
A CIP record for this title is available from the British Library

ISBN 1 84114 205 0

HALSGROVE
PUBLISHING, MEDIA AND DISTRIBUTION

Halsgrove House
Lower Moor Way
Tiverton, Devon EX16 6SS
Tel: 01884 243242
Fax: 01884 243325
email: sales@halsgrove.com
website: www.halsgrove.com

Printed and bound by
Bookcraft Ltd, Midsomer Norton

Every care has been taken to ensure the accuracy of the information
contained in this book. The author recognises, however, that errors and
omissions will inevitably be found, and he regrets any inadvertent mistakes.

Contents

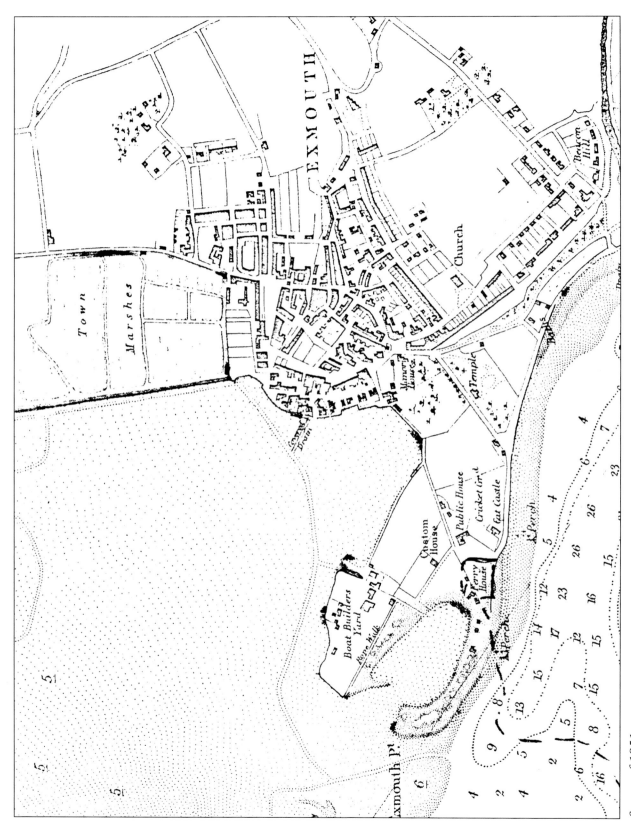

Survey of 1851.

Introduction

From the first little community of fisherfolk at the time of the Norman Conquest (then known as Exanmutha), and its growth inland towards the two villages of Littleham Rural and Withycombe Raleigh, taking in the Bretons who had settled on the Point at Lydnicnaesse as well as folk from Wessex, the enlarged community of Exmouth steadily increased in size. Further growth over the centuries continued, and was compounded at the beginning of the 1700s when a learned judge discovered a great improvement in his health after staying in Exmouth. The town's identity as a resort was born.

The judge praised Exmouth for a multitude of qualities: its bathing and its diversions; its glorious views from the Beacon and the cliffs at Orcombe and beyond; its wonderful bay stretching from Dawlish across Torbay to Brixham and Berry Head; and the landscape to the north reaching across the Common to Woodbury Castle, from where the original Bronze-Age inhabitants had come down the slopes to the lower levels to settle.

From the eighteenth century onwards visitors arrived at Exmouth in their thousands; among them many members of the gentry and nobility, to see and enjoy modern Exmouth. The town thrived as a local community and today over 300 clubs and societies contribute to the vibrant life of the town.

Launch of the Exmouth Life-boat. From a sketch by the Revd J. Parlby, c.1859.

Big rocks at Orcombe, 1936.

View from the Beacon to the west.

CHAPTER 1

Early History

ORIGINS

Exmouth is set at the mouth of one of Devon's most famous rivers, the Exe, and lies at the foot of the wild and impressive heights of Woodbury Common, with its ranging views over miles of Devon countryside and the Channel coasts. It is no wonder then that Exmouth has a centuries-old association with the sea.

It has been said that the history of the town began around one thousand years ago when a ferry to Starcross was established. Another popular belief is that during this period its earliest fishing fleet was located within the haven mouth formed by the sandy spit of land known as the Point. I believe, however, that the settlement's beginnings actually date from prehistoric times; a study of its broad, sandy beach facing the sea and its hinterland provide information about the origins of a small community, ultimately to be called Exmouth, and the time at which it appeared within that haven.

EARLY SETTLEMENT

Around 8000BC Britain became an island, following the melting of the ice caps and the consequent rise in the sea level. Gradually the shape of Devon was revealed. There is evidence of a Stone-Age population during this time – the first peoples present in this area of whom we have any knowledge at all. Indeed, towards the end of the twentieth century it was proven through use of carbon dating that some of the earliest men yet discovered in the world had occupied Kent's Cavern near Torquay, not so very far away. An upper jawbone was found in the area, along with the remains of cold-loving mammals including mammoths, woolly rhinoceroses, giant elks, sabre-tooth tigers and reindeer, to name but a few. These creatures left only their bones as evidence that they once lived and roamed around the West Country.

The Stone-Age folk of the Palaeolithic and Mesolithic periods were hunters who roamed the land for food, but the people of the New Stone Age, the Neolithic peoples, became the first settlers.

They were experienced in forest clearance, they raised domestic animals and sowed the seeds of wheat and barley. As such they were the first agriculturists, as we would consider them. They struck flint flakes to make tools and weapons, thousands of which have been found in East Devon, most notably in the Otter Valley and on Woodbury Common, as well as at Exmouth itself. The inundations of sand in the Exmouth and Dawlish Warrens have no doubt been covering much evidence of the lives of the Neolithic peoples in this region. However, we do know that they created the causewayed camp at Hembury, they settled at High Peak and at Haldon, and were responsible for the original defence works on the heights of Woodbury Common above the 600 feet mark. In addition to the many flints already mentioned, a stone axe of the period has also been found in the area. It is well known, too, that a favourite diet of Neolithic man was fish, particularly shellfish, as the quantities of mussel and limpet shells found in their 'middens',

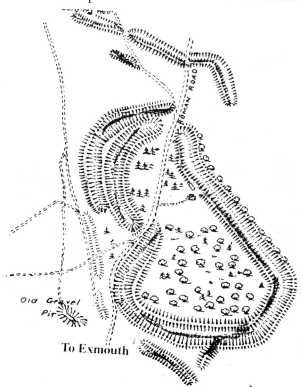

Plan of Woodbury's Bronze-Age castle.

7

Above: *A Bronze-Age sword found on the Pole Sands –
this replica is held in Exmouth Museum.*
Above right: *Bronze-Age pottery.*

or rubbish pits, reveal. Where better to find that sort of diet than the River Exe itself? Certainly the area between the Point at Exmouth, the Warren and the Pole Sands would be rich in this type of fauna. That area also happens to be one of the most abundant wildlife sites in the South West, where the extensive mudflats and grazing meadows are a haven for all kinds of bird life, especially waders and wildfowl; another contribution to the food of Neolithic man.

For centuries, primitive dug-out canoes or boats made from wickerwork frames covered in skins were used (very similar to the coracles or curraghs still in use in West Wales and parts of Ireland). From about 2000BC the Bronze-Age people began to arrive from the Continent and the long Exmouth beach attracted them as it served as a convenient landing place. These folk began to erect more permanent types of dwellings, such as stone huts within large rounds, examples of which may still be seen at Grimspound on Dartmoor and elsewhere. They fortified the mound on Woodbury, and built the huge ramparts with the material excavated from the defensive ditches until an area of over five acres was encompassed. This became a secure place of refuge in times of trouble.

The use of bronze in the manufacture of knives, daggers and swords came a little later with the discovery of copper and tin. With this came the knowledge of how to smelt away the impurities, cast the molten metal and create the bronze alloy which gave this later-Palaeolithic period its name. There was a continuous trade in these metals and metalwork across the Channel. It is highly probable that this extended through the haven at Exmouth and up the river to what is now Exeter, via the base at Woodbury. A Bronze-Age sword was found on the Pole Sands at Exmouth and it is now in the British Museum, with a replica in Exmouth Museum. A double axe of the period was found near Topsham and an axehead dating from approximately 700BC was ploughed up near the Common in 1900, along with fragments of pottery. In the Lympstone direction, a spindle whorl approxi-

mately 1½ inches in diameter was found at Courtlands. This may well date from the Bronze Age or even from the earlier Neolithic times.

These Bronze-Age people preferred to keep their herds of cattle, sheep and pigs grazing in clearings first formed by their Neolithic ancestors. Two of their ancient tracks over Woodbury Common intersect at the Four Firs crossroads. It seems likely that their routes into Exmouth came that way and then down what we now know as Hulham Road or St Johns Lane. The settlers also crossed the river to occupy the highest parts of the Haldon Hills, so establishing themselves in and around the lower Exe Valley. A Bronze-Age society was soon entrenched in that area just as in other parts of Devon. The community was particularly strong here on the Exe where communication and transport were for centuries mainly waterborne. It was these societies, or groups of them, that were collectively responsible for the erection of large stone rows, stone circles and standing stones on nearby Dartmoor and elsewhere. In East Devon there are between 50 and 60 barrows (mounds of earth covering one or more burials) concentrated on the narrow ridge of land between the rivers Sid and Coly. In fact the Farway collection of barrows from this period is the largest in the whole of Britain and there are a dozen or more on Woodbury Common itself. The contents of these barrows when excavated have produced artefacts which suggest they were constructed by a well-organised society, comprised of groups of tribes dividing the land between themselves. Further afield it was the Bronze-Age peoples who built the great temples at Avebury, Stonehenge and similar sites, as well as that huge mound, Silbury Hill, the largest man-made hill in the whole of Europe. There was a great cultural change during the Bronze Age that created an expansion in the population; and so the coastal areas as well as the hilltops became occupied.

THE CELTS

The second and third waves of the La Tene branch of Celts came through France and Brittany to the south-western coasts of this country – they landed in Devon and Cornwall around 500BC. Their arrival coincided with what we now know as the Iron Age. This period occurred a little later in the West Country than in Britain's eastern counties, but stretched roughly from the fifth century BC to the first and second centuries AD. The Celts brought with them the knowledge of working with iron and so were able to manufacture quite sophisticated weapons for hunting and spearing animals and large fish, as well as tools for carving wood and stone for many household uses.

These Celtic peoples lived in round huts in

open settlements, preferring higher ground. They continued to clear forested areas, making way for more and more land to be cultivated. They built field systems with stone hedges and all the evidence suggests permanent habitation. It was a period of comparative peace, for the Celts were well organised into family groups and maintained firm religious practices. Those who settled in the South West became known as the Dumnonii. They lived in tribal groups under their chieftains and assembled at times in larger groups under kings. Their multiple enclosures and forts surrounded the settlements, from which they set out on voyages along the coasts or over to continental Europe. The sheltered waters of the Exe were highly inviting to their small boats, while the haven at Exmouth offered shelter and served as a valuable starting point for their trade routes which had been established with their neighbours.

The Celts had a distinctive style of art, evident on the coins they issued, on their jewellery, and on their tools and weapons. Celtic art and religion flourished and was barely disturbed when the Romans arrived to build their regional capital at Isca

Dumnoniorum (Exeter). Generally, the newcomers were content to leave what was a well-organised community to run itself, and so it was for several centuries. Thus it was the Celtic way of life that developed in Devon.

Some Celtic as well as Roman coins have been found in Exeter and Exmouth. In this period, too, many place names became established in the area. An analysis of 67 Celtic place-names in Devon revealed that about 1½ per cent are related to hill-tops, 34 per cent to spurs, 24 per cent to valley heads, 24 per cent to valley sides and nearly 17 per cent to valley floors. The settlements occur from a little above sea level to nearly 1000 feet, but 83 per cent are below the 600-feet level and 60 per cent below 450 feet. The words Axe and Exe are pre-Saxon words which simply mean 'water'. Hide or Hythe, as in Pratteshyde for example, is a landing place, while 'Cwm' or 'Combe' refer to a valley, as in Withycombe. 'Maer', meanwhile, is a reference to marshy ground. The Celts also settled in places named in devotion to their saints; there are 45 such places in Devon. The best source for the study of Celtic and Saxon names is the Domesday Book.

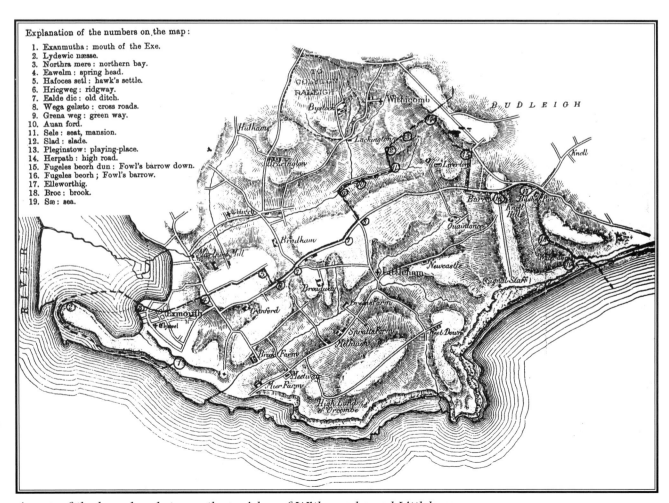

Explanation of the numbers on the map:

1. Exanmutha : mouth of the Exe.
2. Lydewic næsse.
3. Northra mere : northern bay.
4. Eawelm : spring head.
5. Hafoces setl : hawk's settle.
6. Hricgweg : ridgway.
7. Ealde dic : old ditch.
8. Wega gelæto : cross roads.
9. Grena weg : green way.
10. Auan ford.
11. Sele : seat, mansion.
12. Slad : slade.
13. Pleginstow : playing-place.
14. Herpath : high road.
15. Fugeles beorh dun : Fowl's barrow down.
16. Fugeles beorh ; Fowl's barrow.
17. Elleworthig.
18. Broc : brook.
19. Sæ : sea.

A map of the boundary between the parishes of Withycombe and Littleham.

FROM THE ROMANS TO THE CONQUEST

It was in AD50–55 that the Romans arrived in the West Country to establish a large garrison town and regional headquarters at a place they called Isca, which is now known as Exeter. They also built a villa at Topsham and probably others elsewhere yet to be discovered. An aerial photograph taken in 1988 revealed what appeared to be a Romano-British farm building in Littleham parish; a series of lines in an approximate square shape 130 yards by 120 yards. The actual field had been ploughed but its situation was not revealed in the newspaper article about the discovery.

The possible existence of a Roman signal station at the Beacon has also often been claimed, but there is another site at Raddenstile which would have perhaps given an even greater view across the sea. The presence of small fortlets has also been questioned in connection with a house in Raddenstile Lane, where a well exists and many herbs appear to thrive. The need to protect the regional capital at Exeter would explain these coastal defences. Certain excavations at Lympstone near the railway that were made when the branch line from Exeter was being built revealed an ancient slipway for the construction of small ships, possibly of Roman date, by the bridge over the River Clyst. (Topsham has been described as the Roman port for Exeter, even perhaps a Roman naval base.)

It would have been an impressive sight when Julius Agricola, the Roman Governor of Britain from AD78–85, sent his fleet to sail around the whole coast of Britain. It probably passed near to Exmouth, but history does not record how many ships were in that fleet, or whether it may have sheltered in the Exe estuary overnight or visited the regional capital at Exeter.

The discovery of a number of Roman coins and roof tiles, dating from the second and third centuries AD, at diggings in at least five locations in Exmouth, appears to be evidence enough to prove that the Romans had at least established a residence, if not a fortlet, here. The coins were found at Boarden Barn, Marpool Hill, at excavations in Fore Street, Chapel Street and at the site of St Margaret's Chapel; three of them were from the time of Crispus (317–326) and Hadrian (117–138), a denarius and a sestertius. In addition eight Roman burnished sherds with fragments of Roman tiles were found; one sherd was a wedge-shaped voussoir roof tile. A bronze Venus was found in Hamilton Road and it was the opinion of one of the archaeologists that a substantial building with a hypocaust may have once existed in that locality. Ditches found running across the foundations of the St Margaret's Chapel excavations in 1982–84 could also date from the Roman period. Again, on the edge of Woodbury Common at the lower side of the Blackhall Quarries is an embankment, roughly rectangular in shape, which may also possibly be of Roman date.

Roman influences on the everyday life of the Dumnonii were minimal during the years of their occupation, although there was probably a transition into the new building methods, with the streets being built in straight lines after the Roman fashion, and also perhaps in the styles of dress. Otherwise their departure in AD410 left things very much unchanged in East Devon. Roman roads and means of transport had given a pattern to the Celtic people inland, but had little effect on those living on the coast, where the rivers and the sea carried most of the traffic. The so-called Iron Age had already come to an end but Christianity had arrived in Devon and Cornwall direct from the Continent via the old trade routes that had existed from very early times.

The settlements around the Exe estuary were mainly agricultural or related to fishing. The lower-lying lands had already been cleared of woodland and crops were regularly planted after ploughing, or fields were left as pasture for the domestic cattle. The whole way of life was quiet and peaceful and continued as such for two centuries or more, apart from sporadic raids from the sea by the Saxons who, having already invaded eastern England, were now spreading westwards. Later, East Devon was to suffer invasion from the Wessex peoples; they began to move along the old Roman road from Dorchester to Exeter, supported in the journey by their ships along the South Coast which carried their supplies. However, it was not so much an invasion as an infiltration which had reached East Devon from the early seventh century. The newcomers did need to defeat the Celts at the Battle of Bindon above Exmouth, although they were mostly absorbed by them as there was ample

The Church of St John in the Wilderness, c.1900.

room for all, particularly in the wide valley of the Exe. There was evidence that at the time of Athelstan the Celts were on an equal footing with the new English in Exeter. The Celts continued in their old way of life and the Saxons with them began to form the first really settled community in Exmouth.

Many Celtic religious settlements were to be found at or below the 50-feet contour, in the coastal regions. The newcomers also tended to build their churches not too far from the shore. Polwhele, the historian, recorded that there was once a chapel at Chickstone which no longer exists. This Chickstone, or Checkstone Ledge, corresponds with the place Lydwicnaesse, where the Chapel of St Saviour's (mentioned in the *Liber Regis*) once stood, for the use of pilots and seafaring people.

In AD705 the King of Wessex, Ine (688–726) created the Diocese of Sherborne, which firstly served Wessex to the west of Selwood, but was later extended as the Saxons moved west to include East Devon and other places even further west. The Abbot of Sherborne was granted lands, the revenue from which was intended to support his foundation. We know, for example, that he was given the Manor of Maker, then in Devon but now in Cornwall. It lay across the narrow mouth of the River Tamar and so the Cremyll Ferry was created, which still runs from Stonehouse in Plymouth to Cremyll in the parish of Maker. Later, the Abbot was also granted the Manor of Littleham, which included the haven of Exmouth; to save the journey to the other side of the River Exe he created a ferry, like the one in Maker, to Starcross, which is also still running.

The first invasion by the Danes came in AD875; they arrived by sea, foraging and plundering along the southern coasts of England. They landed at Exmouth and sacked the small settlement but, it is reported, failed to capture the fort. Was this fort the remains of the old signal station of Roman times? Polwhele, writing c.1790, tells us that the fort stood on the Bar, the spit of sands that reached out to sea at the end of the Pole Sands. A cannon ball from a later century has been found there as well as the vestiges of some sort of fortification. In AD876 the Danes did succeed in sailing up the Exe and capturing Exeter, and in AD877 they came from Wareham, mounted and by land, for their ships had been caught in a storm off Swanage (see *The Book of Swanage*). They were followed by King Alfred who could not dislodge them from Exeter, but after some months of siege and the giving of hostages, they left for Mercia. In AD894 the Danes sailed south again and came up the Exe to besiege Exeter once more. Again King Alfred and his levies came to face them. These attacks were often renewed over the next century or so, but Exmouth does not seem to have been troubled in a Viking raid in AD982. They came again in 1001 and in 1003 when, under the Danish King Sweyn, the records report the invasion of 'Exanmuth'. This seems to be the first occasion when the name for the settlement at the mouth of the Exe was mentioned.

The *Winchester Chronicle* includes the following:

And thence [from Hampshire] they [the Danes] went westwards until they came to the Defnas [men of Devon] and there to meet them came Pallig, with the ships he was able to collect; for he had revolted from King Ethelred in spite of all the treaties he had made, and notwithstanding that the King had well endowed him with landed estates and with gold and silver. And they burned Tegntun [Kingsteignton] and also many other good homesteads, the names of which we do not know, and there was peace afterwards made with them. And thence they went to Exanmuth [the mouth of the Exe], so that they disposed themselves in one course [made one day's march] upwards till they came to Peenho [Pinhoe] and there Kola, the King's High Reeve and Eadsige, the King's Reeve, were opposed to them, with the force they were able to collect, and there they [the English] were put to flight, and many were slain and the Danes took possession of the field of slaughter. And on the morrow, they [the Danes] burnt down the homestead at Pinhoe and at Gliston [Broadclyst] and also many good homesteads, the names of which we do not know; and then went eastwards again till they came to Wight.

The *Peterborough Chronicle* gives a very similar account, saying that the Danes had left their ships at Exmouth, moored in the inner bay, whilst they raided Exeter, returned laden with booty and then shipped to the Isle of Wight. Doubtless there were dwellings at Exmouth then. The subsequent raids were, however, foiled by the preparations of the local population, who are said to have created a new fortification for the protection of the haven.

It was Athelstan who, completing the work begun by King Alfred to amalgamate the several Saxon kingdoms under one ruler, came in the tenth century to subdue the tribes of the West Country. He rebuilt the castle at Exeter (a tower there still bears his name) and introduced the shire system to the country, encouraging the growth of defined land divisions and boundaries with a system of land tenure.

The gift of half a hide of land at Littleham by King Edward the Confessor (901–925) to a thegn called Ordgar – not to be confused with the Ordgar who was the Earl of Devon – is revealed in the Cartulary of Sherborne Abbey which goes on to describe the boundaries of that land. The parishes of Littleham and Withycombe are deficient in any ancient names, so it is extremely interesting to read this old description of those boundaries:

Exmouth, thence up along stream by the north of Lydewicness to the northern mere – up along the rivulet from the spring head straight east to the Hawks Settle – straight east to the Ridgway to the old ditch – along the ditch from the crossways by the north of the foul land – thence north to the greenway to Aunford – from the ford up along the stream to the mansion, from the mansion north on the greenway to the slade to the playing place, thence to the high road and along to Fowlsbarrow down along it to Fowlsbarrow south to Elleworthy, thence to the brook and along the brook to the sea.

The name Aunford is believed to be Avon ford, Avon being the very early name for a river. It is interesting to note that in the parish of Withycombe Raleigh the font in the Church of St John in the Wilderness bears the date AD911 carved on its base.

In AD970 Thegn Ordgar gave the Manor of Littleham to maintain a Benedictine cell at Horton in Dorsetshire and it was in 1122 that Ordulf, possibly Ordgar's son, was involved in the transfer of the Manor to Sherborne Abbey, together with the rights of the ferry to Starcross. About the same time, another ferry was established to run from Topsham to Exminster, also maintained by the Abbey of Sherborne. It was said that this was to enable a route to Chudleigh to be shortened without going through Exeter. So by 1066 when William, Duke of Normandy, invaded England, the country had for several centuries been maturing into a well-organised and settled community, which the details in the Domesday Book of 1086 reveal under the words '*ea die qua rex Edward fuit vivus et mortous*', meaning 'On the day on which King Edward was alive and dead', i.e. 1066.

The West Country was still subject to occasional raids from the Low Countries and Scandinavia, but William did not have it all his own way in East Devon. King Harold's mother, the Lady Githa, with her two sons occupied the castle at Exeter, having eight manors locally, of which Woodbury was one. Harold and his family also held Topsham and Colaton Raleigh. They roused the local populace to their support and William was compelled to march to Devon in 1067–8 to defeat the rebels and capture the castle. The Lady Githa with her two sons and her daughter escaped to Flanders, possibly by taking ship from Exmouth.

Saxon names began to disappear as the Normans took over the manors gifted to them by the Conqueror and gave them their own names. Withycombe is said to be good Saxon for 'wide valley' and Exton has kept its suffix of -ton. In this early-medieval period too, the records began to improve considerably; people were now using surnames taken either from their parents, their trade or their place of residence. We are soon able to distinguish a place called Exmouth as a separate settlement. The eleventh-century name for the Point was Lydwicnaesse, which is said to mean the ness or promontory where the Lydwiccas lived, a Saxon name for the Bretons who appear to have settled there. There is an alternative theory that the name Lydwicca came from Lyd, a ledge, and Wicca, from a wick or hamlet – the hamlet on the ledge of rock projecting out into the sea and called by some the Checkstone Ledge. The home port of Exmouth itself extended to a certain rock standing off the beach, a little to the east of mid-channel and also called the Checkstone Rock, Chykstone or Cheekstolle.

The Domesday Book does not mention Exmouth as such, but the Manor of Littleham was in the hands of Horton Priory in 1086 and it appears to have been recorded as a large property with 15 smallholders and 20 cottagers, some of whom were living at the Point. It has been demonstrated that Domesday was in fact a statement of Saxon England at that time and it shows that many of the farms listed are almost the same ones that were settled in Celtic times, such is the strength of permanent settlements originated centuries before. Settlements on the valley sides and at the coastal points where the rivers emerged can be identified in the case of the Exe. The streams from Woodbury, for example, flow down through Woodbury village, Ebford, Exton, Lympstone, Withycombe, the Maer and Littleham to reach either the River Exe or the sea.

Windmills had not been invented at the time of Domesday so the grinding of the manors' corn was carried out at the watermills, several of which are mentioned as being on the Exe or its tributaries. Withycombe Raleigh, the northern portion of Exmouth, was held in 1086 by Walter de Claville, a Norman. Domesday tells that the manor had three villeins, six borders and two serfs representing at least four large households in the place. Both Withycombe and Littleham were within the hundred of East Budleigh; adjacent hundreds were Cliston and Wonford to the north, Ottery on the north-east and Colyton on the east, with Exminster across the waters of the Exe on the west – all of these were developing simultaneously under Norman lords.

CHAPTER 2

Medieval & Tudor Times

It is clear that there was an established settlement at a place called Exmouth by the early years of the medieval period – in other words before 1000AD. Indeed, towards the end of the twentieth century, excavations at 3–5 Lower Fore Street in Exmouth revealed the plan of a medieval building. It was initially a timber-framed construction, but was later strengthened and so became a stone-walled structure. The largely clean sands and gravel in the base of the building show that it was close to what was then the foreshore. Several examples of European pottery have been found there, proving the existence of trading practices with northern France and Brittany. In fact it seems that the total number of pottery fragments was exceptional considering the size of the site. This may indicate a continuous occupation over a very long period – right up to the nineteenth and twentieth centuries. Coins found there have been dated from 1280 onwards.

Following the Bull of Pope Eugenius, dated February 1146, Sherborne Abbey was granted the right of ferry from Exmouth to the opposite shore of the River Exe. At this site existed a flight of stone stairs at a place called Woolcomb's Island, which was connected to the shore by a causeway only covered at high spring tides. Thus we can see the derivation of the name Star (stair) Cross. (It is worth noting however that the right of ferry had been held by the Abbot of Sherborne since the eighth century. It may be that for some reason this had lapsed and a new authority was needed from the Pope to revive it.)

In 1147 164 ships gathered at Dartmouth and sailed to France to take part in the Second Crusade. Following this, Richard Coeur de Lion, the newly crowned King of England, set sail from Dartmouth on the Third Crusade in 1190. Although no records reveal whether any of the ships or sailors came from Exmouth on either occasion, due to the numbers involved, it is more than likely that it was so. Indeed, it seems highly likely that all the ports along the South Coast would have had to provide one or more ships to transport the crusaders.

Small fishing fleets were already operating from other tiny havens in the Exe estuary by this time.

In the reign of King John (1199–1226) Exmouth was already becoming a considerable port, and by 1226 Exmouth and Dartmouth were said to be the only Devon ports in communication with France. By the beginning of the thirteenth century, Exeter, which was an important centre for cloth manufacture, was making good quality blue and green cloth. A large amount of this material was exported to France, probably through Exmouth. Later, however, Exeter and the rest of Devon turned to the production of cheap woollens.

This chapter serves as a chronological journey through the sequence of recorded events in the maritime history of Exmouth.

THE THIRTEENTH CENTURY

In 1202, King John imposed a tax called the 'fifteenth', which was levied against all the sea ports of the realm. The return by the western ports was:

Exmouth	*£14.6s.3d.*
Dartmouth	*£3.0s.0d.*
Saltash	*£7.4s.8d.*
Fowey	*£48.15s.11d.*

It is probable that the figure for Exmouth included all the small ports of the Exe estuary, just as Fowey would have included Lostwithiel, the privileged port of the Duke of Cornwall. The following year, 1203, the Manor of Bradham, formerly Brodeham, was given by King John to St Nicholas Priory of Exeter. At this time the river was tidal up through Withycombe village to the foot of the present Bradham Lane and supported two mills in its course.

In 1234, William de Briwere, Bishop of Exeter, granted the church of Littleham with its appurtenances to the Canons of the Church of Exeter. As a result it received 100s. per year for the maintenance of a resident vicar. This is said to have been with the consent of the Abbot and monks of Sherborne, but it seems likely that their consent was enforced, or they got a fair compensation (as we shall see, this particular convent was very

A drawing of Littleham Church.

Six years later, Exeter Corporation began leasing the ferry station to John Pycard for 44s. per year on condition that he maintained both the ferry house and the ferry boat.

In 1270 some Exeter citizens, led by the Mayor, raided Littleham and carried off the contents of a ship which had run aground entering the port. They were endeavouring to enforce a claim to rights over the Manor of Littleham.

King Edward and Queen Eleanor spent Christmas 1285 at Rougemont Castle where the local personages paid court. Not used to welcoming such important visitors, the local peasants no doubt just stood and stared at their sovereigns. Just 15 years later (1290) Exmouth was called upon to provide a ship for Edward I's expedition to Scotland in his attempt to claim the vacant Scottish throne.

THE FOURTEENTH CENTURY

At the beginning of the fourteenth century large quantities of a fairly high quality but undyed broadcloth were being produced in Devon and a thriving trade existed between the Devon ports and the rest of Europe. The Exe Valley was home to one of the main concentrations of the clothing industry; Exmouth was one of the ports through which substantial quantities of grey and russet cloth were exported, so shared in the general prosperity resulting from the trade. Amphorae (wine jars) from the Mediterranean have been excavated in the region, and were probably imported in exchange for the cloth.

In both 1301 and 1302 King Edward I requested that Exmouth ships be provided for the transport of his soldiers to Scotland for the war against Robert the Bruce. The vessel *Seinte Marie* was hired by the Exeter Municipal Authorities for the King's Service in the Irish Sea. She was owned in shares by five local men and carried 28 crew.

During this time Roger Douste was paying 8s. per year for a tenement at Pratteshyde. A quay was built at Topsham in 1313 by landowner Hugh de Courtenay, Earl of Devon.

King Edward's war against Scotland continued to rage, and as a result he continued to request ships from Exmouth. One was provided in 1314, while a further two were given in 1317. The latter two served for one month at their own expense and thereafter at the King's charge. The war was renewed in 1322 and Exmouth, Dartmouth and Plymouth were each asked to provide ships, but this time none responded.

A new challenge came in 1326, with the declaration of war on France. A writ was sent to Exmouth to provide six ships and 144 men. It is worth noting that these numbers were probably

tenacious regarding what it deemed its pecuniary rights). Whether there was a vicar at Littleham prior to this date is difficult to say, but the probability is that there was not, and that the monks, living at a distance, cared nothing for the spiritual interests of the parish. Therefore the Bishop was obliged to interfere, especially as by this time Exeter was becoming a prosperous sea port and its population was increasing. The chancel and chantry in the present church of Littleham appear to have been founded around this date (as suggested by Revd Webb in his *Memorials of Exmouth*).

During the early 1240s a small plot of land on the foreshore at Exmouth was granted to John the Miller, but soon afterwards a lease of that land was purchased by the Mayor and citizens of Exeter for use as a ferry station. It was then known as Pratteshyde or 'Pratt's landing place' (although it became known as Mona's Island in the nineteenth century). It lies in front of the present Glenorchy Church at the start of Exeter Road; the sea at that time came up to this part of the town. By around 1265 the ferry rights had been recognised as a potential source of income and worthy of control. As such, the Abbot of Sherborne granted all rights in the ferry to the Exeter Council in return for the free passage of himself, his monks and his horses and carriages. Then, in 1281, Exeter suppressed all competition against the legal ferry from the other boats and doubled the fare.

designed to include Exeter, Topsham and Lympstone as well.

Two Exmouth ships, the *Cogg Nostre Dame* and the *Rode Cogg* were captured by French pirates in 1329. The *Cog(g)* was the leading merchant ship of Northern Europe in the thirteenth and fourteenth centuries. It had been developed from a flat-bottomed boat design, but had higher sides, little flare, a straight stern and sternpost and a stern rudder. She could carry more cargo and was more suited to shallow tidal waters, hence being used in estuaries such as the Exe.

Following the outbreak of war against France, enemy galleys and other craft appeared along the southern coast of Britain; ports from Hastings to Southampton were attacked and burnt. French vessels then came west as far as Plymouth and it is likely that as a consequence of its exposed position Exmouth suffered as well. The towns of Devon sent a further 30 ships to boost the King's fleet in the summer of 1338, five of which came from Exmouth. These same towns, including Exmouth, were asked to send their representatives to a conference in London to consider the problem of the attacks against the South Coast. In 1341, 1342 and 1344 Exmouth and other ports of Devon sent delegates to a Council of State at Westminster. They had to be men of experience and with a knowledge of shipping, so that they could effectively advise the King in his war against the French.

Meanwhile, in 1336, a licence was granted for a chapel – St Margaret's – at Pratteshyde, as recorded in the register of Bishop Grandisson of Exeter. The site of this chapel was excavated in 1982–84, together with the nearby site of medieval houses at numbers 40–42 Chapel Street. These excavations revealed a ditch under the chapel which possibly dates from Roman times, although the Saxon or early-Norman periods seem more likely. It was filled with sand before the chapel itself was built. Number 40 Chapel Street is the site of what

The Chapel of St Margaret, which later became a butcher's shop.

later became the Old Exeter Inn (built in the seventeenth century). Before that, however, there was a quay on the same site, on which elm trees grew, and being so near to the Pratteshyde site, it was probably an extension of the same quay. The boundary between the parishes of Withycombe, in which the chapel was built, and Littleham ran along a tree-lined path up Crudge's Lane to Margaret Street beside St Margaret's Chapel.

Despite the ongoing threats from the French, records from this period show that there was nevertheless regular coastal traffic and trade. Indeed, a licence was granted in 1343 to allow a Mr Adam Dally of Seaton to unload 20 quarters of salt and a like quantity of corn at a cost of 6s.8d. This fact is also worthy of note as it reveals that the saltpans at Seaton were supplying salt for consumption by neighbouring towns.

Exmouth sent ten ships and 193 mariners for the 1346 expedition by King Edward III to Calais for an invasion of France. Again these totals would most likely have included all the ports of the Exe estuary; these towns were all often described as being integral to the port of Exmouth.

A long suit in the Court of the King's Bench at Westminster determined in the Easter Term of 1348 that:

Quay, Passage and Lastage of Pratteshyde near Exmouth and all the profits arising therefrom were and consequently are now part and parcel of the Fee-Farm of the City of Exeter and as part of the Manor of Lydford, held by the City of Exeter from the Duke of Cornwall at a yearly rent of £20.

The monks of Sherborne as the lords of the manor of Littleham had lost the case. It is possible that other ships used the quay at Pratteshyde; rolls at the Mayor's Court in Exeter record that licences were issued to ships discharging '*apud Prattesyde*' and sometimes '*sine licencia*'.

In the same year, 40 West-Country ships gathered at Plymouth to take the King's daughter, Joan, to Bordeaux. They gathered again in 1355 with ships from Southampton and along the whole coast as far as Plymouth, to ensure the safe passage of the Black Prince, the Duke of Cornwall. A total force of 3,000 men from all over England were assembled under his leadership. He returned two years later, in 1357, with the King of France as his prisoner.

In the late-1340s, Hooker's *Commonplace Book of Exeter* records the beginning of a plague in the city, the notorious Black Death, which lasted for three years. Exmouth suffered as well, for the disease spread rapidly all over the country. Devon lost up to one third of its population by 1352. It is estimated that the country's population was cut back to the level recorded at Domesday, nearly 300 years earlier. During the time of this plague, a Royal Writ was issued to close all ports, in order to prevent the wealthy among the population going abroad to escape the disease and taking their riches with them. In his 1374–5 edition of the *Commonplace Book of Exeter* Hooker recorded that 'throughe the greate and immoderate heate the syckes [sickness] and plague was yn this citie.' Disease had obviously reached this part of the country again and was spreading through Devon.

The Duchy of Cornwall records in 1352 that the English ships paying wine-prisage at Plymouth during this year included some from Exmouth.

The continued threat of invasion by France in 1360 caused the King to order all ships to be drawn up high on the land, away from the water.

The 140-ton ship, *George,* of Exmouth, belonging to Roger Plente, proved to be too large to discharge at Topsham in 1365.

At Bourneuf Bay in Brittany in 1375, 39 English merchant ships were taken by the Spaniards. The largest of these was the 300-ton Exmouth ship, *Christopher,* mastered by Robert Wykford. The ship was valued at £1,695.

Edward III levied a poll tax in the years 1377, 1379 and 1381 in order to finance his continuing war against the French. The level of payment is recorded as being one groat (4d.) per head for all people over the age of 14.

Towards the end of the fourteenth century, there seems to have been a growing interest in the ownership of land – or at least the records of such become more commonplace. In 1377, Isabelle, the wife of William Dupe, died. She was the owner of 30 acres of arable land at Chikeston and two acres of meadow land, and collected 20s. in rents. Also, in 1382, Hille, otherwise known as Rill Manor, was described as being next to Chikston and was the petty manor in which the ferry station at Pratteshyde was situated. During the fourteenth century, Nutwell was a fortified manor house by the river, lying opposite the major castle of Powderham, the seat of the Earls of Devon.

An annual rent of 26s.8d. was renewed for a windmill at Exmouth in 1388, though where it was situated is not precisely known. The 1393 leaseholder of the Exmouth to Starcross ferry was paying Exeter Corporation a rent of 20s. each year.

Similarly, the Church was beginning to feature more prominently in the activities of the town. In October 1381 Bishop Brantyngham of Exeter authorised the Vicar of Budleigh, the parent church of Withycombe parish, to officiate at the Chapel of St Margaret in Exmouth. Then, during 1387, came the last mention of a Chapel of St Saviour's, said to have been erected around 1348. It was probably superceded by Holy Trinity, though it seems that the licence for the latter was the subject of a petition to the Pope in 1414 (q.v.).

The Duke of Lancaster's expedition to conquer his kingdom of Castile set sail in 1386. As part of this force, Exmouth provided *Trinity,* a 130-ton ship.

THE FIFTEENTH CENTURY

Although war continued to rage into the fifteenth century (in 1400–1, Exmouth and Lyme Regis were ordered by the King to each build one barge for the English fleet); the Church appears to dominate Exmouth's history at this time. In 1412, the newly built Holy Trinity Chapel was licensed by Bishop Stafford on 1 June (it was demolished in 1779 and rebuilt). This licence was for its use on weekdays, in consideration of the distance that the people of Exmouth had to travel from their Parish Church at Littleham, the infirmity of many parishioners and the terrible state of the roads. The old road from both Littleham and Exeter came into Exmouth from the top of Long Causeway and down Boarden Barn to Fore Street.

There appears to have been a chapel that once stood on Chickstone Rock. Evidence of this occurs in a notice in Bacon's *Liber Regis,* which states: 'Chickstone St Saviour's olim cap to Littleham Destructa'. Freely translated this means: 'Chickstone, St Saviour's, formerly head church to Littleham destroyed'. Legend has it that the church was destroyed by an inundation by the sea. However, Chickstone was the name of a sub-manor of Littleham, and this chapel was apparently invented at a time when the name of the sub-manor had been forgotten. That the church was destroyed is quite probable, but whether it stood out where the sea now covers is doubtful.

The ravaging sea seems to have been quite a concern for local worshippers. A petition to the Pope dated 1414 for a chapel for the parishioners of Withycombe living in the coastal settlement of Exmouth refers to the dangers of travelling the one and a half miles to St John's Chapel. Potential dangers highlighted in the document include

St Saviour's Chapel.

Looking up Long Causeway – another medieval road going down into old Exmouth.

Boarden Barn, looking down to Fore Street. An old road led into the ancient fishing village.

Looking up Boarden Barn into Raddenstile Lane.

Raddenstile Lane, where there is still a medieval well, capped today.

A sharp bend in the Boarden Barn road.

death from the incoming tide and the threat of pirates taking and burning the town.

By verdict of the King's Bench at Westminster in 1412 (echoing the decision of 1348) it was confirmed that the passage and ferry at Exmouth, along with the Lastage, Stallage and Petty Customs (town duties) of all wares and merchandises landed and discharged within the limits of the port of Exeter were the property of the citizens of Exeter.

In 1426, a French ship was captured by the people of Exmouth and later found at Teignmouth. Spanish merchants appealed to the Chancellor (the Archbishop of York) for the return of the ship and its merchandise. The persons accused were the master, Nicholas Dandy, Payn d'Exmouth, John Payn of Exmouth, Bernard Gavon, Robert Milward of Teignmouth and John Bertons of Exeter, victuallers.

A similar case took place in the 1430s, as an Exmouth mariner, William Keede, was accused with others from Exmouth of taking some ships off Rouen and Brittany in 1431. It was claimed that the men had been involved in attacking a port in Brittany in 1436 and taking goods which they brought back to Plymouth.

Piracy remained rife along the South Coast of Britain during the 1400s. In 1436 the notorious William Kydd (Keede of yore) of Exmouth cut out a Breton ship from the harbour at St Pol de Leon. Similarly, the *Christopher* of Exmouth, manned by Exeter men, was said to have seized 30 packs of woollen cloth off Brittany from a ship called *Marie Landregare* and returned to Exmouth with the booty in 1475. Certain English merchants appealed to the Lord Chancellor (then the Bishop of Lincoln) for the return of the cloth. The case lasted for over two years.

Fast, two-masted ships called carracks were used for trade by the 1430s. However, within two decades the steep bowsprit of the coggs had been raised to become a foremast, giving local merchants three-masted ships, which, with a fore-and-aft rig on the mizzen mast, enabled them to sail closer to the wind and obviated the need to hire the carracks.

During 1435, Nutwell Court had served as a hiding place for the Earl of March (who later became King Edward IV) and the Earl of Warwick (the 'Kingmaker'). They sailed from Exmouth to the Channel Islands, thus adding to the growing list of royal visitors who had come to or through Exmouth during its history.

By this date, St Margaret's Chapel had been in use for over 50 years, rivalling Holy Trinity. The two chapels were ministering to Exmouth's spiritual needs; the boundary between the two parishes ran almost through the middle of town.

In 1437 Exmouth was named as one of the ports that had a regular coastal trade with Plymouth. More specifically, in the 1430s and 1440s the expansion of export trade in kerseys made from Devon's own wool was at its highest.

Exmouth's contribution to military campaigns continued to be made in the form of ships to transport troops. Two ships of over 100 tons were regularly provided between 1439 and 1452.

An *Inquisition Post Mortem* stated that Simon Ralegh died in 1440. He was in possession of wode (woodland) near Chixton Manor which was held by the Abbot of Sherborne as it was part of the Manor of Littleham.

Thomas Marshall made a new millpool in 1476, which he named after himself – Marshall Pool, or Marpool as the area is known today.

Throughout the fifteenth century, ships were becoming bigger and bigger. As a result, towards the end of the century many ships were unable to reach the quays at Exeter and Topsham. Cargoes were therefore transferred to 'lighters' in the Bight off Exmouth and then taken upriver to their destination. An 'industrial revolution' of sorts was taking place and it was spreading throughout the country. There were the improvements in ship design, machinery, tide mills and windmills, the latter now harnessing both water and wind power. Exmouth had two windmills at this time.

Throughout the country, too, pilgrims were being taken to the shrine of St James of Compostella and for more than half a century Exmouth appears in the lists of ships going there, although the majority of travellers embarked on the voyage at Dartmouth or Plymouth.

The Wars of the Roses continued for a number of years after 1453, the disputes between the Yorkists and Lancastrians being fought on many occasions. It fell ultimately to the Welsh Henry Tudor to bring an end to the feud when at Bosworth Field he snatched the crown from the fallen Richard III and was proclaimed King Henry VII in 1485. Henry VII came to the throne as the first of the Tudors. It was the beginning of a dynasty which lasted just over a century, and no other dynasty made such an impact on the history of England.

By the end of the fifteenth century, trade had begun to improve considerably and English ships were roaming far and wide. Indeed, in 1492 Columbus discovered the New World and exploration into previously uncharted waters had begun. Navigational skills and the great improvement in the techniques of shipbuilding had developed. Then, in 1497, John Cabot sailed from Bristol and discovered Newfoundland with its great fishery.

The same year, Perkin Warbeck's rebellion spread from Cornwall into Devon and ended locally when his supporters were cut to pieces in an assault on Exeter.

THE SIXTEENTH CENTURY

By the turn of the century, the country was feeling the strong hand of the new monarch and then of his son Henry VIII, who succeeded to the throne in 1509 when Henry VII died. In the course of this century, sea exploration and the war with Spain became the big challenges facing the nation.

On a local level, however, life was becoming more settled – for example in Exmouth a regular market was being held, known as the Chyxton or Checkstone Market. Between 1516 and 1520 the miller in Exmouth was John Rendell. In 1517 the Earl of Devon challenged the right of Littleham inhabitants to take fish from the sea and the waters of the Exe estuary in Court, but lost his case.

The following year, Walter Raleigh from Fardel, near Plymouth, married Joan Drake of Exmouth, thus forging a connection with what later became Sir Francis Drake's family. The Raleighs then moved to Hayes Barton in East Budleigh.

By 1520 Exeter received the fifth highest amount in trade customs returns and was a regular exporter of wool and fish. Cod brought back from the Newfoundland Banks was at the top of the market. Ships also went to Iceland for cod and the merchant ships were banded together for the safety of the

Iceland fishing fleet, which included at least one ship from Exmouth. It was not until 1530 that William Hawkins became the first man to trade across the Atlantic. He was quickly followed by many other Devon and Cornish men. By 1550 11 West-Country ships were regularly sailing to the Newfoundland Banks for cod. By 1563 this had risen to 26 vessels, the largest being the 90-ton *Bartholomew*. A list of them appears in the appendix, together with some of the dates of sailing.

The sea was still a place of considerable danger and continued to be at risk from piracy. In 1523, the widow Rede of Withycombe had one of her boats taken by the French and consequently claimed from the Withycombe Parish Council that her taxes should be reduced because of the drop in her income.

The sea was also a threat to life on land; the flooding of the lower part of the town was a constant concern, and indeed 1523 must have seen a number of inundations by the sea, as three men claimed from the Parish Council for goods they had lost in floods. At one time the estuary of the Withycombe river was open and tidal to the foot of Bradham Lane. Within the shelter of the Exe estuary, mostly within the area of the Bight,

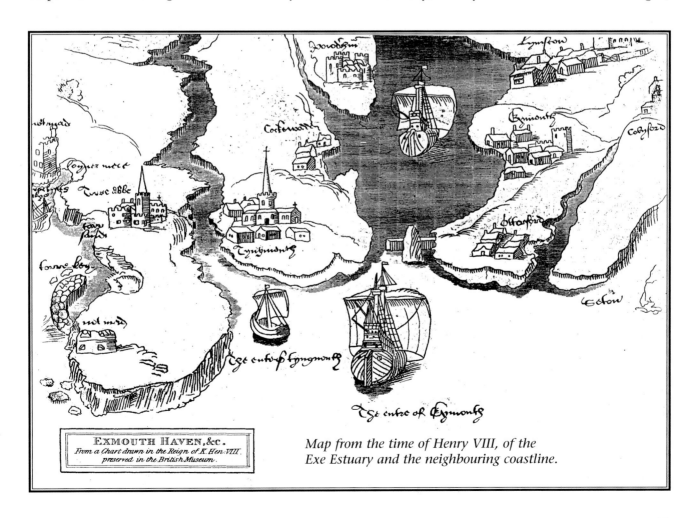

EXMOUTH HAVEN, &c.
From a Chart drawn in the Reign of K. Hen. VIII. preserved in the British Museum.

Map from the time of Henry VIII, of the Exe Estuary and the neighbouring coastline.

there were laid mussel, oyster and cockle beds, but there were many disputes and incidents over their theft. Then in 1545 Woodbury churchwardens contributed 13s.4d. towards the works at Exmouth, then described as 'bulwarks' by Chekystone, at the Point and at the Maer. It has been suggested that this was done in order to raise defences to keep back the sea in rough weather. However, there is also a record of a fort being built in the same year to guard against the entry of foreign vessels. It could well be that the fort was in fact the real reason for the churchwardens' contribution. Serious floods covered the lower part of the town around the quay at Pratteshyde in 1562.

The landscape itself was changing, as Exmouth society became more commercially minded. It is recorded in 1526 that much of the woodland around Woodbury had been cut down and the commons were being grazed by thousands of sheep.

In 1536 John Drake, the son of John Drake of Exmouth, was granted a lease of the Rectory of Budleigh and Withycombe Raleigh for 50 years, at an annual rent of £26.17s.3d. Two years later, in 1538, Henry Courtenay was executed for an alleged conspiracy against King Henry VIII. The downfall of the Courtenays of Powderham Castle freed the river through to Exeter which had been blocked in 1284 by Isabella, the Countess of Devon, building two weirs within the bounds of her Manor of Topsham, so that she could drive a water-mill.

The Abbey of Sherborne was one of those suppressed by Henry VIII in 1539 under his Dissolution of the Monasteries. Any rights to the Exmouth to Starcross ferry that may have survived at this time were assumed by Exeter Corporation.

The same year, Sir Thomas Dennys paid £1127.3s.4d. for the two manors of Littleham and Exmouth. In addition he acquired the Hundred of Budleigh and the Manor of Bicton where he chose to live. This appears to be the only occasion on which Exmouth is referred to as a manor separate and distinct from Littleham. Sir Thomas had thus purchased the right to hold two fairs a year at the Cross in Exmouth, in April and October. The ownership of these manors with the Hundred of Budleigh descended through the family of Dennys until it came to the Rolle family by marriage in 1622.

John Drake took a lease of the ferry in 1542, including the quay at Pratteshyde, a plot of 100 feet by 80 feet, for a rent of 26s.8d. per year, reduced a year later to 20s. The Drake family continued to hold the ferry until 1624.

Henry VIII died in 1547 and was succeeded by a 'weakly youth', Edward VI. However, Edward's death in 1553 at the age of 16 brought Mary Tudor to the throne. The following year Mary married Philip of Spain, but she died in 1558, bringing the threat of a Spanish king to an end.

The year 1549 saw men from Cornwall and Devon rebel against the new Prayer Book. They were met by the King's forces at Clyst St Mary and at Fenny Bridges and were defeated. Many Exmouth men were involved in this struggle.

John Leland, the emissary of Henry VIII, was told to survey the whole country and he came to Exmouth, describing it as 'a fiss-char tounlet a little within the haven mouth'.

Elizabeth, the daughter of Henry VIII and Anne Boleyn, became ruler of England in 1558. She remained in power until 1603, and this is generally regarded as one of the most glorious periods of English history. Men from all over Devon helped to build up an English fleet that proved to be, in due course, a match for that of Spain. Walter Raleigh, born in 1552 to Walter Raleigh and Champernoune, was one who served his country well; he made his first voyage in 1569 at the age of 17. (Champernoune was also the father of Humphrey Gilbert.)

After 1563, the churchwardens of Littleham parish were almost always members of the more important families in the parish. They were the Drakes of Sprathayes, Weekes, Pardons, Crosses, Keedes, Stokes, Days, Perrimans, Woods-Lees, Spisers and Whitrows.

By 1565 Exmouth as a harbour and landing place fell within the Fort of Exeter for jurisdiction and records. However, all the places on the river, including Dawlish, were generally described as being 'within Exmouth Haven'. The building of the first section of 1½ miles of the Exeter Canal, able to take vessels of up to 16 tons, was begun and completed in 1566.

The miller at Exmouth in 1570 was William Browning.

In the latter half of the sixteenth century, privateering was rife in the Atlantic. Spanish ships carrying bullion from the West Indies were often captured very soon after they had set sail for Spain. Using Plymouth as their main base, the great men of the sea of this century, Drake, Gilbert, Hawkins, the Edgcumbes, Grenvilles,

Sir Francis Drake.

Arundells and their kin, were all involved in such action.

The Return of Shipping for 1572 stated that Exmouth had five registered ships. The largest of these was 50 tons. Topsham had a further 14 registered ships. The estuary was obviously a place of great importance in the shipping world during the reign of Elizabeth I, though Dartmouth and Kingswear together had the largest number of registered ships, at 35. In 1577, the Return of Shipping shows that 135 vessels of over 100 tons were registered for the whole of the country. Four of these were from Exmouth.

By 1576 there was a dock area at the mouth of the Exe estuary.

The period 1577–80 saw Sir Francis Drake circumnavigate the world. He was the first Englishman to do so, for which feat he was knighted by the Queen on the *Golden Hind* at Deptford in April 1581.

By the 1580s, many more English ships had turned to the Newfoundland Banks for cod. This was done largely in response to Denmark imposing restrictions on the cod fishing off Iceland.

Richard Whitbourne came from an old Withycombe family and was an intrepid sailor from the age of 12, venturing into the Mediterranean as well as to Newfoundland. On at least three occasions in 1583 he was present when Sir Humphrey Gilbert took possession of Newfoundland in the name of Queen Elizabeth.

In his topographical survey published in 1586, William Camden stated:

Upon this very mouth on the other side (as the name itself witnesses) stands Exmouth, known for nothing but its bare name and the fisher-hutts there.

Shortly after this comment, in 1588, came the first Armada. Richard Whitbourne of Exmouth equipped his own ship, the *Felix*, to join the English fleet in Plymouth Sound, along with two other ships from the Exe estuary. It was a fleet of professional seamen under the command of sea captains of long experience. When the news came that the Armada was travelling up the Channel, Lord Howard, the English Lord High Admiral, came down from the Thames with his fleet and withdrew into Exmouth to await the main body of English ships under Drake. They joined forces and harassed the rear of the Spanish fleet all the way up the Channel until fireships sent in amongst them at Calais broke up their formation and sent them up the North Sea in the hope of escaping to the safety of home via Scotland. Many Spanish ships were wrecked on the way, particularly off the coasts of Ireland.

Richard Whitbourne was commended by Lord Howard for his efforts and those of his men against the mighty Spanish galleons. There were no Armada beacons at Exmouth, the nearest being at Shaldon, near Teignmouth, and the next was eastward at West Down, 250 feet above sea level – it still bears the name of Beacon.

Spain's second Armada began moving towards England in 1596. It was but a small portion of the country's original fleet; numbers had been diminished by English raids on Spain's ports and on their supply ships coming from the West Indies. The Armada was unable to get beyond the Bay of Biscay, as storms sank 20 of the 30 ships in the fleet. Furthermore, the coasts of southern England had been alerted and the English ships were standing by. This did not stop the Spanish from trying a third attack the following year. By 1597 they had raised 136 ships, and intended to land 8,000 men west of Plymouth. However, storms in the Bay of Biscay again damaged the ships and forced them to return home. The English fleets under Lords Howard and Essex with Sir Walter Raleigh had been waiting in Plymouth with 42 ships and 6,000 soldiers.

In 1599 the tithe for fishing at Littleham with the rectory, parsonage and barn at Topsham were leased by the Dean and Chapter of Exeter to William Brutton of Exeter. The rent for the fishery at Littleham was 53s.4d. per year.

THE EARLY-SEVENTEENTH CENTURY

Mary, the daughter of Gilbert Drake of Spratshayes, was married in 1600, but her younger sister Ursula (born 1591) did not wed until 1615.

The Poor Law Act passed in 1601 made each parish responsible for setting its own able-bodied unemployed to work and overseers had to be appointed to supervise the application of the law. The population of Littleham with Exmouth at this time was estimated at 650 and there were about 80 houses in the town.

Queen Elizabeth died in 1603 after a long and glorious reign; the whole country mourned. Nevertheless, maritime exploration continued apace after her death. The ship *Endeavour* of Exmouth (140 tons) with her master Robert Perryman and a crew of 33 men was operating out of the port, her owners being Richard Whitbourne and a merchant called George Troublefylde. The 60-ton *Mayflower* was owned by John Borough of Exmouth and mastered by William Meare with a crew of 15 men and boys.

According to the *Legends of Littleham* (1550) Sir

Hugh de Crevett was said to have acquired the habit of smoking tobacco. It was in his very last year that, returning across Woodbury Common, he found himself surrounded by several spectral appearances, who formed a circle around him and with a grotesque dance, sang:

Sir Knight, Sir Knight, thou ne'er shall lack-o
The smoky weed that's called tobacco;
Thy sons in clouds of noxious fume,
Shall long fulfil their father's doom;
From age to age, from north to south,
Shall pass the day with tube in mouth,
And raise the stupefying vapour,
By morning dawn, by nightly taper,
Mid clouds of smoke, shall eat, shall drink,
And studying, only think they think;
For all that issues from their head,
Shall savour of the noxious weed,
Now, quick Sir Knight, from earth begone
The curse is fixed – the deed is done!

It is said that Sir Walter Raleigh was inspired by this tale to bring some of this weed from Virginia to England. Consequently he is considered responsible for bringing the first tobacco to this country.

With the end of the sixteenth century and the loss so shortly afterwards of her great Queen, England underwent many changes. The most significant of these included the start of a new monarchy – that of a Stuart King, James I of England and VI of Scotland – and the whole of the Atlantic opened up to English ships and navigators, which in turn marked the beginning of mass emigration to the New World. In the next chapter we shall see how Exmouth was affected in the seventeenth century by the beginning of the Stuart line, with all its upsets, and the Civil War.

Primrose Cottage in North Street, the last thatched building in Exmouth.

Sir Walter Raleigh.

Sailing of the Spanish Armada.

CHAPTER 3

The Seventeenth Century & The Civil War

The seventeenth century represents a turning point for the history of England, particularly in reference to the monarchy. This chapter, while tracing the wider events of the nation as a whole, nevertheless includes local milestones in the history of Exmouth and explores how the two are irrevocably linked.

An extreme frost in January 1607 lasted between six and seven weeks. Large blocks of ice came floating down the Exe from its upper stretches, piling up and breaking the gates of the weir. Most of the river was frozen over.

Holinshed stated that at one time Exmouth had a castle, but by 1620 there was little other defence except a barred haven and the valour of the inhabitants. Tradition says that the castle was at Gun Point, at the eastern end of the Beacon Cliff. A contemporary map shows the site as a small circular eminence. It may have been at this point that a beacon was fired in ancient times. Clay tobacco pipes dating from the 1620s were discovered in an excavation at 3–5 Lower Street in 1980.

King James I of England died and was succeeded by Charles I in 1623. This was also the year that the Watts family took over the lease of the ferry from the Drakes, which they held until 1680.

It is believed that a man called Moon once lived in a cottage in Castle Lane, which had been part of the main road from Salterton to Exmouth. He was regarded as something of a wizard and it is said that he could cut off the head of a cockerel and stick it back on again (believed to be an ancient Egyptian feat of magic). He was also the jester for Lord Rolle at Bicton House. Lord Rolle was a big, bad-tempered fellow and it was said that Moon was the only person who could brighten his mood.

FROM EXMOUTH TO THE NEW WORLD

In the late 1500s and the early 1600s, the expansion of the Newfoundland trade in cod-fishing and an increase in emigration there led to a growing number of fishing boats based in Exmouth. No doubt many also came from the other harbours in the river. These boats joined John and Richard Whitbourne of Withycombe in their regular transatlantic journeys, and in all there were over 20 Exmouth boats of up to 90 tons engaged in the trade. It was a long voyage across the Atlantic and the boats were away for months.

In 1615 Richard Whitbourne of Exmouth sailed to Newfoundland, bearing a Commission from the Admiralty to institute Courts of Law in that country. He dealt with complaints from the masters of 170 vessels. The year 1618 saw him sail to Newfoundland again but this time with a second contingent of colonists. His treatise *Discourse and Discovery of Newfoundland* was published in 1620. It was admired by the King and recommended by the Lords of the Council,

Replica of a fire beacon situated outside the Royal Beacon Hotel.

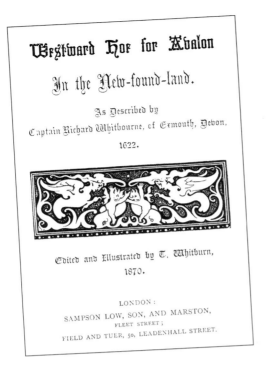

Westward Hoe for Avalon

In the New-found-land.

As Described by

Captain Richard Whitbourne, of Exmouth, Devon,

1622.

Edited and Illustrated by T. Whitburn,

1870.

LONDON :

SAMPSON LOW, SON, AND MARSTON,
FLEET STREET ;

FIELD AND TUER, 50, LEADENHALL STREET.

A reprint of the title page of a book published in 1622 by Captain Richard Whitbourne of Withycombe In the New-found-land. It was published by a descendant, T. Whitburn.

who collected sufficient funds to meet the costs of its publication. He was knighted soon afterwards when a supplement was published in 1622. Edward Drake of Exmouth recommended that Sir Richard be used by the Royal Navy, so in 1627 he was appointed Lieutenant on the *Bonaventure* under Sir John Chudleigh, and later retired to Exmouth.

Emigration from Devon to New England began in earnest in 1623 and emigrants included George Strang and his family from Littleham, who sailed to Boston on the *Regard*. Many left England for the New World, driven by the hope of economic prosperity, as well as a sense of religious destiny.

During the seventeenth century an engineer was sent by the Board of Admiralty to report on the harbours along the South Coast of England. Of Exmouth, he reported that he and his ship 'encountered many inconveniences'. More than likely this was a reference to the sandbanks and the Checkstone Rock, which stood in the Channel for many years. The narrowness of the Exe estuary was most noticeable at its mouth, where it was bound by dangerous rocks on the north side and by sands to the south and west. Consequently shipwrecks were a common occurrence.

The Light of Navigation published in 1612 by Blaeu, shows safe anchorages against the south wind by the 'creek of Tops [Topsham] of Exmouth'. They were described as 'good anker ground... which lyey before the tyde of Exmouth'.

TRADE

Due to the outbreak of war with France, the Exeter cloth trade with that country came to an end in 1627. As such, instead of exporting from Devon ports, the cloth was sent to London for the Dutch and German markets.

The first customs house was built in Exmouth in 1629 – an indication of the amount of trade passing through the port by this time. In fact, during the decade to 1630, over 300 ships sailed from the West Country to the Newfoundland fishery.

By 1660 the previously strict control over the unloading of vessels in the estuary near Exeter had been relaxed, although ships from overseas were supposed to discharge at the 'legal' quays of Topsham and Exeter. Coastal vessels unloaded at Exmouth, Starcross, Lympstone, Cockwood and Countess Weir, whilst colliers and stone boats discharged at their relevant kilns. During the seventeenth century vessels are recorded as discharging goods at Exmouth Strand and on the Quay (probably at Pratteshyde) which was said to be accessible to ships of 60 tons or more. The customs port of Exeter was defined in 1676 as including the whole area between the mouth of the Exe and the mouth of the Teign. This is a clear-cut definition whose legal significance has lasted until modern times, although ports which collected their own customs dues existed from as early as the twelfth century – Exmouth town customs existed at the Check-stone at the river mouth in 1261. Exeter, by agreement with the Abbot of Sherborne, had abandoned any claim to customs on merchandise landed in the Manor of Littleham. However, it became clear by 1685 that contraband was being landed by local smugglers at the Maer rocks and in the caves nearby. Customs inspections revealed that these runs of brandy, canvas and other goods were being made regularly, often with the help of pilot boats.

Indeed, by the end of the century, smuggling was an outward trade as well as inward, and wool was being smuggled out of England to various destinations in Europe in large quantities. It was then converted into cloth and sent back to England. An Act of 1698 sought to remedy this by appointing ships to patrol the coast, which reduced the traffic considerably. At about this time, the majority of Revenue cutters were being built at Cowes and Lymington.

By 1699 Exeter had 34 ships in the Newfoundland cod trade. Dried cod was exported to Catholic countries in southern Europe, and more locally, goods were being loaded and unloaded on The Strand, now The Strand Gardens Centre.

PIRATES

Due to the neglect of the Navy, the Channel was swarming with pirates during the 1620s and '30s. (Rewards were offered in 1665 to recruit men for the Navy.) The Government did little to remedy the situation, but the Lord Admiral in Exeter issued 18 warrants (three of which went to Exmouth ships) authorising them to act as privateers. Three Dutch ships were caught and brought to Exmouth by Captain Crosse.

From 1650 onwards, Prince Rupert was using the remnants of the English Fleet to prey on shipping in the Channel, but was dislodged by Admiral Robert Blake operating out of Plymouth and he escaped to the West Indies.

As well as stealing goods, pirates were well known for taking people as hostages, as a further source of income. For example, collections were made in many local churches in December 1678 for the release from captivity of Thomas Lukas of Exmouth, who had been captured by the pirates of Algiers and Sallee. Similarly, in October of the following year, collections were made in many churches for the release of Edward Woodward of Exmouth. In November 1679 further collections were made for the release of Thomas Swallow of Littleham. Obviously the pirates had been busy in the Channel and many Devon ships were captured. On one occasion 15 sails of Turkish ships were sighted in the Channel off the South Devon coast, so few local ships ventured to leave harbour. Three Topsham ships were taken and their crews held for ransom.

PLAGUE

In 1628 Exmouth suffered badly from a severe visit of the plague. Exeter and other towns in Devon also suffered from this dreadful scourge in the seventeenth century. Particularly bad years for the region included 1624, 1626, 1628 and 1639. The disease was brought to this country from time to time by ships trading abroad; for instance the plague of 1646 which ravaged several towns in Devon, first broke out in Bideford where, as Pevsner informs us:

... in June a vessel from Spain, laden with wool, having landed her cargo at the Quay... diffused itself to so shocking a degree, that in a few weeks the houses there were filled with horror and the street covered with grass. Some children who had been playing on the woolsacks were the first who caught the infection.

Below is a list of Exmouth people who were killed by the plague in 1628–9. Their names have been taken from the Parish Register of Burials.

Nich. Whitcombe; Jane Pitford; Edwd. Pitford; Abram Gilbert; Geo. Pitford; Benedic Blatchford; Abram Pitford; John Pitford; Thos. Day; Geo. Pearne; John, son of Wm Kemp; Benedict, son of Jane Temple; Mary dau. of Geo. Pearne; Joan Pearne; Simon, son of Nich. Pearne; Robert Brayne; Thomas, son of Wm. Temple; Ellen Mappin; Richd. Pearne; Catherine, dau. of Thos. Jolly; John Adge; Richard ?; Mary Hambridge; Wm. Temple; Geo. Cheny; Catherine Peeke; Abigail Drew, wife of John Drew; John, son of Henry Warren; Dorothy Jolly; Emeline, wife of Christopher Adger; Nicholas, son of Wm. Blatchford; Margaret Peeke; Alice, wife of Robt. Turpin; Richd. Palfrey; Elizabeth Weekes; Elizabeth, dau. of Jno. Turpin; Christopher, son of Roger Hellier; and John Weeks.

THE CIVIL WAR

In October 1640 the Civil War broke out. When Charles I came to the throne in 1623, his policies were set against the feelings of his subjects. As a result, he faced considerable opposition, which was expressed in the House of Commons. Cornwall was predominantly Royalist, but Devon in general was only partly so. Plymouth had declared for Parliament, but Exeter was Royalist. Exmouth supported Exeter and built royal forts and gun emplacements at the mouth of the River Exe to prevent the forces of Fairfax and Cromwell from attacking upriver. The church at Littleham purchased 'a sword, bandolier and a rest, for 6s. and the parish musket was fetched from Ottery at the cost of ninepence.'

In 1643 four Parliamentary ships were trapped inside the Bar by contrary winds. They came under fire from the guns at Exmouth and Starcross. The following year Charles I placed his family in the care of the Earl of Bedford, in Exeter. However, the successful defence of Plymouth against the Royalist forces meant the family had to be moved elsewhere.

Gun Field near the Beacon. This green area of garden is kept as a place of leisure because tradition says that a fort or castle once stood there. Fortifications were said to date from Napoleonic times to command the narrow entrance to the river. It held out for six weeks in the King's name in 1646, until forced to surrender to Col Fairfax's men on 1 March of that year.

Cannon balls found in Exmouth, probably dating from the Civil War.

By 1645, Prideaux at Nutwell House had declared for Parliament and was facing the Royalist garrison at Powderham Castle across the river. On 14 December the Prideaux garrison crossed the river to attack the castle, but only succeeded in occupying the church. The garrison at the castle was later reinforced by men from Exeter, which meant the Prideaux men were forced to withdraw across the river and back to Nutwell.

One year later, in 1646, General Fairfax, the Parliamentary Commander, came by land to attack Exeter. In February he sent Colonel Shapcote to blockade the Exmouth forts. They held out under Colonel Arundel for 46 days, before finally surrendering on 15 March to Sir Hardresse Waller. As a result of this victory, Waller had captured 16 pieces of Ordnance with ammunition, 72 muskets and various other weapons and ammunition. Nutwell Court was fortified by the Parliamentarians and the Castle at Powderham again besieged. Ultimately, however, the Parliamentarians were forced to surrender to Colonel Hammond. The Committee of Public Safety met weekly at Exeter in the troubled years of the late-1640s. It comprised members from all Devon's major towns.

Charles I was dethroned by Parliament and beheaded in 1649.

THE STRUGGLE FOR THE THRONE CONTINUES

The Duke of Monmouth was in the West Country in 1680 to gain support for his cause (as the illegitimate son of Charles II he became the focus of a Protestant claim to the throne). He came to Topsham to rally men and, indeed, people from Exmouth were persuaded to join him. However, he was defeated at Sedgemoor five years later, after which time Judge Jeffreys issued his 'Bloody Assize'. There is no record of anybody from Exmouth who suffered at his hands.

In 1688 William of Orange landed at Brixham assured of support from many of the Devon ports, an event which is still commemorated at Brixham. Some of his transports are known to have discharged at Exmouth.

Following the defeat of the English and Dutch fleets by the French off Beachy Head in 1690, a number of warships sailed from the waters near Exmouth to the Channel Islands, in order to find safety in 1691.

THE GROWTH & DEVELOPMENT OF EXMOUTH

Since 1628 there had been a distinction between the 'land' and the 'town' in the parish of Littleham. Robert Duke was the land warden and John Heman was warden for the town of Exmouth (1654). Different parish rates were being charged for each area at least until 1688. The parish completed some work on the causeway in 1657. In total it cost £4.19s.6d.

The Restoration of Charles II to the throne in 1660 was a reason for the people of Exmouth to celebrate. The fort was repaired and brought into use again as part of the coastal defences against foreign landings. Then, by 1677, a further half mile of the Exeter Canal was completed. By the end of the century it was able to accommodate craft up to 150 tons. Exeter Corporation provided 12 pilots for ships entering the estuary in 1587. All ships of a draught exceeding five feet had to use a pilot. The Corporation also agreed to erect a tower on the Checkstone rock to aid navigation.

Engineers from the Court of Admiralty visited the harbours on the South Coast in 1698, with a view to the construction of what would be 'safe harbours'. Exmouth was, however, reported as being encumbered with many inconveniences, the entrance to the harbour being filled with rocks and shoals. (Indeed, Thomas Westcote had written in his 1630 publication, *View of Devonshire,* that there were two huge stones at the mouth of the Exe – called the Checkstones.)

Key industrial developments for the town at the end of the seventeenth century included the construction of a sugar refinery at Countess Weir, the sugar being imported from the West Indies. Additionally, a glass factory had been built.

After the year 1700, visitors began to come to Exmouth – which is discussed briefly in chapter four, and in more detail in chapter five. Exmouth was no longer a 'little fisschar town'.

We whose names are heare unto Subscribed Doe heareby testifie that Edmond Daye of this p'rish hath ever bene a Layall Subiecke unto his Late Ma[tie] King Charles the first of Ever Blessed memorie. And of knowen Integritie and for that his Loyaltie and Integretie hath Suffered by plunder and other Callamities Incedent to Loyaltie. And hath for many yeares paste And at present is An Able and Dilligent Schoolmaster and Tuter for the bringing up of Youth In Teaching Them English Writinge and Sipheringe which is most usefull and Requisit for this place Where he Doth Reside.

In testimonie Whereof we have hearunto Subscribed our Names Dated at Exmouth the 16th of March 16621

John Drake.

Michell Spicer)		Clement Weekes)
)Counstables.		)wardings.
Tho: Ebdon)		Richard Kayman)
Richard Watts.	John Basse.	John Therber.
John Elson.	William Newcombe.	Robert Lovering.
Tho: Weekes.	John Lee.	Daniel Moore.

Robert Withall)
) Collectors.
John Crosse)

A Civil War document of 1662.

TRAGEDY IN EXMOUTH

As well as the plague, people of the seventeenth century were at risk from a variety of untimely deaths. Not surprisingly perhaps, the sea claimed the lives of many people in this coastal town. The following are extracts taken from the Parish Register of Burials.

On 21 May 1631 John Halse was drowned and on 9 August a William Nicholson was hanged. [After each of these entries in the Register of Burials at Withycombe Church, the word 'pridie' appears, which seems to indicate that the death occurred only the day before the burial.]

The Starcross ferry boat was wrecked on 4 September 1633, three men being drowned – Andrew Pully, John Rynnicke and William Waite, the last being buried in the sands.

Six Exmouth men were drowned off the coast of France from their ship Dieu Grace *in 1634. They were named as Osmund Fawster, Bennet Crosse, Leonard Frisson, John Hussey from Littleham and Richard Cheyney and Alexander Hodder of Withycombe Parish.*

On 9 October 1656 George Drake, 'who died from the shot of a gunne', was buried at Withycombe Church.

On 24 October 1656 a number of men from Lympstone were drowned in the Bight.

Two Exmouth men, Symon Crutchett and Robert Withall, were drowned in 1658.

Returning from Torbay on 6 February 1660, Arthur Horring, Thomas Stile and Thomas Brancome were drowned.

Peter Hiddell fell from the cliffs at Bikiny and died in 1668.

A fall off the cliff at Orcombe killed Thomas Jolly in 1672.

A pilot, William Elzon, was drowned on the Pole Sands in 1674.

Thomas Avis, a ship's master, and William Hooper, a pilot, were drowned in an accident on the Bar in 1675.

Alice Molland was the last of a number of Exeter women accused of witchcraft and sentenced to death. She died on the scaffold in 1684.

CHAPTER 4

Queen Anne to Queen Victoria

The coronation of Anne as the Queen of England marked a new departure in Exmouth's development, which meant the town and port became one of Devon's top coastal towns. Supremacy at sea enabled England to develop her foreign trade, particularly with India and with her colonies. Trade with India and the Far East had begun in earnest – all English subjects had been granted that right in 1694 by Parliament – but the East India Company soon held the monopoly of that trade.

Although having a queen reminded people of Good Queen Bess and the great times of the Elizabethans, exploration and trade were now more important than mere discovery. Exploration was by this time driven by the merchants' expansion of their trade to foreign lands.

This chapter follows the growth of Exmouth from 1703–1901.

THE GROWTH OF OVERSEAS TRADE, 1703–31

In 1703 the Board of Customs informed the Collector of Dartmouth of the list of vessels appointed to cruise against 'owlers' (an old name for smugglers). The *Dolphin* and the *Hastings* were to serve in the area from Milford to Exmouth, and the *Woolwich* and *Swan* were to cover the Downs to Falmouth.

Gibraltar was captured from Spain in 1704 and retained by the Treaty of Utrecht, by which Britain also retained Hudson's Bay, Nova Scotia, Newfoundland, St Christopher and Minorca.

The Devon serge trade grew to a peak around 1710. Wool was being transported to the Exeter area from Ireland via the ports of North Devon and Somerset, and from the Bodmin and Dartmoor uplands, as well as by sea from Rye in Sussex. The serge was then manufactured and exported to Holland, Germany, Spain and Portugal. By 1720, however, Devon's serge was slowly declining and the business was passing to Norwich. It was one of the county's major exports, chiefly to Spain and Portugal, and

through these countries to their colonial empires in Central and South America. The imports were of wine, fruit, olive oil, salt, iron and dyestuffs, as well as gold and silver bullion. The exports abroad also included fish and grain.

The Newfoundland fishery trade had declined by 1718 due to the impressment of seamen for the Navy, according to a master in the trade, Henry Peardon of Exmouth. By 1722–31, the average annual import of tobacco into the Exe estuary was 293,000lbs, mainly from Virginia, Maryland and the West Indies. Sugar was also being imported from the West Indies and going to the refinery at Countess Weir.

> The short reign of Queen Anne (1702–14) preceded the reigns of the four Georges:
>
> *George I: 1714–1727*
> *George II: 1727–1760*
> *George III: 1760–1820 (including a Regency period from 1811–20 due to the King's illness)*
> *George IV: 1820–30*

EXMOUTH, 1714–60

According to a Captain Peacock of Starcross, lecturing in 1869 about the history of the Warren, there was a 'memorable gale of 1703' which swept away part of the Warren to create a new channel for the River Exe. It was noted in 1716, however, that at half-tide the Warren became an island due to the heavy storms having washed away much of the sand. It was thus possible to walk across from Exmouth to the Warren fields on stepping stones. By this time the Warren had farmhouses on it and the maps of this century show the narrow passage through the Warren called Paradise Lake, usable only by small boats. It was later said (1730) that it was no longer possible to cross to the Warren over the stepping stones.

The 1712 parish accounts of Littleham show a payment for 2,000 slates and 15s.6d. for the landing of them.

Sir Francis Drake, a descendant of the brother of the famous Sir Francis, came to live at Nutwell Court in 1731.

On 15 May 1733 Matthew Lee, aged 18 of Ebford Barton, sailed to Rotterdam to learn about his father's business with that port, and to learn the language. He sailed from Exmouth with Captain Bishop on the *Friendship* and returned in the same vessel the following year.

From 1737 the Littleham Poor Relief system gave money to the travelling poor, which included some people from Ireland, seamen who had lost their ships, men released from Dunkerke or Turkey by pirates, poor and maimed soldiers and persons travelling home on what were called 'Authority' passes, many of whom had been landed at Exmouth. Up until 1737, bridge money was also paid under the Poor Relief system. Gaol or Hospital money was also paid under the Poor Relief system. In 1739 a parish doctor called Thomas Gooch was appointed for the Littleham part of Exmouth, and he signed an agreement to look after the poor of Littleham and Exmouth.

From 22 December 1739 the South West endured the 'Great Cold' – everything was frozen hard until the end of the following January. Even the sea froze and many trees and shrubs were killed.

A new Customs House was built on the Point in 1740 and the port of Exeter had its first Customs Boat, the *Cholmondeley*. It was an 80-ton ship – easily the largest in the service. A new ship called *Joanna* was also registered at Exmouth the same year.

As a result of the short distance across the Channel to continental Europe, smuggling mostly took place in Kent and Sussex (although Exmouth saw its share). At the peak period, around 1745, there were about 20,000 people in England who were employed in the smuggling business. The most common items imported in this way were tea, brandy, muslins, silks and tobacco. One half of the tea consumed in England had not had duty upon it, and the loss to the Crown was enormous.

The period 1745–48 saw instances of rival boatmen fighting against the lawful ferry service for passengers who wished to cross the Exe to Starcross.

It was reported in the 1748 *Replies to the Visitations of the Bishop of Exeter* that a chapel near the New Inn was converted into a dwelling house in 1724 (q.v.). This was St Margaret's Chapel, which had an upper floor inserted with a window in the gable end. The piscina or stoup was moved to the outside wall facing Chapel Street and it remained there for over 200 years.

It was Sir John Colleton, a local resident, who first brought to this country the famous Exmouth Magnolia, then called a Tulip Tree. He died in 1754 at the age of 76.

In the mid 1700s the Ship Inn in the High Street was the favourite haunt for the fishermen of the town.

By 1753 the Port of Registry at Exeter had over 10,000 tons of ships registered there.

The Topsham to Exmouth road was begun as a turnpike and by 1753 it had reached as far as the Bronte House at Lympstone, where a gate was erected.

The Newfoundland cod-fishing trade was lost entirely for 1754, though it picked up again in later years. Instead, a group of Exeter merchants joined forces to found the Exeter Whale Fishery Company. They acquired a ship of 346 tons in 1755, which they called the *Exeter*. It was fitted out on the mudflats at Lympstone and anchored in the Bight off Exmouth in the spring of the same year. She had a reasonably long life in the trade, being still afloat in 1783, despite an attack by the French when a Ben Courtenay was killed. Exmouth must have seen her often during that long period, for the ships of the Company set off for Greenland every spring, returning in July or August. One ship, the *Worthy Shepherd*, was lost in the ice in 1759. The catch averaged six whales and some seals on each voyage. The base port was at Lympstone, and for the winter the whaling ships were quartered at Parsonage Stile, a small shipbuilding cove on the Exton side of the Lympstone Cliff. Two other ships engaged in the trade were the *Lympston* (328 tons) and the *Alcyone*, who made her last voyage for the Company in 1787. The former was put up for sale at Exeter in 1790.

Exmouth Market was held in the area known as 'The Cross', where a ruined stone cross stood for many years, and around which the butchers erected their stalls. No inscription could be deciphered on the cross.

High Bank was built of gravelly sand to protect the quay of Pratteshyde in 1758. It is now called the Parade.

In 1759 it was reported that smuggling in Devon was on the increase, and in the larger estuaries every small creek, inlet or harbour was being used for landing goods. One of the larger smuggling boats in this area was the *Swift* from Bridport; she was of 100 tons and armed with 16 guns and a crew of 50. Even larger was the *Ranger*, built at Cawsand near Plymouth, of 250 tons, 22 guns and nearly 100 crew. Both made many runs that landed near Torbay and other ports on Devon's south coast. The fishing boats of 18–25 tons also had a very successful time landing cargoes to the east of Torbay, in the Exmouth and Dawlish areas.

EXMOUTH, 1760–1820

The two Customs boats for the port of Exeter in 1760 were the *Wren* and the *Shaftesbury*.

A plan made in 1761 from a survey shows a slight growth in the number of houses in Exmouth. It had 11 houses around Trinity Chapel as well as a large house a little distance away called Sacheverell Hall. The Great Tree Inn (called the York after 1790) was in existence by this time – it was a long thatched building near Manchester Quay. (The 1698 survey showed that the little town of Exmouth consisted of Trinity Chapel, six trees and just three houses.) There was also a change in the course of the river at this time as it was altered in order that it entered the sea by two channels – the main flow was at right angles to the shore, just east of the Checkstone, and a subsidiary flowed through the Warren.

A Spanish oak, sometimes called the Luccombe oak, was introduced into Exmouth in 1762. It stands near the present Council House in the Manor Gardens. A 'Rejoicing' was held on 5 November 1762 for the capture of Havana and the Honourable Peace concluded between England, France and Spain.

REJOICING DAYS

The escape of Charles II on 29 May after the Battle of Worcester in 1650.

Guy Fawkes Day, 5 November 1605.

The Duke of Marlborough's victory at Oudenarde in 1708 and Elpaquet.

Prince Ferdinand's victory over the French in 1761.

The taking of Quebec by General Wolfe in 1759.

The Coronation Day of George III and Queen Charlotte in 1761.

The 1770s saw many improvements to the infrastructure of Exmouth. A Mr John Brindley designed a canal to start at Exeter and reach the Bristol Channel at Uphill via the towns of Tiverton, Wellington, Taunton and Glastonbury. However, the Act was never obtained, although a section of this design, from Tiverton to Taunton, was completed under the name of the Grand Western Canal by an Act of 1812. Additionally, between 1770 and 1790 many turnpike roads were built. Before then most of the local goods traffic

Glenorchy Church Tower in Exeter Road before the new church hall was built. In front lies the area known as Mona's Island, formerly Pratteshyde ferry terminal.

travelled by water. As a result of the new roads, by the end of the century several of the smaller ports on the Exe had lost a significant amount of business. Another development was that of a new Assembly Room, built by Robert Wood as an extension to his Globe Hotel. There was also a bowling green on the edge of the Strand. The first yacht club in Britain was founded at Starcross in 1772. It used the broad waters of the Bight and soon encouraged yacht racing and regattas at Exmouth and other coastal towns in the area. The first regatta on the Exe was held by the Starcross Society in 1775. An Exmouth boat won the race to Teignmouth. One of the largest regattas at Exmouth was held in 1820.

The Countess Weir bridge over the Exe was completed in 1774, while the Exeter Corporation purchased the Quay at Topsham in 1775. In 1777, the Glenorchy Chapel was built on what was formerly the Ferry Quay at Pratteshyde. There was much opposition to it in the town, for a gentleman in Exeter called it 'a wicked place'. There was a flourishing congregation by 1783, which numbered several hundreds, according to

Lady Glenorchy herself. Just south of the Pratteshyde Quay, at 40 Chapel Street as it became, was the old Exeter Inn, in front of which a number of elm trees stood, beside 'Mr Broom's Quay'. This was also the site on which the London Inn was built in the early-nineteenth century.

The records of the landings of Newfoundland cod at Oporto in Portugal for the three seasons up to 1770 show that the Exe estuary had 11 ships in the trade. All the cod trade in Oporto was handled by English firms there. By 1771 39 ships from the West Country were regularly sailing to the Newfoundland cod fishery. Exeter and the Exe estuary had 56 ships in the Newfoundland cod fishery trade by 1774, while Dartmouth had 74. English firms in Oporto were still handling the dried cod imports.

War broke out with France in 1776 and Spain in 1779, in connection with the growing colonies in America. This led to many Naval conflicts in the Channel and inevitably involved Exmouth – soldiers were recruited from the area. The Volunteer Inn in Chapel Street was named after the site where the recruitment took place.

The stables which comprise the present Exmouth Museum were built in Sheppard's Row in 1779, with horses for hire to the residents of the town. This activity provided enough work for two blacksmiths, whose smithies were in the Row. There were then 19 cottages, nine of which were later demolished when the Salvation Army Hall was built. There are only two left at the time of writing. The Chapel of the Holy Trinity, first licensed in 1412, was taken down and rebuilt in 1779. A Chancel was added to the Holy Trinity Chapel built in 1823.

The *Sailing Directions* for Exmouth Harbour published in 1779 stated that at the south end of Exmouth beach a ship might ride in seven or eight fathoms of water.

Exmouth had little to offer in the way of social amenities; there were no public rooms or assemblies, and lodgings for visitors were generally in the cottages of the fishermen (see letter overleaf, written 1778). According to Walpole's *British Traveller* published in 1784, Exmouth contained only a few cottages inhabited by fishermen and the vices of the working people included drinking and smuggling. The public house, North Country Sailor, at the top of High Street (now the Heavitree Arms) was named after the crews of the colliers who came into Exmouth in their dozens.

The Port of Registry at Exeter had 130 vessels registered with a total tonnage of 10,423 in 1786. It is from this year that the Registers for the Port survive. A large number of 'sub-ports' came under Exeter, whose area covered the southern coast, from Hope's Nose off Babbacombe in the west, to

Manchester House, built 1795.

Windmill Cottage on the Point.

Seaton and Beer in the east. They included Sidmouth, Budleigh Salterton, Exmouth, Topsham, Kenton, Lympstone, Chudleigh, Starcross, the Warren, Dawlish and Teignmouth, as well as Parsonage Stile, Glasshouse Cut and Gullpit in the Exe estuary. In the period from 1786 to 1823 the number of vessels registered was 1,332, but by the period 1855 to 1899 there was a drop to only 218. It is interesting to note that an Exmouth ship was included in the Port of Fowey Register in Cornwall for the period 1786 to 1802.

A building was erected in 1787 on the site of an old farmhouse below Beacon Cliff; it was later given the number 1A, The Beacon. This may be regarded as the first stage in the development of the Beacon itself. In this year also, newly-erected houses in Fore Street, on the site of medieval properties, were advertised for sale.

Three young men, John Ashford, Henry Franks and Mr Clapp, were burnt to death in 1793 when the premises of a Mr Langsford, a builder in what is now Margaret Street, caught fire.

In the same year, John Connett completed the *Dolphin*, a privateer at the Point, while Robert Connett finished a 47-foot cutter. The following year, 1794, they launched another cutter, called the *Friends Goodwill*.

A yeoman army was raised to meet the threat of a possible French invasion in 1794, and a new battery was constructed at Gun Point. However, it was washed away by a storm two years later. A signal station built on West Down Beacon at this time continued to be used until 1816.

By 1795 there were 33 registered lighters operating on the Exe, the largest being of 72 tons. In 1799 the ships registered within the port of Exeter amounted to a combined figure of over 11,000 tons.

Samuel Eyre of Balcony House, a well-known benefactor in the town, died in April 1795 and an immense crowd followed the coffin to the Parish Church at Littleham. In 1772 he had given the church a silver flagon.

As a result of the Napoleonic Wars, Exmouth Volunteer companies were formed. They held drills on Woodbury Common. Captain Ducarel was at the head of the local volunteers for the defence of the town during the Napoleonic Wars. On the Gun Cliff before Trefusis Terrace, fortifications were built to command the narrow entrance to the river and harbour. In 1800 a band of escaping French prisoners of war stole a yacht in which they intended to return to France, but it ran aground on the Bar and they were recaptured. Shortly afterwards John Ball's fishing boat was taken by some other French prisoners who this time made good their escape over the Channel.

A windmill was erected on the Point by Charles Webber at a cost of £300. However, almost as soon as it was finished, in 1797, one of the workmen, a Mr Champling, was hit by one of the sails and killed.

The same year, Revd Richard Polwhele, living as a curate in Exmouth, wrote the monumental *History of Devonshire* which is still regarded as one of the standard works on the county. The section

about Exmouth praises it well, referring to the town as the best frequented watering place in Devon. He describes the view and the good houses occupied by the genteel families, who have the pleasure of meeting in a good assembly room (at the Globe Hotel). The climate, he says, is remarkably mild, proven by the '... fresh verdure of luxuriant trees that border the water'.

Two miles north of Exmouth, just off the road to Exeter, there is an unusual house called A La Ronde, built by the Misses Jane and Mary Parminter. They chose the site because of the view over Exmouth and beyond towards Brixham, which was said to remind them of the Bay of Naples. From there they travelled by boat to attend services at Glenorchy Chapel, but because they were only able to reach it at high tide, they later built their own private chapel nearby, called Point-in-View.

The raised wall bordering the Parade had been built as an embankment to prevent the sea from flooding the lower parts of the town. Originally the top was a gravelled walk, but the building of houses later began there. At the end of this raised wall a new quay was constructed near Manchester House (hence its name, Manchester Quay) where vessels and lighters were unloaded. The quay was destroyed in the 1860s when a new road to the docks was made. Various goods, including coal, were also discharged directly onto the beach and at a slipway.

A lease was granted to Charles Webber for a new lime kiln to be built on the Maer. A quarry at Orcombe was built by Staples, an Exmouth builder who was also responsible for building Staples Buildings in 1810, a row of cottages now demolished. The parish of Littleham paid £18.14s.0d. in 1800 for 8,000 Tavistock scantle slates for the church, probably brought by ship from Plymouth to Exmouth.

By 1800 there was a fixed scale of tolls on the Starcross ferry and a new ferry house had been built.

Around 1800 Jack Rattenbury, the famous East Devon smuggler, was eventually allowed a pension of 1s. per week by Lord Rolle – perhaps the latter had cause to thank Rattenbury for his services and supplies rendered. It is worth noting that in East Budleigh Rectory the walls were thick enough to contain two secret passages, each 18 inches wide.

Inset: *A close-up of the windmill on the Point.*

A letter written in 1778 to the Revd Richard Polwhele, historian and rector of a neighbouring parish, describes Exmouth as follows:

... The village is a pretty one and composed, for the most part, of cot-houses, neat and clean, consisting of four or five rooms, which are generally let at one guinea per week – no public rooms, save one card assembly in an inconvenient apartment at one end of the inns. The company meet at half-past five, and break up at ten; they play at shilling whist or two-penny quadrille. Principal parts of Exmouth are: North Street, the entrance to the town, the Parade, a fine range of buildings with pleasant gardens behind and a broad gravelled walk in front. Johnson's Place, pleasantly situated near a fine elm called the 'Round Tree'. Contiguous to the Mudbank are some good houses, particularly those of J. Hill and F. Rowe, Esqs. By this embankment a fine tract of pasturage has been rescued from the overflowing of the Exe. The Square, with stately trees with the Market House, erected at the expense of Lord Rolle, Mr Hill's classical and commercial boarding and day school and the Globe Hotel (Mr Bastin). Mr Bastin also has his Marine Hotel on Beacon Hill. On the Strand are good shops and lodging houses. The Dolphin Inn is near the Cross (Mr James Foster). The London Inn by Mrs Gifford, the Swan Inn by Mr P. Clode and also good secondary houses. The Vicarage is on Chapel Hill (Revd J. Pratt) and near to it the Mansion House (now demolished). On the western beach are the baths, the houses of the preventive men and beyond them Shell Cottage, the residence of H. Spence Esq. The extensive beach to the northward is studded with villas, e.g. The Temple (Revd Joseph Gattey). On Beacon Hill, a very elegant display of houses. The two family hotels of Mr Bastin and Miss Ewins, Louisa and Trefusis Terraces, built in the Bath style, Adelaide Terrace on the New Road, Bicton Place, Bicton Terrace and rows of genteel houses are near the new church. Then Castle Park Terrace, Fore Street, Southtown Street, the Chapel Street and Tower Street.

Taken from *Beauties of the Shore* by D.M. Stirling, published in Exeter, 1838.

THE RISE OF EXMOUTH AS AN INTERNATIONAL PORT

It is important at this stage in the history of the town to consider the merchant traders of Exmouth. Shipbuilding had been taking place in the town since the early-eighteenth century, but as ships grew larger and the shipbuilding yards became larger too, with the need for craftsmen in the several branches of the trade, we can identify the shipbuilders and their ships much more easily. The appendices list most of the ships built in the town by the various established shipbuilders of the eighteenth and nineteenth centuries, as well as a few built in the twentieth century.

One of the busiest periods in the development of Exmouth as a port was from around 1780 to 1880, during which time a large number of persons owned and traded with over 200 ships in and out of the port. Of that number, only 13 were actually built in Exmouth, but Lympstone and Topsham also built ships and 31 of them were represented. Another 50 were built in the ports of southern England, whilst from Wales, Scotland and northern England came 38 ships. It should be noted that Exeter had no shipbuilding industry of any merit. Surprisingly, the remaining 52 ships came mostly from Canada. In fact, 25 per cent of the whole number of ships trading out of Exmouth in that period of 100 years had been

brought across the Atlantic and were possibly used in the transatlantic trade. The main shipbuilding area over there was on Prince Edward Island where West-Country men had settled over a century earlier. Another link with that island was established when the timber supplies from Norway failed and instead were imported from Prince Edward Island.

In these decades of piracy, privateering and war, it is not surprising that 12 of the ships trading out of Exmouth were converted prizes taken on the high seas. Correspondingly, of course, losses by storm, shipwreck and possibly capture, were heavy and over 100 vessels were lost through one or other of these causes. We know that the *Dart*, an 81-ton sloop built at Brixham in 1803, was captured by an American privateer in 1814. Many names of the ships are repeated under different owners, showing that they had been sold within the port of Exmouth. They ranged from the 13-ton *Owners Delight* to the 370-ton *Lord Raglan*. Some were sold out of the port, were hulked or simply broken up as they became worn out.

Many of the owners were master mariners captaining their own vessels; others were the shipbuilders and some private individuals involved part time in general trade. A few were coal merchants, no doubt trading with South Wales or the Tyne for coal and going out with sand as ballast. Local merchants were also involved in the import/export trade – Charles Webber, for example, was in partnership with a master mariner who skippered the ship from 1825 to 1853.

In fact, in this busiest 100 years of Exmouth as a port, 206 ships were operating out of the harbour, owned by 135 persons who, in several instances, were members or descendants of the same family. The names of the ship-owners of this period, residents in the town, are listed in the appendix with any dates relating to them where known. It is possible to identify the ship-builders among them: John Adams, Thomas Dixon, John Hayman, John Walters and James Wishart. A master mariner owner was Andrew Beer who, in 1861, was drowned when his ship, *Magyar,* was sunk.

Obviously Exmouth had become a very busy port over this particular period and had also become 'one of the most frequented watering places on the Devonshire coast' as has already been quoted. There were bathing machines on the beach which were drawn backwards and forwards with the tides by means of ropes attached to a windlass. There was much for the visitors to see and so they continued to arrive in their hundreds.

At the end of the eighteenth century, George III was still on the throne but was very ill. The Napoleonic Wars continued to rage and there was rebellion in Ireland (though the new century began with the union of Great Britain and Ireland in 1801). These events seemed to be very far away for the people of Exmouth, even though sailors were still being recruited for the Navy.

THE NINETEENTH CENTURY

This was an exciting new century, one of great activity and many changes with the spread of the British Empire across the whole world.

There were several gentlemen's seats in the country around Exmouth. In Plymouth the Freedom of the City was given to Lord Nelson in recognition of his outstanding victories in the Napoleonic Wars (he was killed at Trafalgar in 1805).

In 1802 one of the boats bringing limestone from Berry Head for the lime kilns at the Maer, sank on the Bar together with two of the town's fishing fleet. The following year, September 1803, the first lifeboat, 27 feet long with a 10-foot beam and 10 oars, appeared at Exmouth. The cost was defrayed by Lord Rolle. A boathouse for the lifeboat was erected near the Passage House. In December 1813 a severe storm washed away the old Lifeboat House, and the lifeboat itself was taken away from Exmouth. There is no evidence that she was ever launched in the 11 years she had been stationed at Exmouth.

PIRACY

A French privateer captured the ship Delight *off Exmouth as she was on her way from London to Exeter in 1746. The Stafford family were prosperous merchants in Exmouth at this time, through their trade with Newfoundland and other foreign parts. They owned much property in the town.*

The ship Exmouth *under Captain Withiel was taken by the French in 1756.*

In 1803 a French pirate ship seized the sloop Peggy *off the mouth of the Exe when she was en route from London to Bristol.*

As a result of the attacks on Turkish and Algerian coasts by Lord Exmouth, the numbers of pirates terrorising the shipping in the Channel were very much reduced in 1816.

On 15 July 1819 a French row-galley was chased into Exmouth by a Revenue cutter, the Sprightly *from the Dartmouth station, and six crewmen, five of them French, were caught after jettisoning 200 casks of spirits overboard, of which 68 were recovered and taken to the Customs House at Topsham for safety.*

Mrs Drake sold the Spratshayes Estate to a John Drewe in 1803 and so ended the long association of the Drake family with Littleham and Exmouth.

A *Guide to Watering Places* was published in 1803. Under Exmouth it was noted that bathing in the sea was popular and bathing machines were placed within the Bar, making it a secure place to swim:

... protection is afforded [so] that there is seldom a day when ladies may not bathe at Exmouth with safety. Bathing in the sea from the machines with two guides costs 1s. each person the first time and 6d. after.

Gun-brigs were being built all over the country to a particular design for use in the Napoleonic Wars and several were built at or near Topsham. The largest, the *Medina,* was 469 tons and was launched in 1811. No record exists of any built at Exmouth in the first decade of this century, although *Weazle,* a sloop of war, was copper-bottomed there.

A lease to rebuild the Maer lime kiln was granted in 1806. At high water, lighters loaded with limestone came up through a gap in the sand

The ferry house on the Point in 1867.

dunes to unload immediately below the kiln. Later, in 1825, the kiln was owned by a Mr Davey (who also owned the cutter, *Surinam*) and rated at £10 per annum. However, the docks were built in 1806, and so dock dues became payable for the whole of the foreshore. As a result, lime kilns were built by the docks and those at the Maer and at Straight Point fell into disuse.

On 15 September 1807 several French officers, having broken their parole and armed with cutlasses, endeavoured to take a boat from the beach to escape to France. They were prevented at their first effort but seized another smaller boat and put out to sea.

The same year, a Topsham-built sloop, the *Porcupine,* was brought to Exmouth to be rigged prior to sailing to Plymouth.

The Exmouth Bank was established by Matthew Lee Yates in 1809, but it failed in November 1812. Two examples of the notes it issued are in Torquay Museum. Hundreds of the notes could not be honoured when the Bank failed and much distress was caused to Exmouth and district.

The same bank leased nine acres of the Point on which to build a repairing dock on the southern shore and a shipbuilding yard on the northern side with a warehouse and a coal yard. A large three-storied building was erected as a sail loft near the windmill. It still stands and has the year '1810' cut into the stone wall.

In 1806, two coach-houses on Beacon Place were converted into Exmouth's first congregational church. Meanwhile, sittings in Exmouth Chapel were rented at 7s.0d. each to raise money to effect repairs to the roof and other various improvements.

On 28 March 1811 the shop of R. Pinn, a watchmaker of Exmouth, was broken into and 14 gold and silver watches stolen.

Mr W.H. Hull of Marpool Hall began reclaiming

the marshland fronting the river on the line of the present Exeter Road. The Mudbank, as it was called, enclosed approximately 40 acres of the marshland away from the river. The road from Exeter into the town had nearly always been via Marpool Hill, Boarden Barn and Fore Street, and sometimes by way of North Street or Albion Hill.

The year of 1811 was important for the children of Exmouth; a national school was opened under the patronage of Lord and Lady Rolle. In August there was general rejoicing at the Duke of Wellington's victories. The war with France ended two years later, in 1813. Edward Pellew, a Cornishman and a celebrated Admiral of the wars against France, took the title of Baron Exmouth in 1814 and was created a Viscount in 1816.

During August 1813, large shoals of mackerel came over the Bar, many being caught by the bathing machines. This was a repetition of an event 30 years previously.

For six months during 1813 nine coasters were discharging grain, stone, glass and wine. The

The old sailing loft of 1810.

lighters brought coal from the colliers in the Bight and the Exeter Collector of Customs admitted that the colliers and other vessels were now lying considerably nearer to Exmouth than Starcross, so that the dues could no longer be collected at the latter.

Napoleon was taken on board the ship *Bellerophon* which was in Plymouth Sound for a short while in 1815. Thousands of people from all over Devon and Cornwall came to see the Emperor of France before he was taken to St Helena for internment.

Ships built for the Navy by Robert Davy of Topsham, the *Adder* and *Clinker,* sailed from Exmouth in 1813 with the bomb-ketch *Terror,* under escort to Portsmouth for fitting out. The last two warships built by Davy sailed from Exmouth in 1814. He moved to Exmouth in 1818 to benefit from the sea bathing and to consult a well-known physician.

In April 1816 the good sloop or stone boat called *Bicton* of 83 tons and upwards was put up for auction; it was about three years old and well calculated for the coasting or limestone trade.

On 19 September of the same year, five large buoys were placed along the length of the Bar and 1d. per ton was levied on all vessels entering the harbour to meet the expense of providing and maintaining them. The channel of the Exe was buoyed up as far as Topsham by 1829.

On 23 August 1816 a craft crossing the Exe from Starcross capsized and one man was drowned. It was claimed at the time that passengers waiting for the ferry were catching colds because of the lack of shelter. The old ferry quay had fallen into disuse, being finally cut off from the river by an embankment built by William H. Hull, along which the railway now runs. It was vulnerable to high tides and strong winds, being affected in 1796 and again in 1815, before being almost totally washed away in 1816.

The violent gales of March 1818 carried the sails of the windmill on the Point around so fast that the works within caught fire and the vanes were ultimately blown off and broken into pieces.

As a result of the many complaints about the insanitary state of the town in 1818 (pigs were permitted to wander, drains and sewers ran into the streets, and there was riotous and disorderly conduct among the rabble every Sunday evening) individual persons and premises were recommended to clean the streets and remove all dung and filth at least twice a week by means of a scavenger. The same year a fire engine was presented to the town by the West of England Fire and Life Insurance Company.

The *Flower,* a sloop of 76 tons, was built at Topsham for Captain Richard Court Treatt of Exmouth and was completed in October 1818.

EXMOUTH, 1820–1837

A smuggler, the *Lyme Packet,* was seized off Sidmouth by the Revenue cutter, *Scourge,* lately arrived from the Deal Station. The cutter's commander was Captain M'Lean with a crew of 30, whilst the smuggler's captain was John Cawley, who alleged that a John (Jack) Rattenbury had arranged the whole trip to Cherbourg and back with casks of spirits. Rattenbury was also said to have gone ashore at Sidmouth to arrange for the landing. While he was ashore the Revenue cutter arrived and took the *Lyme Packet* into Exmouth. The *Scourge* also caught smugglers in 1822, whose booty included tea and spirits. Among the men caught were some from Beer. From this year on, the Exmouth Coastguard was established and the three arms of the Customs, the off-shore Revenue cutters, the in-shore Waterguard and the on-shore Riding Officers, became active in the area. Exmouth became one of the Cruiser Stations. However, this does not appear to have stopped the smuggling. The sloop *King George* owned by Robert Hooper was captured in October 1822. Those on board were the brothers Thomas and George Gibbs, and John Waldron. Each was fined £100.

Trade generally must have been slack at this time, as several ships were put up for auction. On 28 May it was announced that 500 prime Norway spars from 22 feet to 45 feet in length were up for sale, while on 22 April 1823 a pleasure yacht named *Cawsand* was put up for auction at Lympstone, having been built at Exmouth 'of the very best materials'. In May 1828 the schooner *Neptune* of 79 tons, lying near the windmill, was put up for sale with all her materials. Interested parties were to 'apply to Messrs Walters & Wishart, boatbuilders of Exmouth'. John Walters had taken over the Point boatyard and was joined by James Wishart in a partnership that was to last over 40 years. An appendix gives a list of the ships they built. The 15-ton yacht *Cherub* was put up for sale in April 1832. It had 'very commodious accommodation with two beds in her cabins.'

Mrs T. Tillman, landlady of the Jolly Sailor Inn, was married in March 1822. By June she decided to leave the trade and the inn was put up for sale.

In May 1823 the Plymouth and Starcross Cockfighting Clubs met at Starcross to pit 19 birds each at 3 guineas a battle and 20 guineas on the whole main. The ferry from Exmouth must have been very busy that day. Exeter was one of the centres of the sport and there were pits at Ottery St Mary and Honiton as well.

In October the ship *Exmouth* arrived at Plymouth under Captain Evans after a long voyage from India.

By 1823 there were two boatbuilders on the Point. John Hayman and George Hook began

SHIPWRECKS

The Charles *from Rye, laden with wool, ran aground on the Bar in 1784.*

A Topsham sloop, captained by Thomas Radford, was wrecked on the Bar in February 1795. All drowned.

In November 1795 a boat capsized when crossing the Bar and Joseph Perriam, aged 60, and two lads of 16, Thomas Bence and John Madge, were drowned.

The sloop, Fancy, *became stranded at Hallsands, having been driven there on 26 January 1797 by a heavy gale. The owner, his boy and a dozen passengers were drowned but six were saved.*

During a storm in 1807, the vessel Fox *and the privateer* Thornborough *were wrecked off Plymouth, losing her captain and three crew.*

In November 1810 the ship Widdicombe *sailing from Dartmouth to Exeter ended up on the Maer Rocks.*

The ship Brothers, *a Welsh collier of Poole, ran aground on the Pole Sands in 1812.*

In February 1815, three pilots of Exmouth (Charles Perriam, William Perry and Michael Hooper) were drowned whilst attempting to reach a grounded brig on the Bar. On 16 August a servant girl who had been on a pleasure trip was drowned after the boat was driven on to a collier's hawser and overturned.

In January 1817 five acres of the Warren were washed away in a storm. The ship Moon *was wrecked at Orcombe Point.*

In October 1820 the Exmouth ship John *was lost on the Bar at Padstow (Cornwall). All the crew drowned.*

The French boat Marie *was wrecked on the Bar in 1830 and a local gang attempted to plunder it.*

In December 1830 the brig Unity *was wrecked on the Bar and seven of her crew were rescued by the efforts of the Preventive Boat. The coastguard, Lieut J. Sargeant, was awarded the silver medal of the RNLI.*

The Nimble *hit the harbour wall on 30 September 1831. Three of her four-man crew drowned.*

There were several wrecks in the storms of 1836. One was a French vessel whose crew were all saved by Exmouth boatmen, each of whom was presented with a silver medal by the King of France.

Mr Pring and four boys were drowned when returning to shore from the brig Hinde *anchored in the Bight.*

In January 1851 the schooner Mary *was wrecked and a local pilot, Thomas Pincomb, was awarded the silver medal of the RNLI for his brave efforts to save the crew.*

The Exmouth schooner New Ann *was lost among the rocks near Guernsey. The crew was saved but the cargo, belonging to Messrs Redway and Mitchell, was lost.*

The Fleur de Marie, *owned by F. Thierens of Exmouth, was off Dawlish in 1853 when one of her seamen was drowned in attempting to swim ashore.*

A Norwegian barque Habaut Aujer, *laden with timber for Exeter, was wrecked on the Pole Sands in November 1855.*

Captain Bricknell of Exmouth was drowned on the Newfoundland Cod Banks in 1856.

In August 1857 the Naparima *of Exmouth, owned by Mr Sheppard, was grounded near the Maer Rocks.*

In March 1860, the 283-ton vessel Sir Alexander *was wrecked on the Pole Sands.*

In January 1894 Swedish vessel, John Gronsund, *went aground on the Pole Sands. The crew was rescued by local men, John Bradford, Uriah Bradford and George Prowse, who were awarded the RNLI silver medal.*

shipbuilding and their boats won many prizes in the regattas. A list in the appendix shows several of the ships they built. The Exmouth Regatta in August was a great success and was followed by an excellent dinner and ball at the Globe Hotel.

At the end of November 1823 following a great gale, 50 ships were blown out to sea and much destruction was caused in the town. On 22 November the following year a severe storm caused many roofs to be blown off on the Beacon. It came at the same time as one of the highest spring tides ever seen. The Embankment gave way and two-thirds of the town was flooded. The Warren was also submerged and when the waters receded several boats had been left stranded.

The mid to late 1820s saw a significant amount of construction work take place in Exmouth. Houses for the Preventive Officers were built near the Customs House in 1824 and were later taken over by the Coastguards. (There is now a boating lake on the site.) Additionally, Shell House was a decorative new building on the sea front, being erected that year by George Abbott and sold on a 99-year lease by the Rt Hon. Lord Rolle. A copy of the Temple of the Winds at Athens was erected by the same builders. This is the only building of the 1820s remaining today and it stands in the grounds of the Imperial Hotel.

The new Holy Trinity Church on Chapel Hill was completed at a cost of about £12,000 and was consecrated by Bishop Croxey. It took the place of the old Chapel of Holy Trinity which had stood on Chapel Hill since 1412. It was, however, rebuilt on a new site between 1905 and 1907.

On 1 February 1825 a meeting in the Globe Hotel proposed that a basin or quay be formed and a railroad laid down from Exeter to cope with the greatly increased business in the town and harbour. A pier at the Point was also suggested. The final stage of the building of the Exeter Canal took it a further two miles, to Turf Lock. It had a depth of 14 feet and was able to admit craft of up to 400 tons. Towage on the Exeter Canal by horse from Turf Lock to Exeter was charged at 2½d. per ton by 1865. In April 1828 some black marble from a Torbay quarry was delivered to Exmouth Harbour for 2s.4d. a ton in order to build a wall at the entrance to the town.

In 1828 Mr W. Board was appointed to the office of Superintendent of the Pilotage and Buoyage Department at Exmouth by the Corporation of Trinity House in London.

In June 1828 an advertisement for the letting of No. 14 The Beacon described the view from it as including:

... a vast expanse of sea and in front the broad and rapid Exe covered with vessels of almost every description and as a watering place Exmouth stands unrivalled.

In January 1829 there was an advertisement for a superior cargo of American pine timber, birch and lathwood, with 100 pairs of Quebec oars of ash from 14 to 20 feet long, all of which had just been landed at Exmouth and were to be sold on reasonable terms. Potential buyers were advised to apply to Mr R. Webber, merchant of Exmouth. Another such cargo arrived in October.

It was said that this year the Point Windmill was working again, driven internally by a horse or donkey.

In late July 1830 a French schooner-rigged pilot boat arrived at Exmouth with the body of Admiral Nesbit, the son of Lady Nelson by her first marriage. He had died in Paris of pleurisy. The ship also contained the bodies of three of his children. Due to their late arrival the coffins were

Examples of the shipping charges imposed in period 1824–27 can be quoted as follows:

Coal	*10s. per ton*
China Clay	*12s. per ton*
Flour	*8s.6d. per ton*
Hides	*4s.0d. per ton*
Salt	*14s.0d. per ton*
Rock Salt	*6s.0d. per ton*
Common Salt	*10s.0d. per ton*
Fruit from Spain or Portugal	*£5.5s.0d. per ton plus a gratuity of £10.10s.0d. to the captain*

A complete list of the tolls for 1829 comprising over 300 items may be seen in Priestley's Navigable Rivers *& Canals of 1831. By 1988 the port of Exeter controlled the Exeter Ship Canal and commodity dues as well as those for the use of the canal, the opening and closing of locks by commercial and other vessels (e.g. pleasure craft, boatmen and the Topsham ferry). A booklet listing all the charges is issued by the Exeter City Council through its Director of Leisure and Tourism.*

laid in the Cats Castle, a round building on the Esplanade which for some years afterwards was known as 'Corpse Castle'. In September unreserved sales were held of yacht stores, boats and ships' stores; the property of the late Admiral Nesbit. The auction was held by Mr G. Tupman on his premises near Manchester House. Lady Nelson herself died in 1831. She had lived on the Beacon for many years and was buried in Littleham Churchyard.

A new Market House was opened on the western side of the Strand, built to replace the old one in Fore Street. It had been financed by Lord Rolle and it was taken down in 1869 when a new one was erected. A Town Customs Collector was appointed in 1830, he supervised the discharge of vessels arriving in the port. Casks of spirits were discovered in the sand beneath the Customs House in September 1831. Some of the casks bore the names *Sprightly* or *Nimble*, both Government cutters kept on this station in the Preventative Service. A Court of Inquiry was appointed.

During this decade, the Mutter family seem to have become involved in smuggling, particularly in the distribution of the smuggled goods, even partnering the well-known Jack Rattenbury in more than one adventure. Abraham Mutter and his brother Sam were deeply involved as were Abraham's sons John and William. The family kept a public house in Exmouth which customs officers visited on occasion. It was said that many a gentleman's house around Exmouth, Sidmouth and even Exeter received additions to their cellars when Abraham's cart, ostensibly laden with wood and turf for fuel, arrived.

In the area to the north of the new Market House there was a general garden and bowling green lying beside the Globe Hotel. The Estuary bounded the north-west side and so gave the Strand its name. The Deeds of Property in this area often refer to 'Exmouth Strand' as being by the water's edge where the cottages of the fisherfolk were situated.

The hot summer of 1831 brought cholera from Exeter and Woodbury and was the cause of many deaths in Exmouth.

A vessel which had lain for 40 days in the Bight during 1833 had on board a young apprentice from East Budleigh who, it is said, acquired a settlement in the parish of Kenton, within whose boundary the waters of the Bight notionally fell.

Captain John Parker of Exmouth had ordered the schooner *Vansittart* from Davy's yard at Topsham and she was launched in 1834. His family also owned two other Davy schooners, the *Mary* and the *Britannia*.

By 1836, a steam packet boat left from Exmouth for London once a week.

VICTORIAN EXMOUTH, PART 1 (1837–67)

King William IV died on 20 June 1837 and was succeeded by his niece Victoria. She was aged just 17 and ruled Great Britain and its fast-growing Empire until 1901; the longest and in many ways the greatest reign the country had ever known.

In February 1837 heavy gales and high tides which had not been expected combined to cause much disaster in the harbour as well as in the town. The ship *Lady Louisa* of Exmouth, whilst anchored in the Bight, was surprised to find a fine salmon of about 8lbs, which had apparently leapt aboard from the river.

The Plantation below the Beacon was enclosed to prevent any erosion by the sea by 1837, and a pleasant walk had been created there. The square holes in the red sandstone cliff below the Beacon once held long spars on which fishermen held an open-air Fish Market as well as hanging out their nets to dry. This suggests that the sea at one time reached up to that area, possibly at high tide.

The 170-ton brig *Exmouth* was launched in 1839 by Messrs Walters and Wishart before a crowd of about 3,000 people. Later a ropewalk was built nearby and Mr Walters began the manufacture of ropes. In the following year great shoals of herrings were driven into the Bight by dogfish, many of them being caught in nets put out opposite Powderham Castle. It was in this year (1840) that a new road, later called Carlton Hill, was cut through from the beach to the Beacon, and the windmill on the Point was demolished, having been there since 1797.

The Exmouth Docks Bill was at last brought forward before Parliament in 1841, but no definite action was taken at that time.

The Beacon Hotel held its opening dinner on 6 May 1840, possibly acquiring its title of the Royal Beacon Hotel when the King of Saxony stayed there in 1844. It was also known as Bastin's Hotel. It offered to its visitors:

... a superior stud of horses and a variety of modern carriages for wedding parties; also offering wagonettes and drags for posting, excursions, etc.

On 20 August 1841 the foundation stone for the new sea wall was laid by Lord Rolle amid tremendous celebrations. Processions were followed by a public dinner at the Dolphin Hotel with tea and cakes in Webber's field for the children.

Thomas Redway was a ship's chandler at Windsor Place as was John Start. John Parker was a sail and ropemaker in Tower Street. Two boat owners are named at this time as Mrs Jane Hore of

A postcard showing Exmouth Warren at the time when a very high and stormy tide broke through the sandbank and let the River Exe through. The wooden bridge across the gap remained there for several years.

The Beacon, Exmouth, c.1900.

E.S. Gosling

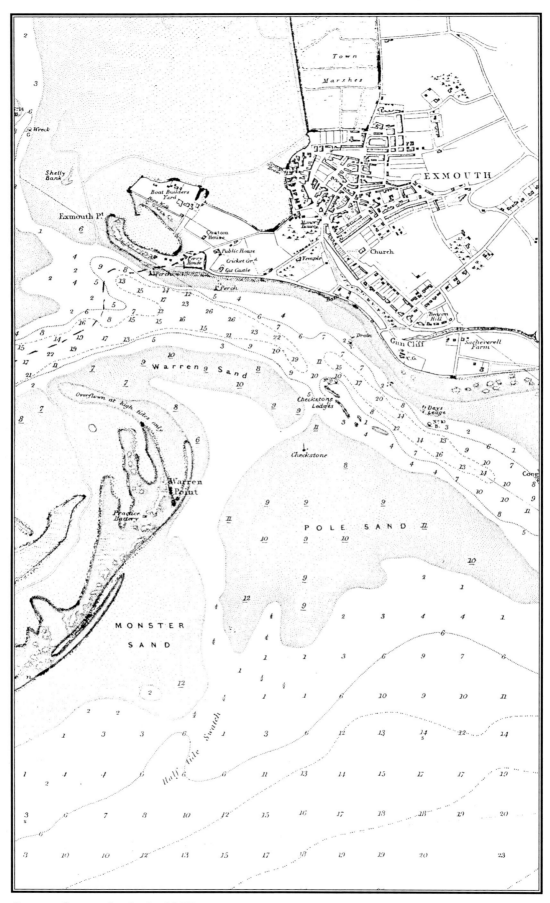

Survey of water depths in 1857.

12 Bicton Street and 'Geo.' Scoble of 8 Bicton Street. Boatbuilders were Thomas Dixon at the Sea Wall, John Hayman of 8 Parkers Place and George Hook and James Wishart at the Point. There were 25 Master Mariners and 17 inns or taverns with five beerhouses. Regular coaches ran to Exeter from both the Globe Hotel and the London Inn, with two turnpike roads for the main route into Exmouth; one via Courtland Cross and the other via North Street. The ferry boat took passengers at 6d. each to Starcross for those wishing to catch trains to Plymouth. At least 300 Exmouth inhabitants were regularly engaged in the making of Honiton lace which was obviously a thriving trade. (This industry had practically disappeared by the late 1880s.) The new Coastguard Officer was Lieut John Walker.

Henry Perriam, Master of the *Vansittart* belonging to Mr Parker of Exmouth, was adjudged a bankrupt in 1851. Meanwhile, the members of the crew of the *Speculator* of Exmouth were charged with smuggling tobacco and spirits.

There were strong easterly winds in February 1852 and the yacht *Coquette* belonging to Lord Godolphin sprung her mast in attempting to leave harbour and was obliged to put back for a new one. The yacht *Lily of the Exe* (26 tons) was launched from Mr Hook's yard. It was a splendid vessel, fitted out by Mr Bence of the town. Captain Tippett of the sloop *Flower* was summoned for failing to pay for the pilotage of his vessel from Exmouth to Topsham; the pilot at the time was John Litton. A large brig *Empire*, intended for foreign trade, was launched by Messrs Redway and Bickford. In early April 1855 the *Matford*, a schooner intended for the coasting trade, was launched from the yard of Mr Walters.

The crop of potatoes brought from France sold very well and Mr Redway it was said, 'may be encouraged to import another such cargo soon'. In October 1854 the *Eleanor* arrived from Jersey under Captain Denning with a cargo of apples consigned to a Lympstone merchant, the second such cargo of the season. The trade of the town was improving vastly; four or five years previously there were only six small vessels registered at Exmouth, whereas there were now about 50, some of them being of heavy tonnage. Seamen's wages were increased to £2.15s.0d. a month instead of £2.5s.0d.

The Queen's birthday in 1853 was celebrated with flags flying from the Customs House and from all the various yachts and vessels in the harbour. Exmouth's first newspaper, the *Exmouth Mercury*, began publication the same year.

The first ship to be described as 'built of iron' was entered in *Lloyds Register of Shipping* in 1853, although the rules for the construction of iron vessels were not to be framed until 1854. However, it took many years to phase out the wooden-walled ships. A boat moored near Parker's Dock had materials stolen from her in 1854. Just the next day Constable Hall apprehended the culprit, a William Osborne.

In February 1855 mysterious footprints appeared overnight on roofs and walls, made apparent by the fresh fall of snow. They spread from Exmouth to Topsham and crossed the River Exe to appear as far away as Teignmouth. No explanation has ever been furnished as to what caused the marks, nor how such gigantic leaps from house to house were achieved.

A Russian vessel, the *Ackbar*, was seized locally by the Government cutter *Francis* of Lyme with the aid of the Exmouth Customs boat. It was towed into the Bight, and the Captain and his ten-man crew were taken into detention. The ship was later towed to London by a Government steamer.

The Crimean War with Russia had begun in 1854 and lasted until 1856. In June 1856 the Exmouth Rifle Corps with other corps from neighbouring areas assembled for a target practice at the Maer Rocks. The return of peace was celebrated with roast beef and plum pudding – almost 4,000 people joined in and they had tea and buns in the evening.

Francis Danby's painting 'Dead Calm, Sunset at the Bight in Exmouth' was exhibited in London in 1856. (At the time of writing it was displayed in Exmouth's Council Chamber in the Town Hall.) Living in Shell House on the Maer, Francis Danby was also able to indulge his hobby of building small boats and yachts.

A new slipway was built in 1856 at the Point for ship repairs. The schooner *Eliza Jane* was lying at anchor off the Bank when an apprentice fell from the masthead, later dying from his injuries.

For the sum of £75, some speculating townspeople purchased the vessel *Independent*, which had been wrecked off Salterton. From the salvage they recovered as much as £600–£700.

In November a low flat boat, apparently French, was found at the Maer by Revenue Officers with French brandy still on board.

On 27 November 1856 the first sod of the

THE 1837 FERRY TOLLS

Passengers	2d.
Horses	4d.
2-wheeled carriages	1s.
4-wheeled carriages	1s.6d.
If drawn by more than one horse	3s.

All tolls were doubled after sunset.

proposed Exmouth Railway was cut – another cause for celebrations in the town.

A fine schooner, the *Eleanor*, belonging to Mr Sheppard the postmaster, was launched early one January morning in 1857 and was described as a 'pleasing and beautiful sight'.

The emigrant ship *Calcutta* of 1,000 tons was in the harbour for a few days, bound for Quebec. Emigrants could secure their berths immediately.

A number of windbound ships, laden with coal, arrived together in late April, providing welcome work for the labourers in the town.

In 1858 Mr Walters launched the schooner *Carmel* which was the largest he had built. In August of that year, a Starcross boatman called Garnsworthy fell overboard, being drunk at the time, and was drowned.

By 1858 the S.S. *Royal Princess* was running out of Exmouth three times a month to the Channel Islands, taking eight hours for the trip.

The *Exmouth Journal*, the town's second newspaper, was founded by Mr T. Freeman.

The opening of the dry dock at Lower Yard, Topsham in May attracted merchants and shipowners from Exmouth and elsewhere for the ceremony.

On 25 September 1858 a tremendous storm hit Exmouth. A couple of schooners were driven ashore at Bull Hill, several bathing machines were smashed and the sea wall strewn with wreckage. The whole space in front of the Strand was flooded as were the quays and the lower parts of the town. Across the river, the railway line between Starcross and Dawlish was littered with wreckage and a large bluff on the Warren was swept away.

During the 1840s and '50s the fine houses which had been built on the Parade since 1790 were occupied by fashionable people, one being a

The Swan of the Exe, *designed by Captain G. Peacock and built by Dixon of Exmouth. This vessel's crew was able to catch and cook fish whilst out in the river.*

surgeon, Thomas Eustace. Manchester Quay lay opposite the western end of the Parade and there the Great Tree stood.

There was much emigration during the 1850s, mainly to North America. Advertisements in newspapers and on handbills in 1850 sought passengers at £3 per adult over 14 years of age and £1 per child. Ships sailing from Exmouth were the *Sarah Fleming* and the *Margaret*. There were 53 sailings altogether in 1851, many of the emigrants going first to Canada and thence into the States.

The *Swan of the Exe*, designed by Captain George Peacock, FRGS, was launched in 1860. She was over 17 feet long, 7½ feet in beam and the top of her head was 16 feet above the waterline. She was exactly four times the size of a Bewick Swan. The large cabin had a facility for several persons to sit and fish directly into the water through holes in a table. She soon bore the name *Peacock's Folly*. In the same year the fishing industry expanded; there were 58 small boats involved in crabbing; hooking and drifting with trawlers out of Exmouth.

Smallpox reached Exmouth during 1860. One consequence of this was that Mr Hull of Marpool Hall was fined 2s.6d. for refusing to have his children vaccinated, after the disease had raged in the town for several months.

In 1860, an artillery battery was erected nearer the sea than the coastguard's cottages and just east of them. Two years later three 32-pounders and an 8-inch mortar manned by the Exmouth Volunteer Artillery Company were installed.

Exmouth's first hospital, at 5 Clarence Road, was opened in 1862 and founded by Mrs Hume-Long. It was run entirely at her expense up to the year of her death in 1899. Maud Hospital was then kept open by voluntary contributions, but a decision was eventually made to build a new Cottage Hospital for Exmouth. In May 1862, Prince Arthur landed at Exmouth on his way to visit Exeter.

Beginning in 1862, Richard Redway leased a plot of land from the Rolle estate in order to begin shipbuilding. His sons Edwin and Walter worked in the offices and later Richard's brother Thomas also began to build ships at Camperdown. There were several areas of activity – the shipyard itself, rope- and sail-making, the blacksmith's and fitting shops, block- and spar-making as well as a coal business. A great amount of coastal shipping business took place with the ports of London, Liverpool, Swansea, Middlesbrough, Sunderland, Hull, Grimsby, Cardiff, Milford Haven and others, as well as a prosperous West African trade. At the height of their prosperity, the Redway yards were employing nearly 300 men and built 37 ships. Edwin Redway, who was trained in the technical side of shipbuilding under Scott Russell, became a

A gun emplacement dating from the Second World War.

Member of the Institute of Naval Architects and then the Chief Constructor of a yard in Milford Haven.

Trade in Exmouth had developed considerably and in only one month seven ships arrived which had come from as far afield as New York, Kronstadt, Greece, London, Sweden, Romania and from the River Plate in South America. They brought cargoes of wheat, timber, currants, manure, rye, maize and hides.

In 1863 Exmouth secured confirmation of its order to build a pier and a dock by the end of the sea wall at Ferry Road and work was due to begin in the following year. It was inevitable that Exmouth would one day get its dock; for centuries ships had been beached and built on slipways, and loaded and unloaded on the beach itself as well as repaired there, particularly on the inner and sheltered side of the Point.

Across the river the Earl of Devon claimed the right to control the fisheries in the Bight as Lord of the Manor of Kenton, and he was leasing that right to a new company called the Exe Bight Oyster Fishery and Pier Company. The Pier was to be erected off Cockwood; oysters were to be laid and a dam built across the end of the Greenland Lake on the Warren to protect them.

Withycombe village had a church of its own which was completed in 1864 and dedicated to St John the Evangelist.

The first buildings to appear on Exmouth seafront were Gertrude Terrace.

In 1865 Nancy Perriam, whose house in Tower Street still stands, died at the age of 98. She had accompanied her husband, a sailor, into action with the Royal Navy because of her ability to repair shirts. She had been on active service with HMS *Crescent* and HMS *Orion* and when the ship was in action she was a powder monkey, working in the powder magazine preparing flannel cartridges and filling shells. She served with Admiral Lord Bridport at L'Orient on 23 June

1795; at the Battle of Cape St Vincent under Admiral Sir John Jervis on 14 February 1797; and at the Nile under Admiral Lord Nelson on 1 August 1798. Her brother and 13 other Exmouth men had served in these ships at the same time. On retirement she was awarded a small pension and settled in Exmouth as a highly respectable citizen of the town.

A wooden pier was erected at the Ferry Station on 15 June 1866. In July of that year a fire burnt down some dilapidated thatched tenement houses in Bird's Court, some of which had already been demolished to allow for the development of the new Rolle Street. In fact many of the little old courts and streets disappeared over these years to make way for this fine new road.

The year 1867 proved to be quite an eventful one. On the negative side, bread riots took place in the town and Clapp's Bakery at the foot of Rolle Street was damaged (the first shop to be opened there). Then on 3 August Henry Brutton was drowned off Dawlish Warren. As an Exmothian he was a highly respected businessman who worked in the West of England Insurance Office. On the positive side, however, in April 28,000 oysters were laid in the Bight over an area of 80 acres. By October water was being brought into Exmouth from a new reservoir at Squabmoor, four miles away in the hills to the north-east.

Thus ends the first 30 years of Queen Victoria's reign. Exmouth had become a thriving town, growing and improving with every year. Many vessels were now discharging at Exmouth to avoid the difficult passage upriver, delays on the canal and the expenses of pilots' lighters, towing and the dues of the canal.

Nancy Perriam of Exmouth who served with her husband on Nelson's ship as a seamstress and acted as powder monkey in times of battle.

VICTORIAN EXMOUTH, PART 2 (1867–1901)

The town now possessed one of the largest coast-guard stations on the English Channel coast with a force of 18 men, including the chief officer. Exmouth was also a station for the Royal Naval Reserve, which came up for drills in the area for 28 days each year, mustering about 350 men.

With the completion of all that the Exmouth Dock Company set out to do, the area around the Point changed in character considerably. The Pier became a centre for entertainment and amusement for a number of years. The Pavilion built thereon could seat 500 people and there were concert parties, musical concerts and various other forms of entertainment in season. At times a fair visited and occupied part of the Pier for quite long periods.

The dock, however, had difficulties in attracting a sufficient amount of trade, partly due to the awkward entrance from the river (emphasised by a pilot's guide book published in 1863), so by 1891 the Dock Company had to be financially reconstructed to solve the problem. In 1873 the principal creditor, Richard Turner of Fleet House near Weymouth, petitioned in the Court of Chancery for a winding-up order, but it was refused because 48 shareholders opposed the petition. Turner held the total Debenture Issue of £15,000 having advanced the money to the contractors on the advice of the Dock Company. By then £16,000 had been spent on the works but the gross receipts of the Company were only £600

p.a. The Court found the Dock Company's behaviour most disreputable, but it could not wind it up because it was formed under an Act of 1861, which governed piers and harbours.

The Manager at this time was John Howard and because of the economic pressures on the Company he tried to raise opposition to the proposed Exe Bight Company of the Earl of Devon among the fishermen of Lympstone and Exmouth, and by early 1869 750 people had signed a petition and memorial against the project across the river. The Dock Company endeavoured to battle on, despite all the opposition.

The new dock's completion in that year enabled it to accept ships. There was a depth of 17 feet at high spring tides by the entrance to the docks. There were 58 fishing boats and four trawlers registered in the town, which had become one of the busiest fishing ports on this part of the Devon coast.

In January and February spring gales and high tides combined to devastate the coast. The Warren was seriously breached and sand filled the oyster beds, most of which were destroyed. The new parapet on the sea wall (completed in April) was swept away for several hundred feet north of the Temple Steps. The Bight Company claimed that its pier was not damaged by the gales and so it was open to traffic from the South Devon Railway via the station at Starcross. Furthermore it was not subject to the dock dues. A Mr Garnsworthy made use of the pier, but he was charged by the Dockmaster for mooring a vessel without informing the Harbourmaster. He was convicted, but an appeal to the High Court quashed the sentence.

Ice-cream vendor on the Esplanade, c.1930.

THE LIFEBOAT

Following several shipwrecks in the years preceding 1858, the RNLI established a station at Exmouth and provided a new lifeboat. This was the first since 1814 and the first to be supported by the RNLI. Lady Rolle generously presented both the new lifeboat, a 30-feet vessel called Victoria, *and the new boathouse together with a special launching carriage. The coxswain was Edward George Tupman. The captain was paid £8 a year and the coxswain and eight oarsmen got 10s. for every day call-out and 20s. by night. The cost to Lady Rolle of both boat and boathouse was £350. The town raised another £60 by subscription to buy the lease of the ground on which the boathouse stood. Charles Dickens visited Exmouth in the following year and he mentioned the new lifeboat in a short article in his magazine* All the Year Round.*

The new lifeboat received its first call-out in March 1866 to assist the brig* Congo. *However, it turned out that the lifeboat was not actually required. Similarly, the French lugger St Luc ran into difficulties in a heavy sea off Dawlish in 1867. The lifeboat was launched but the French ship's crew refused to be rescued and so she returned home.*

The first serious call-out of the lifeboat Victoria *was on 5 January 1867 to the ship* Julia, *a brigantine of 148 tons belonging to Mr Jos Norris of Exmouth. However, the* Julia *was lost on the Pole Sands with six lives. The lifeboat was then only a six-oared vessel and she was unable to reach the* Julia, *so the RNLI decided to provide Exmouth with a larger vessel.*

The new lifeboat was also named Victoria *and was 32 feet long, 7 feet 6 inches in beam and 3 feet 4 inches draft, being self-righting and carrying two coxswains and eight hands. She was also donated by Lady Rolle at a cost of £253. She was soon in action when in July the brig* Ranger *of Newcastle was in difficulties off Budleigh Salterton. By the time the lifeboat reached her, the brig had been beached and the crew taken off by rocket apparatus.*

In December 1872 Victoria *was called to the schooner* Flora *of Exeter which was in distress off the Bar; the vessel and her crew of six were saved.*

On 29 March 1878 the lifeboat was called out and taken by a team of horses through the narrow country lanes to Budleigh Salterton where a fishing smack, the Lady of the Lake *from Portsmouth, was in distress. It was finally the Sidmouth lifeboat that saved the crew of three, but she had to go to Exmouth to land them. The* Victoria *was launched off the beach at Budleigh Salterton.*

The French lugger Marie Elisabeth *ran aground on the Pole Sands in 1874. The lifeboat rescued her crew of four.*

In December 1880, the lifeboat Victoria *saved a fishing boat in distress with her crew of four.*

Edward Tupman, coxswain of the lifeboat for about 20 years, retired in 1880. He was succeeded by Edmund Knight, who was coxswain for nearly 17 years, before Henry Squire took over.

In November the Victoria *was launched to rescue the schooner* Lady Elisabeth *but was unable to find her. Suddenly the lifeboat herself was capsized by a huge wave; she righted and the crew got back on board, but it took them over five hours to row back to Exmouth.*

A new lifeboat arrived in February 1884, 34 feet 6 inches long, 7 feet 6 inches beam and self-righting with 10 oars. It was the gift of Mrs Joseph Somes of Annery House in North Devon in memory of her son, who was the MP for Dartmouth. The new boat was named the Joseph Somes *after him. It had its first call-out in October 1889 to attend the fishing boat* Topsy *of Torquay which was in trouble off Langstone Head near Dawlish. She was taken in tow and brought in over the Bar to the docks.*

In July 1867 John Prout, master of the barge *Friendship,* was accused at Woodbury Sessions that 'he did bring up and discharge within the limits of the Dock Company other than at the Docks.' In fact he had gone to the pier owned by the Exe Bight Pier Company. The Dockmaster, H. Pyne, produced a plan showing the limits of the Exmouth Dock Company. John Prout was fined a total of 30s. The Dock Company had won this time.

The face of Exmouth's industry was changing. On 18 October the *Memento,* a fine barque, was launched from Redway's Yard, this being the last of the many vessels built there, as Richard Redway moved to Dartmouth. With the *Silurian,* built by John Holman & Sons at Topsham in 1870, these were the last big sailing ships to be built on the Exe. A list of the ships built by Richard Redway and his brother Thomas at Exmouth appears in the appendix. The younger brother, Thomas, purchased over 20 acres of land from Mr Hull on which he erected extensive brickworks to begin a new industry in the town to meet the demands of the local house-builders. These brickworks were followed by two others, the Exmouth Brick and Tile Company and the Architectural Brick and Tile Works run by H.H. Cooper. (W.R. Redway took over the shipbuilding yard which had previously been owned by his uncle Richard Redway in 1873.)

The opening of the Suez Canal in 1867 gave an immense impetus to the building of steamships, resulting in the closure of yards which had tried to stick to the old 'wooden walls'.

Coal was still being imported; one of the colliers was the *Tabitha* which brought cargoes of coal for the Otterton Tilery owned by the Rolle Estate. It was unloaded on the beach at Ladram Bay and carted up the valley to Otterton. Richard Redway remained the coal merchant for Exmouth until he moved to Dartmouth. In the docks area a stem saw-mill was established by a builder called C. Cowdery.

The late 1860s and early 1870s brought many changes to the town. Some of these included: a Public Dispensary opened at Manchester House on 7 May 1867; the Imperial Hotel which was built on the Esplanade (and an Assembly Room was added to it in 1883); the Trinity Chapel which was re-opened after some renovation work.

In 1870 plans were put before Exmouth Council to enclose the Strand with iron railings and to lay out the interior with turf and ornamental shrubs. The total area of about half an acre was to be completed at the expense of the Hon. Mark Rolle for the benefit of the town and would cover the site of the former Market Place. The enclosure of the Strand Gardens was completed and opened to the public on 6 April 1871. A bath house was built on the Esplanade (now known as the Deer Leap) in the same year. A new Market House was also erected on the site of the Church Hall in 1870.

The company operating the docks was wound up and its assets were acquired by the Devon Dock, Pier and Steamship Company, which also took over the Exmouth and Great Western Ferry Company

Withycombe Mill in 1904, and inset; *the mill wheel, now sited below the Beacon.*

and the Teignmouth and Paignton Piers, Dock and Ironworks, along with the assets of a company running launches in Torbay. Expansion under the new control continued at Exmouth.

Morris's *Directory of Devonshire* for 1870 states that the market days at Exmouth were Tuesdays (corn market day) and Saturdays. Annual fairs were held on 25 April and 28 October. The street listings in this directory show that out of 33 master mariners mentioned, ten lived in Albion Street and eight in Bicton Street. The gentry and private residents were separately listed but they also lived in Albion Street and Bicton Street, revealing that they ranked equally in society with the master mariners. The Exmouth Board School was opened in the Exeter Road in 1877. Mr Henry Mann was the headmaster.

During this period, too, the building of sailing ships ceased because steamships were taking their place. The rapid improvement in the design of steamships and in the building of iron-and-steel-hulled vessels also helped to bring about a decline in the building of even the smaller wooden ships.

A gale destroyed 60 feet of the dock's west wall in 1874. As a result, the sea wall, originally built

EXMOUTH CENSUS

In Exmouth's first Census return (1801) the population of the town was almost 2,000 and the number of individual houses, 406.

The 1851 Census revealed that the population of Exmouth exceeded 5,000.

In 1860 the population had risen to 6,049.

In 1871 the population of the parishes of Littleham and Withycombe, now including the town of Exmouth, had increased to 6,478. The proportion relating to Exmouth alone is estimated to be 5,614.

in 1842, was extended further to form an Esplanade over 3,000 feet long. The steamship *Ossian* hit the dock jetty and cut it into two parts in 1875. The Customs House was destroyed in a violent storm in 1877.

By 1877 Thomas Redway had acquired a fleet of ships, building up a very busy trade with West Africa. The Redway's best-known vessel, *The Belle of the Exe*, was launched in 1878. She was a fast and powerful barquentine 120 feet long and purchased at the end of the year by H.J. Stabb & Co. to be used in the Newfoundland trade. Walter Redway began to trade as a wholesale fish merchant in 1880. The Redways were also shipowners and by this year had nine vessels varying from the little *Cyprus* of 60 tons to the *Rajah of Sarawak*, a barque 122 feet long, built at Bideford in 1850. Richard Redway's old ship-building yard caught fire in 1880, destroying a lot of valuable machinery and a vessel on the stocks was badly burned.

In 1880 G.W.D. Lavis began as a boatbuilder, a business which has continued in Exmouth until the present day.

From 18 January 1881 great gales swept the area and ships in the harbour were badly damaged. It was a very severe winter. After a bad storm, 100 tons of herrings were swept into the bay and it took two special trains to take the thousands of fish to London.

In May 1881 the Duke and Duchess of Edinburgh came to inspect the Coastguard Station and the men's cottages. During the same year, St Saviour's was opened as a Mission Chapel, having been built at a cost of £500.

In 1882 and the following year, improvements were made to the dock because of storm damage, enabling timber ships to enter. New dock gates were fitted when the old ones collapsed because of the weight of water held in the dock.

The *Exmouth Chronicle*, another newspaper in the town, was started in 1882.

Sharp's Timber Yard was opened in 1883 (still going strong at the time of writing) and in the same year a new outfall for the sewerage system was completed at the Maer Rocks, and Captain Upton paid for lights to be erected at the summit of the Beacon and at Trefusis Place on Gun Cliff.

The fishing industry employed 369 men by 1883. Most cargoes coming into the dock were of coal, stone, cement, timber and slate, reflecting the increased building activity in the town. Limestone from Berry Head was delivered to the foreshore for 2s.6d. a ton and the coal from Newcastle was sold for 1s.2d. per cwt. A load of bricks from the Withycombe Brickyard cost 2s.6d.

During this decade much development was being carried out in the town, sponsored in many ways by the Rolle family. What became the Elizabeth Hall was built for the Exmouth Club for the gentlemen of the town and it survived as such until the 1950s. It became an aquarium later. The building now called the Harbour View Café was first erected as a sea-water bath house. It then became the headquarters of a sailing club. The new Public Hall was opened on the Strand (it is now called the Savoy complex). The focus then, as now, was on leisure activities.

The Queen, and the rest of the nation, celebrated her Golden Jubilee in 1887.

View of Imperial Hotel grounds, c.1906.

The docks office with two unidentified dockers.

The Sailors Rest in St Andrew's Road after removal from the original site down by the docks. This larger building was erected in 1895. The foundation stone was laid by the Marquis of Aylesbury, the President was Mr J. Stuart, the architect was Mr Ernest D. Ellis and the builder W.H. Parry. There are a number of other names on the stones either side of the entrance.

The seafront in the early 1900s.

The bottom of Exeter Road but much changed now – note the old lamps on the right.

The clock tower on the Esplanade. This tower was erected to celebrate the Diamond Jubilee of Her Majesty Queen Victoria. The Hon. Mark Rolle provided most of the £350 needed to meet the cost. A foundation stone was laid on 15 September 1897 by Lady Gertrude Rolle. A tablet on the front of the tower is now rather worn but reads: '1897 – Erected by public subscription to Commemorate the 60th year of the reign of our most gracious sovereign QUEEN VICTORIA.'

The Starcross ferry was being operated by Mr Bruton in 1887, who used a converted fishing smack.

In 1888, Messrs Ellett and Matthews, Directors of the Dock Company, organised the first regularly-scheduled pleasure steamers sailing out of both Exmouth and Torquay. They had purchased the iron paddle-steamer, *Prince*, from Cosens of Weymouth, a 61-ton ship built on the Thames in 1852. She was 128 feet long with a 13-foot beam and her new owners gave her an extensive refit before putting her into service. The town crier canvassed and bill-posted the times of the steamer trips and soon she became very well known in the area. A specially-designed 'landing apparatus' enabled the ship to land and pick up her passengers directly from the beaches of the bay, such as Sidmouth, Budleigh Salterton and Seaton.

Also established in this year were the Sailors' Rest, financed by public subscription, and the YMCA in Rolle Street. Whilst superintending the construction of the baths at the Point, Thomas Redway died suddenly at the age of 63. (Richard Redway died at the age of 67 in 1881.) The pool was never completed. By 1890, the Imperial Hotel had stabling and lock-up coachhouses for guests' horses and carriages.

There were by this time large storage sheds around the docks to handle the various imports. Vessels usually left in ballast with sand from the sandbanks in the river. The branch railway to the docks was half a mile long and was linked to the South Western Railway at Exmouth Station. A new iron bridge was fitted to the dock entrance in 1894. The Exe was described as a fair river for salmon and it was also said that the enthusiastic algologist (seaweed collector) could not afford to ignore the claims of Sidmouth and Exmouth, among several other places.

It was extremely cold in the winter of 1890/1. By January 1891 the Exe was frozen over at Topsham and Exeter and several ships were frozen in at the entrance to the canal. The great blizzard of March affected the whole of the South West. A snowdrift at Littleham had to be tunnelled through to relieve the villagers and the heavy falls of snow covered large areas, blocking all movement of transport. The ketch *Sunshine* on her way from London to Exmouth with a cargo of manure was blown a long way off her course, being ultimately towed into Brixham with her mainmast lost but the crew safe. Although the *Sunshine* was saved, there were a number of vessels that were totally wrecked and many lives were lost. The winters of 1893 and 1895 were also very cold.

The Dock Company was once again reformed in 1881, this time being renamed The Devon Dock & Steamship Company. The steamer *Prince*, having made a good return that year, was sold to a London firm and ran out of Lee-on-Solent before being scrapped some six years later. A new paddle-steamer was ordered and delivered the following year. It was named the *Duchess of Devonshire*. She was licensed to carry 687 passengers and was of 221 tons gross, 170 feet long with a 20-foot beam and a draft of 8 feet, and cost £12,000. She became an immediate success. The paddle-steamer *Duke of Devonshire*, slightly larger than the *Duchess*, was ordered from the same builder in 1894. After a successful five years with the *Duchess*, the new *Duke of Devonshire* entered the service from the pier at Exmouth. She was very similar in design, but was 257 tons, 175 feet long, 20 feet at the beam and with an 8-foot draft. Captain Bert Page handled the *Duke* and Captain Tom Helyer the *Duchess*. They operated from any of the ports between Weymouth and Plymouth, and became a familiar sight for many years. The operation of pleasure steamers was suspended in 1914 with the coming of the First World War. Meanwhile, the Starcross ferry boat *Melita* was built especially for her duties in 1894.

Wilson's boatyard was opened in 1893 for boat-building and as a timber merchant. Exmouth was now importing more timber than Exeter.

In December 1893 the schooner *Conquest* of Padstow was stranded on the Pole Sands but refloated on the next tide and was taken into harbour.

The Manor House, dating from the seventeenth century and standing below the Beacon cliff, was demolished in 1894. Its grounds, the Manor Gardens, came into the ownership of the Exmouth Council around 1908 and a bandstand was then erected there.

In 1895 the marshland fronting the Exeter Road into the town was reclaimed to create the area on which the houses now known as the 'Colony' were built. A total of 50 acres was reclaimed in this way and building was not long in starting. The Wesleyan Church in Tower Street was built at a cost of £8,000 during the same year.

Sprague's Beach Hotel in Ferry Road was burnt down and Alston terrace was built on the site.

In 1896 the new church of St Andrew's was consecrated in the road of that name which ran parallel to Victoria Road. Before that, the services were held in a large tin hut known to all as the 'Tin Tabernacle'. It was removed to the docks and used as a warehouse. The present Beach Hotel was built on the site of a coal dump. That end of Victoria Road was also built on a soft dumping material and was naturally difficult to cross in winter when it was a sea of mud. The new All Saints Church built in Exeter Road was consecrated in 1898, while in 1900 the Baptist Church in Victoria Road was built for the members who had first met together in 1891.

KELLY'S DIRECTORY, 1889

Master Mariners:	*Charles Breading, George Gray, G.E. Harris, Thomas Hoodless, John Langsford, Robert Norman, Thomas Parker, John St Perriam, George Phillips, George James Phillips, Samuel Richards, Josiah Soloman, Thomas Stokes, Henry Tupman, George Weeks and Christopher Hugh Young.*
Chief engineers:	*John Cooper and Thomas Richards.*
Marine engineer:	*Theophilus J. Brend.*
Boat builders:	*William Bricknell, Thomas Dixon & Sons, John Hook and George Lavis.*
Sailmakers:	*John Thomas Horn, Luther Martin Knight.*
Fishermen:	*Edwin Bridle, George Hawkins, Robert Pym, Thomas Slocombe and Thomas Smith.*
Ships chandlers:	*Ellett and Matthews.*
Marine store dealers:	*Chas. Gosling.*
Fish merchants:	*Samuel Horn, Warwick R.R. Redway, Thomas G.N. Sapter.*
Pilots:	*George Parnell, John Perriam, William Henry Stockman.*
Timber merchants:	*R.W. and F.C. Sharp.*
Ferry boat owner:	*John Carder.*
Customs officer:	*James Pym.*

The increased number of place names in the town, where most of these people lived, reflects the growth of Exmouth in the nineteenth century:

Albion Terrace, 1; Albion Street, 1; Beach, 2; Beacon, 2; Bicton Street, 2; Brunswick Square, 1; Clinton Square, 4; Ferry Road, 2; Gertrude Terrace, 1; Hamilton Terrace, 1; High Street, 1; Johnson Place, 1; Montpelier Road, 4; New Street, 1; The Point, 7; Queen Street, 1; Raleigh Terrace, 4; Strand, 1; Trinity Square, 2; Trinity Terrace, 3; Union Street, 1; Victoria Street, 1.

To celebrate the Diamond Jubilee of Queen Victoria's reign, the Clock Tower was erected on the Esplanade where the Queen's Drive was also constructed as an extension. At first it was just a footpath 14 feet wide extending over the sand dunes to Maer Road. In honour of the Jubilee, the *Duchess of Devonshire* attended the Naval Review at Spithead on 26 June 1897.

In March 1898 the Devon Steamship Company was reconstituted, the new company taking over all the assets of the old at Exmouth, Teignmouth and Paignton with the pleasure launches in Torbay. The takeover included the iron works called Exmouth Foundry, which cast lamp standards, two of which are still standing as far afield as the town of Glastonbury. The directors of the new company were G. Ellett, A.L. Darke, Captain Luke and Captain Davey, the last named having been the Master of the *Duchess*. Alfred Augustus Carter, Chairman of Exmouth UDC, a dentist, and an accountant amongst other things, founded the Carter Steamship Company in Exmouth in 1899.

The total in the Ship Register of the Port of Exeter for the period 1855–99 was 218 ships. Doust House on Mona's Island which belonged to Exeter and where the port dues were collected in previous centuries was finally pulled down in 1899.

Following the actions in other local places, a Co-operative Society was formed in Exmouth.

By 1900, the rooms at No. 1A, The Beacon were being used by the priests of St Andrew's Church as a Boys' Club and it continued to be so used until 1914 when the membership was about 250.

Queen Victoria died on 22 January 1901. Although she had not been well for some time, her death came as a shock to all her people, since she had ruled for so long (even though she had been in virtual retirement for her latter years). King Edward VII came to the throne at the age of 60.

The battleship *Exmouth* was launched to act as the flagship to several successive Rear-Admirals. It became a gunnery training ship and remained in service until 1919.

The Exmouth Water Company which had been established in 1864, was purchased by the District Council of Exmouth in 1901.

So ended the great nineteenth century; expansion and growth of the British Empire was its main theme and Britain literally ruled the world, or as much of it as it believed was important. From purely physical achievements, the nation now moved into a century of technical mastery with the coming of the motor car, the flying machine, radio and telephonic communication.

ENTERTAINMENT IN THE NINETEENTH CENTURY

On this subject it is interesting to read Eric Delderfield's book entitled *Exmouth Yesterdays* with all its references to the days when children made their own entertainment and played their own games. He lists the many activities which occupied their leisure hours – they played on the streets, of course, which served as their playground. There was skipping, running with hoops, spinning tops, marbles in the gutter, hopscotch and chestnuts in season. There was kite-flying and of course there was always the river for fishing.

He also refers to the Carnivals and to the Annual Cart Horse Parade when the horses were beautifully groomed and the brasswork on the harness was polished until it shone. The one-man band lost its popularity to the occasional visiting fairs. Towards the end of the twentieth century tastes changed again; Exmouth currently has two Carnivals (one in the summer, the other in the winter) and the youngsters have turned to television, cinema and other indoor activities.

A problem arose as a result of the number of visitors around the town, especially during the fine summer days, when even the attractions of the beach were not enough. Entertainment was an essential ingredient of a holiday as the years rolled on and the numbers of visitors increased every season. The South Devon coastal resorts were favoured because they were not as commercialised as those of the growing resorts of Blackpool and Southend, so they attracted those visitors who were dedicated to the 'purest of pleasure'. In 1890, the average number of Bank Holiday visitors was 4,000 at Exmouth, compared with 2,000 at Dawlish and Teignmouth and 3,000 at Torquay. The record, however, occurred on August Bank Holiday in 1897 when Exmouth's visitors exceeded 6,000. However, for some time Exmouth had not been the sole resort in East Devon, Sidmouth having attracted several members of the Royal family to stay for long periods.

In the field of travelling entertainment, Barnum and Bailey's 'Greatest Show on Earth' came to Exmouth in 1899 and was followed by Buffalo Bill's Wild West Show, attended by the famous Colonel Cody himself, in a field near the Lympstone Road. The more genteel entertainments of soirées, whist drives, dances and annual balls with regular concerts, still survived and were popular. There was also the Exmouth Town Band, and a Salvation Army Band, which played regularly outside the London Hotel. Slowly, as interest began to develop, there came the Jollity Boys once the Pier Pavilion had been built. In addition, Operatic Societies were formed and played the Gilbert and Sullivan operettas which were becoming popular in the early 1900s. Concerts were given regularly by the Exmouth Entertainments Association.

The population growth as well as the increase in the number of visitors coming almost daily in the holiday season also stressed the need for more forms of sport; sport was always a major interest and clubs were being formed. Swimming in the docks was very popular from 1880 onwards. Swimming clubs, sailing regattas and regular sports days were held in the sea.

The swimming pool on the Esplanade, 1937.

FORMATION OF CLUBS & SOCIETIES

Cricket Club	1860
Swimming & Life-Saving	1885
Football Clubs	1892
Bowls Clubs	1894
Tennis	1881
Golf	1886
Rugby	1888
Archery, Croquet & Swimming Pool	1889
Swimming Pool on the Front	1893
YMCA	1889
Sailors Rest	1889

This is thought to be a photograph of a meeting of the Working Men's Club in Market Street, c.1955.
E.S. Gosling

The YMCA had been meeting from 1889 in the Public Hall on the Strand, but moved to its own building on Victoria Road in 1907–8. Additionally, many of Exmouth's churches were fully established during this period: the Baptist Church (1891), Evangelical Church (1895) and St Andrew's Church (1896).

As early as 1809 there was a well-appointed theatre in Exmouth on the site of what was the Brethren's Rooms. Until his death in 1816, Samuel Fisher was the manager of many theatres in Devon and Cornwall – certainly at Teignmouth and Falmouth as well as places elsewhere, including Exmouth. He is said to have been a brother of a Bishop of Bristol. Edmund Kean, the tragedian, once said 'I gave readings from Milton three times a week at Exmouth.'

The earlier chapters in this book have also referred to many other places of entertainment in Exmouth over the years (most notably public

houses!). On the more serious side, there were fortnightly lectures in the Church Hall by some of the leading lecturers in the country, including Bransby Williams, the cowboy Escott North, the naturalist Oliver Pike, and many others of note.

There was also a choice of rather more sophisticated entertainments for the social elite that began to throng the town from the late-eighteenth century onwards. The Assembly Rooms opened in 1817 for cards, dances and social gatherings, while the theatre performed tableaux. In short, most interests were catered for from the early-nineteenth century.

In about 1870 came the periodic visit of Harry Wright's Theatre, pitched within the market area under canvas. The naphtha flares for all the illumination was supplied locally by Peter Partridge. It began the four-horse carriage procession which led the circus parade of Barnum and Bailey's 'Greatest Show on Earth'.

In 1895 the Myriorama with animated pictures was shown in the Pier Pavilion. Gradually cinemas took over – one even claimed to show over 40 miles of film on a visit of the St Louis Animated Pictures in the Public Hall with the aid of the Gaumont Chronophone.

Exmouth Rifle and Town Band gave concerts, having been revived again in 1898, and selections of music were given in different parts of the town. Then Mr W.B. Havill was the bandmaster.

It is comforting to find that so much of the information about events in the eighteenth and first half of the nineteenth century can be found in the book by the Revd William Webb called *Memorials of Exmouth* published in 1872. For example, he quotes from a newspaper on 23 November 1816:

The favourite watering place [Exmouth] *has never been more favourably attended than this year. The new ballroom* [Ewen's] *attracts rank and fashion twice a week, the elegant little theatre continues to have overflowing audiences and the dinner parties are numerous; in short, nothing can exceed the harmony, sociability and good humour which reign among us.*

It is fitting to end this chapter with the following, written by Sir Walter Raleigh (1552–1618):

Even such is time; that takes in trust
Our youth, our joys, our all we have,
And pays us but with earth and dust;
Who in the dark and silent grave,
When we have wander'd all our ways
Shuts up the story of our days;
But from the earth, this grave, this dust,
My God must raise me up, I trust.

CHAPTER 5

Devon's First Resort

Exmouth's famous seafront.

It seems that Exmouth has always been a venue for visitors over the centuries, whether wanted or unwanted. From the beginning of the Stone Age, the Copper and Bronze Ages, into the Iron Age when the Celts came and settled, all were contributing to the population of East Devon in its villages and small settlements. Not all left evidence of their existence in the area, although evidence of a Roman building of some sophistication was provided by a fairly recently discovered fragment of hypocaust.

Next, according to the *Anglo Saxon Chronicle*, was the coming of the invaders from Wessex under King Ine. They left us with a ferry across the Exe to Starcross from the spot later called Pratteshyde ('Pratt's landing place'), which itself became home to a number of fishermen. Access to the cottages here was by a steep lane now called Long Causeway and into Boarden Barn, Fore Street and Chapel Street. Bretons had landed on the Point and settled there for a while. Then in AD1000 came the Danes or Vikings under King Sweyn. Although this was an era of rape and pillage, these newcomers did not stay. Parish churches had been built well inland to avoid the coastal invaders, so it was the little fishing villages which suffered from these unwanted visitors.

It is not really sufficient to merely list the names of all the visitors found in local records. The town and its inhabitants had to somehow accommodate them all. Hotels and lodging houses were built to take over from the little cottages which had at first tried to receive them, especially when in addition to their families, the more important visitors brought their suites as well. Accommodation may be regarded as being not only a place to lay one's head, but also the provision of entertainment and entertainers, the planning of functions, balls, concerts and parties as well as simple social events. Exmouth rose to the occasion in no small way; the building of those fine houses on the Beacon is a good example.

The story of visitors over the years must take into account these factors. This chapter reveals some of the ways in which many of the visitors were received, looked after and entertained at this, Devon's first resort.

THE TOWN GROWS TO MEET THE VISITORS

Around 1715, the Lord Chief Justice came to Exmouth to bathe in the waters. He afterwards spoke of 'the natural beauty and excellence of climate' which he enjoyed there. This was sufficient to encourage many people of quality to visit the town and its beach. They came mainly to bathe as the Lord Chief Justice had done, but some stayed for a while, lodging in the little cottages with the residents. At first they came mainly from Exeter and other Devonshire towns, most often just for weekend breaks. Gradually, however, the reputation of Exmouth's beaches and beauty spread further afield, mainly through travellers on the Exmouth to Starcross ferry or by the newly started coach services from Exeter to Exmouth.

In 1720 Sir John Colleton (1678–1754) arrived in the town. He was the son of the Sir John Colleton who had been raised in rank in Charles I's Army during the Civil War, at the end of which he had fled to Barbados. He was knighted by Charles II and given an estate in the Carolinas (then a British possession). The son wished to return to England and so he came to Exmouth, bringing with him a large collection of tropical plants and trees. He is credited with the introduction of the magnolia into this country, but he also brought many other plants. These included:

Carolinas Sword Blade Aloe;
Trumpet Tree;
Carolinas Raspberry Tree;
Anemone Tree;
Carolinas Kidney Bean Tree;
Artichoke or Orange Myrtle, the flowers of which are in clusters and of a reddish hue;
Turncap of Carolina matayon, which is red and white;
Mottle-leaved Tulip Tree, which seems to be the only occidental plant;
Serpentine Euphorium, the coat of which resembles the scales of a serpent, but is very much raised.

Sir John purchased the Manor of Rill, a sub-manor of Bradham. The manor house still stands at the bottom of North Street. Before it, on the site of the present library, he established a large garden in which these plants were grown. He was also a large benefactor to the new chapel in Withycombe village (demolished in 1870). He died in 1754 and his grandson inherited the baronetcy. A monument to Sir John was placed in the chapel in Withycombe and an altar piece donated by him was moved to the Church of St John-in-the-Wilderness.

In 1739 a parish doctor was appointed to Littleham and he signed an agreement as follows:

I, Thomas Gouch, do acknowledge to have agreed with the Vestry here this day of May 1739 to look after the People of this Parish of Littleham and Exmouth and supply them with all Fissickes and Shergossy as fully and as often as they or any of them shall require and for so doing I am to receive Three Gennys per yeare and for three Yeares to come from this Date in case of amputation then it must be considered to have another assistant upon the parishes charge.

Given under hand at this Vestry per me,
Thomas Gouch.

Gouch was obviously a visitor to the town who was prepared to accept this offer made by the Church for three years.

In 1750 Dr Richard Pococke visited Exmouth and said that it was largely a fishermen and publicans' place that catered for day trippers. There was a primitive swimming bath at the Maer cut out of the rocks in 1755, which was in regular use.

Then in 1753 Miss Catherine Wrey, the sister of Sir Bouchier Wrey of Tawstock (1714–84) was married in Littleham Church to Sir William Pine, the Clerk of Heavitree in Exeter. From 1758 until 1797 the North Country Sailors public house (now the Heavitree Arms) was frequented by the crews of the colliers bringing coal from Durham and Yorkshire. They were sometimes recorded as having married local girls and taken them back to the North East.

George Zorn had by 1760 staged concerts in Rill Manor House, which had apparently been sold following the death of Sir John Colleton. The Littleham registers show the burial in 1762 of Elizabeth Ford, the daughter of Charles Ford and the granddaughter of Sir Henry Ford of Nutwell and also of the Pollexfen family.

In 1763, the sea bathing off Exmouth was described by one James Burrow as 'in the nature of a Brighthelmstone but of inferior estimation'. However, the number of visitors continued to increase. By 1768 the 'Exmouth Machine' was in operation; a daily coach service that left Southernhay in Exeter at 8a.m. to drive to Exmouth. The cost per passenger was 2s.6d. Two years later a larger vehicle was needed, thus reflecting the rise in popularity that Exmouth and its beach were experiencing.

By 1765 the lodging houses were getting full every year. Exmouth had two Assembly Rooms (Rupert Wood had built a new one as well as a bowling green near the Globe Inn). Exmouth was visited by Sieur Rea, the famous conjuror who used a swarm of bees in his act in 1772. The same year Sarah Morris' Exeter Inn had a fresh assortment of fine wines delivered. A year or two later Exmouth held its first regatta and the visitors demanded entertainment and enjoyment. The

The 1777 foundation stone of Glenorchy Chapel in Exeter Road.

growth of trade generated by regular visitors was evident by this time.

By 1770, ships arrived regularly laden with wines. They had, until this time, been unloaded at the landing place called Prátteshyde. (However, by about 1780 the estuary had become very silted up and so goods were unloaded at Manchester Quay.) In 1771 the Exeter Inn advertised that 'the best wines are laid in for the nobility and gentry'.

In December 1776 Lady Wilhelmina Glenorchy (widow of John Campbell, Viscount Glenorchy, who was son and heir of John, third Earl of Breadalbane, died 1771) came to Exmouth, staying for several days. Following her husband's death, she travelled to the various resorts along the South Coast, and writes of her visit to Exmouth:

My Chaplain preached at different places to crowded auditories, some of whom seemed very impressed. Here we met with much opposition from a neighbouring Justice (Mr Samuel Eyres) who sent a press-gang to the Long Room to disturb the congregation and ordered the Landlord to give no more admission to such preachers on pain of taking away his licence. This made me wish much to have a house licensed in the town, large enough to contain the people who were willing to hear.

At this time Exmouth was considered to be a 'very wicked place'. Not surprisingly then, the first Dissenting place of worship in the town was erected by the following year. The foundation stone bearing the date 1777 may still be seen on the corner of the Glenorchy Chapel in the Exeter Road. The first sermon was preached there by Revd Sir Henry Trelawney, Bart., who later became a Prebendary of Exeter Cathedral.

In 1779 John Festing, the brother of Michael Christian Festing of London, a member of a very talented musical family, was responsible for many compositions and for the founding of the Royal Society of Musicians. He came to Exmouth that year, but the reason for his visit is unfortunately not known.

While England was at war with the Dutch, Exmouth and other ports along the Devon coast were being visited by Dutch warships. In 1782, many people of the town were drawn to the cliffs at Orcombe to witness a fight between an English ship and a Dutch ship. It ended with the beaten Dutch ship being towed into the estuary as a prize. Those Dutchmen killed in the battle were buried in the sands of the Warren, while the body of the one Englishman killed was buried in Littleham cemetery. For a long time afterwards the Warren was looked upon as being visited by ghosts; no doubt involuntary visitors to Exmouth.

A gentleman's magazine published in July 1783 included an ode addressed to the bathing machines on Exmouth Beach. The second and third verses run as follows:

... Far from the ignoble tribe, I silent hail
Th'amphibious buildings of this sea-close vale,
Temple of health, which graces Exmouth's shore,
Sole sovereigns of these wide watery fields:
To whom the sea her daily tribute yields
Of ciral shells and wild fantastic ore.
Your priestesses each early morn
Salute the fragrant wine
While in your sacred robes of snow
Fair nymphs their limbs entwine,
And beauty from your portals wide
Re-ushers more divine...

An even earlier quote, taken from *The Compleat Angler* by Isaak Walton (1653), reveals:

Look to your health, and if you have it,
Praise God and value it next to a good
Conscience for health is the second blessing
That we mortals are capable of
A blessing that money cannot buy.

VISITORS OF EMINENCE

Charles Baring was a member of the important Baring family of bankers and was descended from Johann Baring who settled near Exeter. His son, also called Charles, married Margaret Gould at St Leonard's Church in Exeter in 1767 and very soon became known as 'of Courtlands'. This referred to a large estate at the north-west corner of Exmouth in the parish of Withycombe Raleigh. In 1790 he lived on Chapel Hill, now called Baring Place. From the heights of Courtlands there is a view which Dr Richard Pococke described:

... which with the fine country to be seen on the other side, is where persons of condition have come to live – the place which they are improving by a grand walk to the river.

Lord Nelson.

Captain Horatio Nelson met and married Frances (Fanny) Nesbit, a widow, in the West Indies in 1787. Less than a year later he wrote to a friend in April 1788, saying '... we are going to Exmouth on a visit for a month.' As a result of that visit, Nelson's health was much improved, for in May 1788 he wrote to the same friend saying 'My health is much got up again, after the doctors telling me they could do nothing for me, Dame Nature never has failed curing me.' The couple returned to Exmouth in the following November, staying then at Brontë House in Lympstone. Nelson was promoted to Rear-Admiral on 20 February 1797. Some time afterwards he met Lord and Lady Hamilton and it was his association with Lady Hamilton, which led to her bearing his daughter in January 1801, and in turn led to his separation from Lady Nelson. He nevertheless gave her a generous allowance, and she settled at their London address.

The year 1788 was when the celebrated Mrs Piozzi (depicted as Mrs Thrale in Boswell's *Life of Johnson*) came to reside in Exmouth. She became so favourably impressed with the climate of the area that in her *Prologue*, written that year for the Exmouth Theatre, as it was then known, she claimed:

... By many a wave, by many a tempest toss,
Our Shipwreck's hopes are cast on Devon's coast,
Where the soft season swells the ripening grain
And verdure brightens with refreshing rain,
Where lightnings never glare, nor thunders roar,
And chilling blasts forget their freezing power.

Some 32 years later, after retaining a very vivid memory of another hot summer spent at Exmouth, she wrote to Sir James Fellowes in 1820 from the Royal Crescent, Bath.

Gerard Gustavus Ducarrel was one of the principal gentry who by the year 1790 had arrived and settled in Exmouth. He had become a church-warden of the church at Littleham by 1796. Initially, he lived in the Manor House on Chapel Hill, which gave its name to the Manor Gardens.

Left: *The old cedar in the Manor gardens.*

Below: *Looking along the houses to the Beacon today.*

His son Philip built a house opposite for his mother, a house which became the business premises of Richard Webber & Sons, and today is known as Tuckers. The family continued to live in the town well into the next century.

John Staples was the builder of the New Square in the Strand and in 1791, under the sponsorship of Lord Rolle, he began to erect large houses on Beacon Hill; the first six were completed by 1795 ready for occupation by the gentry. At the top of the Beacon a Posting House was built, now known as the Beacon Hotel. The Rolle family were beginning to develop the town.

The accent on sea bathing for the sake of one's health had gone a step further when doctors began to advise the drinking of it as well. A diet of a quart a day was recommended, prior to the recital of this little rhyme:

Hail! Hospitable Wood: to thee I owe
Whate'er of Exmouth's beauteous scenes I know
In this salubrious draught thy Health I wish
May'st thee in life ne'er want health, cash nor fish!

(Wood was the builder of the new Assembly Rooms in 1790.) Another recommendation of Exmouth for recovery came from King George III's physician, Dr Jebb, who proclaimed that the pureness of Exmouth's air was above that of the South of France.

In 1790 the principal gentry resident in Exmouth included Charles Baring, Gerard Gustavus Ducarrel, Samuel Eyre and Edward Iliff. Mr Iliff lived in Sacheverell Hall, which stood on a site behind what is now Louisa Terrace. Two years later the population of the town was about 1,900, with about 400 houses. It seems that many families came to pass their winter in this pleasant place.

Admiral Sir Richard John Strachan (1760–1828) had joined the Navy in the East Indies in 1772, serving with Admiral Hotham and Admiral Howe, as well as under other commands. Before gaining his promotions, he returned to Exmouth in 1793. He finally rose to the rank of Admiral in 1823.

In December 1794, Trewman's *Flying Post*, published in Exeter, reported that in Exmouth the place was full of company: 'Earl Abergavenny and his band of music play every day twice in the New Square as well as at balls and assemblies in the season.' The Earl was also in Exmouth as the Lt Colonel of the Monmouthshire Militia, in order to revive the Exmouth Voluntary Infantry who had assembled in Shepherd's Walk. From there they marched to New Square to review their new Colours being presented by the Ladies of Exmouth. Among their numbers were Ladies Abergavenny, Haye, Campbell and Mallett, and the Hon. Mrs Hide, Mrs Montgomery, Mrs Chanter, the Misses Baring, two Miss Elliotts, Miss Williams, Mrs Ducarrel, Mrs Megral, Miss Acland and Miss Guvinian. They had all assembled at the ballroom of the Globe Hotel.

A la Ronde. The first design after the thatched roof was removed – its most decorative look.

Point in View, built to support A la Ronde in 1905.

The next year, 1795, appears to have been quite a year for visitors. Evidence for this comes from a number of visiting cards that were found in a house being demolished. Most of them were for tea and there was even one from the landlord of the Globe informing the two Lady Butlers who had lived there that a ball was to be held on 21 December. That Exmouth was in fact extremely busy in this year was also confirmed by a report in Trewman's *Flying Post* of 20 August which stated:

… Exmouth fills fast with the most fashionable and respectable families. The Theatre opens three nights a week and balls are held every fortnight. The first of them was held on Monday last August 17th at Mr Pomeroy's Globe Inn where nothing could excel the fashion and beauty which were assembled.

The newspaper was apparently paying close attention to those who were arriving in Exmouth, for more entries relating to them appear often over the years. In April 1798, for example, the house that had been occupied by Lt General Bland was to be sold; in June of that year Hugo Mair, a London merchant, was married at Withycombe to Miss Mary Baring, the daughter of Charles Baring of the famous banking family; in July, Major General Simcoe reviewed the local Company of Volunteers on the Point; and in October Mr Laud Carrington, surgeon of HM Brig *Mentor*, married Mrs Elizabeth Thomas, a widow.

It is probably true that the war with Napoleon in Europe was a contributory factor to the increase of visitors to Exmouth that started at the end of the eighteenth century. Indeed, many failed to go on the Grand Tour of Italy, Spain, Germany and Austria. In fact, the reverse happened; some of the residents abroad returned to England. Jane Parminter, who had spent many years living in Portugal and touring Europe, came to Exmouth in 1795 with her cousin, Miss Mary Parminter, whom she had adopted. They aimed to settle in the area and so bought a piece of land on the outskirts of the town in a high position overlooking the bay. There they built an unusual house of an octagonal shape and called it A la Ronde. The design was based on the Church of San Vitale in Ravenna. It was completed by 1799 and attracted much attention. The two ladies then spent many years decorating the interior with shells and feathers. They went on to build for themselves a small chapel with houses for the servants and the priest. It was called Point in View and is now a National Trust property.

On 9 October 1799 Mrs Young died at the age of 59. She was the wife of Owen Young Esq. of the County of Rosecannon in Ireland, and the sister of Sir Anthony Brabazon, Bart. On 20 June of that year Samuel Cave, MD, FRS, physician to the Army and to the Sheffield General Infirmary, married Mrs

Theodosia Lucy Williams, daughter of the late Sir James Barrington of Penponds, Abergavenny.

As the eighteenth century drew to a close there was an announcement in the *Exeter Flying Post* that a mistress of one of the Exmouth bathing machines had died; it appears that these attendant ladies had achieved some degree of notoriety.

There is a fine description of the scenic beauty of Exmouth's town and surrounding area by a Marion Densford of Tiverton, who wrote:

> *... Exmouth is one of the most frequented watering places on the Devonshire coast; it is irregularly built in groups of houses, some of which are good modern buildings, erected of late years chiefly by the inhabitants of Exeter, several of whom have their summer residences there. Many elegant and convenient houses have been built also to provide lodgings for the numerous families that yearly visit this place; there are some pleasant walks shaded by high trees, in what is called the Square, a large open place in the centre between the scattered groups of buildings.*
>
> *Tho' the walks to the river and sea shore, over the loose sand are troublesome to invalids, those in the cliffs are highly pleasant and salutary and easy of access; they afford an extensive sea-prospect – much of the south coast of Devon – the course of the river with its variegated beauty and the amusing view of the passing vessels of trade – Powderham and its Belvedere – the village of Starcross and distant view of Halsdown Hills on the opposite side of the river, exhibit grand, interesting and diversified pictures of nature and art beautifully combined. We find nothing of Exmouth in antiquity, but of its being a small fishing town composed of mariners' and fishermen's dwellings, which are now chiefly confined to one or two narrow streets on the side of the hill, where the females are generally employed in the manufacture of lace.*

A drawing of the lady dippers who cared for the lady bathers.

NINETEENTH-CENTURY EXMOUTH

The start of this century brought many changes, as will be seen. The first arrival in 1800 was the Rt Hon. John Lord Teignmouth with his wife, Lady Elizabeth. He had been the Governor General of India and had retired to Exmouth to write his memoirs. His brother, the Revd Thomas Shore, was the Vicar of Otterton who came to Littleham in 1801 to baptise their son. He later joined the Army as a chaplain.

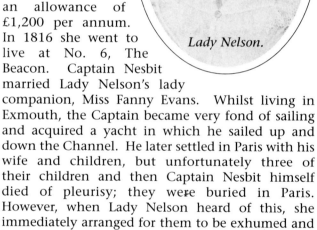

Lady Nelson.

In 1807 Lady Nelson, who had quarrelled with her husband after the Lady Hamilton affair and separated, came with her son by her first husband, Captain Joseph Nesbit, to stay in Exmouth. At that time she received an allowance of £1,200 per annum. In 1816 she went to live at No. 6, The Beacon. Captain Nesbit married Lady Nelson's lady companion, Miss Fanny Evans. Whilst living in Exmouth, the Captain became very fond of sailing and acquired a yacht in which he sailed up and down the Channel. He later settled in Paris with his wife and children, but unfortunately three of their children and then Captain Nesbit himself died of pleurisy; they were buried in Paris. However, when Lady Nelson heard of this, she immediately arranged for them to be exhumed and brought to Exmouth for re-burial here. It was late at night when the ship arrived and so the coffins were temporarily placed in Cats Castle, a building unoccupied at the time. This event earned it the unfortunate name of Corpse Castle. The bodies were interred the next day in Littleham Churchyard.

Lady Nelson en-joyed many of the social activities of the town, even more so after moving to The Beacon from Brontë House in Lympstone. Her friendship with Lady Byron, who lived at No. 19, was

Nelson House on the Beacon.

renewed and on the grass forecourts to these residences there strolled all the titled people: Admirals, Generals and notables of all kinds. The Globe Hotel had gained in reputation because of the balls which were regularly held there, even though there were other venues equally as popular. Lady Nelson herself favoured the London Hotel, a modern building at the foot of Albion Street.

Exmouth was also favoured in 1803 when the Duke of York (he who marched 10,000 men to the top of the hill and then marched them down again) came to the town. His mistress, Mary Anne Clarke, came with him and lived at a 'grace and favour' house – Manchester House, which had been built in 1795. It stood on the waterfront of the river and had its own little quay which was used for a while by the Exmouth to Starcross ferry. Whilst living there, Mary Anne joined in many of the social activities locally. Many years later, a lady writing about the life in Exmouth of that time, under the nom-de-plume of 'Cousin Alice', said that Mary Anne made a considerable stir in St Stephen's Chapel and:

... many a walk we had on the Warren together and many a hearty laugh (for her drollery was irresistible) and I enjoyed at her hearty repartee. She was pretty but her face lacked expression and altogether not unlike the Mrs Jane Wellesley; fair complexioned, with a lively laughing eye... I shortly learned the truth from Lady Nelson.

As a result of the Duke's arrival in the town, a local hostelry changed its name from that of the Great Tree to the York Hotel. The establishment retains that name today. Mary Anne was tried in 1809 for libel and for acting as a broker in obtaining appointments to Government offices through her friendship with the Duke. She later moved to Paris.

Also at the beginning of the century, an interesting marriage took place on Sunday 11 March 1801, when at Exmouth Chapel W. Baring Gould Esq. of Lew Trenchard wed Miss Sabine, the daughter of Joseph Sabine Esq. Their son was the Revd Sabine Baring Gould whose name connected three families: the Barings, the big banking family; the Goulds of Lew Trenchard; and the Sabines. Joseph Sabine (1770–1837) was a lawyer who became Inspector General of Assessed Taxes until 1835, one of the original Fellows of the Linnaean Society in 1798 and a prominent writer on horticulture.

Many visitors came to the town in July 1801. They came to see Viscount Courtenay from Powderham Castle give prizes for a sailing race from the castle to Exmouth and back again.

In May 1803 the conjuror, Mr Moon, purchased part of the West Down estate in Littleham parish, an area of about 100 acres mainly of pasture on which he was prepared to graze young cattle for the season. For this he needed several farm labourers and he also sought 'a clever young man as coachman,' 'perhaps he can also play the violin,' Moon noted. 'The greatest encouragement will be given to him.'

The Rt Hon. the Earl of Orrery and Osfory came to Exmouth to be married to Miss Price Clarke on 17 March 1805. She was the only surviving daughter of and sole heiress to the late Godfrey Clarke Esq. of Sutton Hall in the county of Derby. The service was by special licence and conducted by the Revd John Lombard.

In the following year, on 25 April 1806, Her Royal Highness the Princess of Wales paid a visit to 'that salubrious watering place, Exmouth'. She was brightly pleased with the extensive sea and land prospect from Beacon Hill, as well as the delightful scenery on the banks of the Exe.

Writing of his time in Exmouth in the years 1807–8, George Prynne Esq., MA, Fellow of Trinity College, Cambridge, Professor of Political Economy in the University and MP for the Borough, claimed:

I passed the winter at Exmouth – where there were above twenty other young valetudinarians at Exmouth besides myself – I then formed a friendship with Hudson Gurney, now in his ninetieth year, and Joshua Spencer, who was the elder brother of General Sir Brent Spencer (1760–1828). He introduced me to his sister, Mrs Drewe of the Grange, Devon. Joshua was an Irish landowner and afterwards MP for an Irish borough. Having crossed the Rubicon I was admitted to the exclusive excellent society of Exmouth. I became a member of the Whist Club and frequented the card parties and dances. We went to them in sedan chairs, an admirable invention for an invalid – returned to London in the beginning of May 1808.

For a very short time in 1808, five French officers were visitors to the town. They were prisoners of war but had escaped from a camp at Moreton and in attempting to sail back to France they grounded on the Bar at Exmouth and were caught. They were brought back into custody by the pilots of Exmouth – which made them involuntary visitors! Perhaps they had not seen the advertisement in Trewman's *Flying Post* on 14 September 1809: 'Lodging houses to be let unfurnished, calculated for a genteel family commanding a delightful view of the Exe.' In the next few issues of that paper there were several cottages advertised to let through the winter from October onwards. Each year, too, game certificates were granted to several visitors who no doubt enjoyed the chase up on the Common.

Miss Marianne Starke (1762–1838) was a writer of guide books, having spent her early years in

India and seven years in Italy, and she had written many plays. After a stay in Exeter, she came to Exmouth in January 1832 to attend a public entertainment at Ewen's Rooms. Her exhibition of tableaux of Raphael's sibyls and fresco paintings were described at the time as 'a unique and sublime representation'.

In 1812 Dr Bell arrived in Exmouth to open a National School to operate under his own system with the patronage of Lord and Lady Rolle. The residents subscribed generously to its support, collecting over £40. In the same year Captain John Carpenter (1760–1845), who later became an Admiral, came to live on the Parade where unfortunately his young son fell from the top of the house and was killed. He is mentioned as one of the guests in the poem of 1823 (q.v.). Another visitor in this year was Major-General Desbrisey of the Royal Artillery, and it was his son Charles, aged 11, who was found drowned and picked up by a local boatman. The lad was buried at Lympstone.

In 1813, Mrs Towill was running the Ladies Boarding School and her fee was 40 guineas per pupil per annum; she was taking 12 young ladies at a time. By September of that same year, a Mr John Gifford had arrived in Exmouth and chose to stay at the London Hotel.

It is worth noting here that in 1814 Admiral Sir Edward Pellew (1757–1838) was created Baron Exmouth of Canon Teign. His estate was in the valley of the River Teign. After his expedition to bombard the port of Algiers in North Africa, he was made Viscount Exmouth, but the title came not from the town but from the name of his ship.

Beacon Congregational Church, founded in 1810 by Richard Staples and rebuilt in 1893.

On 13 April 1816, Mrs Starke died at her home in Exmouth aged 81. She was the widow of the late Richard Starke Esq., former Governor of Fort St David and Madras in India. In the same year, George Crabbe, the poet, came to Exmouth, following the death of his wife in 1813. According to a newspaper report '... his favourite bathing place had never been more fashionably attended than that year.'

In 1817, Cliff's End House, which later became the Park Hotel, was put up for sale. The new road opened and the New Rooms began to advertise and hold balls. That held on Friday 17 October had Lady Gifford as the patroness, with W. Hull Esq. and Major Langton as Stewards. Tickets were available from the Library. The New Rooms were also opened on 15 January 1818 for the weekly dance and cards, which were continued every Wednesday until 1 May.

In June of 1818 the Rt Hon. John Leslie, Baron Lord Newark of North Britain, visited Exmouth. He was the lineal descendant of General David Leslie, the first Baron Newark who commanded the Scottish forces under Charles II at the Battle of Worcester. For many years, his Lordship was the Colonel of the Third Regiment of Buffs and

In October 1814 the Ladies Association for the Relief of Institute Orphans in Germany was collecting in the area of Exmouth and the subscribers from the nobility and gentry were as follows:

Lady Rothes: £2.2s.0d.	Mrs Harris: £1.0s.0d.	General Mercer: £1.0s.0d.
Lady Rothes' Servants: 8s.0d.	Her children and servants: 0s.6d.	His servants: £1.0s.0d.
Mrs Parker: £1.0s.0d.	Miss Lampton: £1.1s.0d.	Miss Parminter
Mrs Hobbs: £1.0s.0d.	Lady Mills: £1.1s.0d.	A la Ronde: £1.0s.0d.
Mrs Trorman: £1.1s.0d.	Miss Mills: £1.1s.0d.	Miss T. Fisher: £1.0s.0d.
Mrs and Miss Webber of North Street: £1.5s.0d.		
Lt Col Mills: £1.1s.0d.	Mrs Hosch: £1.1s.0d.	Mr Jackson: £2.2s.0d.
Servants at North St:		
Mr G. Porcher: £1.0s.0d.	Globe Inn: 6s.0d.	Mrs Wyatt: £1.0s.0d.
Miss Warren: 10s.0d.	Mrs Jarvis: £1.0s.0d.	Mr R. Webber: 10s.0d.
Mr Reynolds: £1.1s.0d.	WI: 10s.0d.	Mrs Russell: £5.0s.0d.
Sundry sums: £0.1s.6d.		

Aide-de-Camp to his Majesty. The year 1818 was described as 'having an extra allowance of climate'. One reason for this was that in an orchard at Withycombe an apple tree was seen to be in blossom while some of the apples were strongly set.

In 1819 Edward Iliff, Esq., a well-known coach proprietor who lived in Sacheverell Hall, died at the age of 91. Sacheverell Hall was one of the largest houses in Exmouth and was named after the notorious Dr Sacheverell (1674–1724), a preacher at St Saviour's in Southwark. He delivered two sermons against Dissent, advising the Whig ministry against jeopardising the safety of the Church. He was impeached in the House of Commons, tried in the spring of 1710 and suspended for three years. He was regarded as a martyr and after the suspension period was over he was presented by Queen Anne with the rich living of St Andrew's, Holborn, but he then fell into obscurity. Many houses all over the country were named after him by admirers, but there is no evidence that he ever visited Exmouth. The house was demolished soon after the death of Edward Iliff.

Lady Lyndhurst was the daughter of Charles Brunsdell Esq. and the widow of Lt Col Charles Thomas, formerly of the First Regiment of Foot Guards who was killed at Waterloo. She later married Lord Lyndhurst on 31 March 1819. In this year the Annual Regatta was held in August as before. The newspapers gave reports on the races and the winners and told of the ball held in the evening at the Rooms on the Beacon. Mrs Admiral Carpenter was the Lady Patroness with Sir Digby Forrest, J. Sweetland Esq., Captain Young and Wm. Webb Esq. as the Stewards. Tickets were available at the Rooms: breakfast, 3s.6d. and, for the ball, 5s.0d. However, the ball to be held on 27 January 1820 was cancelled because of the death in Sidmouth of the Duke of Kent.

At the close of the first 20 years of the nineteenth century, it is clear that Exmouth had become extremely popular as a resort for the nobility and the gentry and was being developed to suit them and their tastes. A number of larger houses had been built to suit such visitors and the buildings were often used as hotels as well as lodging houses. Parts of the Esplanade were also developing along similar lines, particularly along the western front. The coming of Lady Nelson in particular to live on the Beacon had immediately attached other members of the gentry, as well as her own friends.

But Exmouth was not the only resort being developed along Devon's south coast; Sidmouth to the east and Dawlish to the west were also growing to attract visitors, and as such began to rival Exmouth.

GROWTH & DEVELOPMENT

It was on 31 January 1821 that Lady Nelson gave a most splendid ball at the London Hotel. All the nobility and gentry of the neighbourhood were invited and supper was included. Among the company one might mention Sir S. and Lady Young, Admiral and Mrs Carpenter, W.T. Hull, Mr T. Simpson, J. Sweetland Esq., and the Misses Roberts of Courtlands, with many other distinguished personages. After supper the health of Lady Nelson with Captain Nisbet and family was drunk with enthusiastic applause and the merry dancing was kept up until the early hours. In order to coincide with the event, Sarah Gifford of the London Hotel had advertised the excellent stabling, lock-up coach-houses, a neat post-chaise and dickey chariot with able horse and careful driver.

During the 1820s the building of new larger and comfortable houses in Exmouth was proceeding apace and Bicton Street and Louisa Terrace were growing. A touch of the classic was apparent when the temples of Theseus and Athena, probably influenced by visitors to the town, were erected on the foreshore. The former still remains in the grounds of the Imperial Hotel.

The company for the new Theatre in Exmouth had arrived in January 1821 from the Channel Islands by a new steamboat service. In the same year, extra coaches were put on from Exeter's New London Inn, and by 1825 there was a coach to Exmouth from Exeter every day, Sundays excepted, at 3.45pm. Among the gentry to arrive were Lord Ellenborough and Lord Gifford, who was a frequent visitor, for his family owned property in the town. His brother Charles lived in what was familiarly known as Brimstone House (which has since been demolished). His Lordship was born in 1779 and educated to the Bar. He was appointed Solicitor General in 1817, Attorney General in 1819 and Lord Chief Justice of the Common Pleas in 1824. This last office, however,

A view of Bicton Street.

he resigned in the same year for the Mastership of the Rolls. He was described as a great lawyer and in 1816 he married Henrietta Maria, the daughter of Revd Edward Drewe of Broadhembury, Devon, who later became the Squire of the Grange. Lord Gifford died suddenly in 1826.

Guests and visitors to Exmouth over this period were obviously well catered for, judging by the contents of a sale near Manchester House on 11 February 1822 which advertised '700 gallons of fine Madeira Port; and Cape wine in pipes and hogsheads; the sale to start at 3 o'clock precisely.'

Bishop Carey of Exeter came on 14 October 1824 to consecrate the new chapel dedicated to the Holy Trinity and built at the expense of Lord Rolle. It was consecrated as a Chapel of Ease to the Parish Church in Littleham village. The Revd John More, Archdeacon of Exeter, preached the sermon to over 3,000 people who had assembled to witness the ceremony. Lord Rolle gave the charity children a meal of roast beef and plum pudding.

The weekly assemblies at Ewen's Rooms on Beacon Hill commenced on Tuesday 22 October 1822 under the patronage of almost all the families in the neighbourhood.

The dancing was kept up with all the spirit and gaiety that youth and beauty could muster. The continuance of these agreeable parties will greatly enhance the pleasure which every visitor derives from the natural beauties and salubrity of this charming place.

The attendance was maintained by the regular appearance of the Countess of Guilford and Mr Justice Holroyd with Lord Howard.

On 31 January 1823 at Ewen's Rooms, there was an Assembly at which many notable people were present:

*When the clock of the chapel struck seven
at night,
The fiddles were tuned and the candles
burned bright;
The floor shewed the labour of mops and
of brooms,
And all things proclaimed it was the night
of the Rooms.
Oh! then came the bustle; 'the gath'ring
of clans,'
Some walked on their feet, some arrived
in sedans
While the grandest and wealthiest made
their approaches
In all the gay splendour of cars and of coaches.*

*Oh! vain it would be to attempt to declare
The names of even half of the quality there,
Oh! vain it would be so I hope it will do
If I only just mention the names of a few.
There was Admiral Carpenter,
Lady and daughters,
With his son (one of those who have sailed
on deep waters),
There was the agreeable, gay Mrs Worth,
And her daughter, the fairest of creatures
on earth,
All brightness and sweetness and beauty
and mirth.
There were Richardsons too with the Guerins
their guests,
There were Williams and Comptons, and
Sweetlands and Wests,
There were Bradshawes (the Lady was drest
very choice),
There were Pagets and Spekes and the whole
race of Boyce;
There were Hulls just returned to sweet
Devonshire's plains;
There were Giffords and Youngs, there were
Kirkbys and Paynes;
There were Ditchers and Norrises – with the
last came
A young lady, but I could not find out her name,
Though her eyes made me ask it, for oh! they
were such
As but seldom are seen, but when seen,
are lov'd much!
There was Shephard, the chief of satirical jokers,
There were Luscombes, Bartholemews, Webbers
and Cokers;
There was grave Dr Ferris (to learning no
stranger)
There were Messrs Burch, Fortescue, Glascott
and Granger;
Mr Houritson, too, and I'm sure 'twould be hard
To omit Mr Pering, and Captain Bomgard.
There were Blacks and Devismes, and, among
those that dress well,
Conspicuous in neatness appeared
Mrs Cresswell,
By her husband attended, and, life of the whole,
Mesdames Oliver, Drew, Spencer, Barnewell
and Molle;
There were Roberts, from Courtlands; from
Nutwell, the Mills,
From Bicton Place, Mr and all the Miss Hills;
Miss Gilbert was there, and to join the gay set,
And add harmony, too, there was Mrs Divett
And her daughter – and last but not leastworthy
remark,
The famed, and the gifted, and the talented
Sparke.*

Also in 1823 the Countess of Guilford with two or three friends came with her husband, Frederick, the Fifth Earl of Guilford (1766–1827). She was a great traveller throughout Europe. He was MP for Banbury in 1792 and 'Comptroller' of Customs for the Port of London in 1794, being elected FRS in the same year. He held several other appointments in later years and the Prince Regent awarded him the KCMG in 1819.

In February 1823 Mrs Agnes Ibbetson died at Exmouth. She was a most remarkable woman; the tombstone in Littleham's churchyard described her as:

... gifted with high talents which have associated her labours with her literary records [and] eminently distinguished by a judicious and unbounded charity. She likewise displayed that unchangeable attachment and undeviating friendship which will ever endear her memory to her family and to her friends.

The Chapel of Holy Trinity mentioned above had long proved of insufficient size to accommodate the many visitors arriving in the town, so Lord Rolle financed the building of the new Holy Trinity Church in the fields behind Beacon Hill with a convenient access behind the Royal Beacon Hotel.

In 1825 an active Lodge of Freemasons appeared in Exmouth. At the same time, there were various sales of properties in the town and the advertisements all appeared to stress the advantages of having stables as well as standings for the carriages. There was news in November of a light coach running from Exeter to Exmouth before 8a.m. each day.

On 30 August 1826 the Bishop of Exeter's health required a change of air, and he came to Exmouth to 'effect that restoration that all classes of society must desire'. He returned to Exeter on 20 September to confirm 475 persons in the Cathedral, but immediately returned to Exmouth!

The Annual Christmas Ball, held in January 1827 with Lady Rolle as Patroness, boasted a very numerous assembly of nobility and gentry, among whom were: Sir J. and Lady Duckworth, Sir Trayton and Lady Drake, Sir Digory Forrest, Mr and Mrs Hortopp, the Misses Hull, Mr and Mrs Divett, Mr and the Misses Buller of Downes, Mr and Mrs

Lord Rolle.

Lady Byron's house on the Beacon.

Buller, Admiral Cumberland and family and the Misses Dacre to name but a few.

In November of that year, the Revenue cutter *Nimble* operating off the Devon coast, captured a smuggling boat with 135 cases of spirits aboard. It was crewed by two Frenchmen and three men from the Devon port of Beer. Surely these visitors were not welcome?

Among the visitors in 1828 were the Marchioness of Bute, and Lady Byron with her daughter Ada (born in 1815) who lodged at No. 10, The Beacon, which was then a boarding house run by Bastins. Lady Byron's marriage to Lord Byron in 1815 (his second wife) was at Seaton in County Durham. They settled in London in March 1815 at Piccadilly Terrace, but there were troubles from the beginning and Lord Byron moved to find his attractions abroad. Lady Byron left London in 1816 and stayed with her father, later travelling the South Coast and staying in Exmouth for a time before finally moving to Brighton.

The new market was opened on 3 January 1828 when a band of music attended and two hogsheads of cider and some penny loaves were given away to welcome customers.

The 'Toute Ensemble' consisting of Mr Kendall's beautiful Temple and the delightful drives and walks through the grounds close to the shore, renders the view from the Beacon the most finished and magnificent which could be well conceived, while the easy access of the sea and specially soft water the climate offers to the valetudinarian, advantages which few situations can offer.

Such was the description advanced for the visitor to choose Exmouth as his holiday venue.

At the end of 1828 it could be said that both Gifford's London Inn and Ewen's Beacon Hotel could boast that during the present and past few seasons, they had accommodated many of the most distinguished families and that the constant daily arrival of visitors spoke well of the comfort and service provided by these establishments.

A Christmas Ball was held at Chapman's Rooms on 8 January 1829 with Lady Rolle as the Lady Patroness. On 14 January, however, Mr Charles Baring died, the younger brother of the late Sir Francis Baring, former head of the banking family. By July of that year, Exmouth was at the height of its attractive and fashionable summer season, with company arriving daily. Lady Nelson occupied a house in Louisa Place, not No. 6, Beacon Hill as she had done on previous occasions. Exmouth proclaimed its advantages of being a good, reasonably priced place with excellent inns and entertainment. On 9 October, Samuel James Hallard, Esq., Admiral of the Blue, died at Exmouth.

The need for caterers to maintain the supply of food and drink to the hotels and their guests was apparent and led to the establishment during 1829 of the growing business of F. Perriam & Son in East India House on the Strand. The business ran for very many years, and its site may still be distinguished on the Strand today. It was reported as supplying General Roche at Trafalgar House, Sir Charles and Lady Kernick of Louisa Terrace, Mrs Hunter also of Louisa Terrace and Mrs Gordon of Miramar, who drove to the shop in a handsome carriage and pair.

At the end of 1829, on 31 December, another Christmas Ball was held at Chapman's Rooms, attracting many of the fashionable people in Exmouth that year. It was more numerously attended than any such preceding event, and in addition to those residing in the town:

> ... the circles of their friends created a brilliant gathering and graced the festive season with the large number of nobility and gentry residing in different parts of the county, signifying their desire to be present. This Christmas event will doubtless be increased by the proposed introduction of the elegant Gallopade en Quadrille arranged by that eminent Professor Mr Thomas Mason who attends by particular desire.

The event was a great success.

By August 1830 there was a big demand for houses and accommodation in the town. A brilliant season was forecast, with families of the first class among those visiting the town, plus an influx of travellers from Europe. The hotels were thronged and the reports in Trewman's *Exeter Flying Post* list the names, many of them familiar from previous years. Some came and went for short periods but returned when the season got into full swing.

Finally for this period a *Pigot's Directory* for 1830 records the visitors on Beacon Hill as including Lt General Charles Boyce, Lt General Broderick, Edward Carpenter Esq., Revd Whitworth Russell, Revd William Cones and Mrs Cresswell. General William Edwards was at 19 Bicton Place and Sir Digory Forrest in Louisa Terrace; other gentry were accommodated in houses nearby. Altogether it was a very busy decade for Exmouth.

This section ends with an ode by Lord Byron, possibly written to Lady Byron who resided in Exmouth at the time.

EXMOUTH STAKES 1866.

No. 1.---PARSONAGE HORSE.
A rather dark steed, possessing good points, his chief weakness lies in the pertinacity with which his friends match him in races to which he is not suited; did they confine him to courses which his early training suits, he would no doubt come out a first class.

No. 2.---LITTLE CHAMPION.
A plucky colt, full of fire and mettle: there is great confidence in this colt, his friends feel certain he is just suited to the work and that he will be a winner.

No. 3.---EXMOUTH HERO.
Rather full of flesh, comes up bouncing, scarcely known so much as his good points entitle him to be.

No. 4.---OLD ENGLISH GENTLEMAN.
A very fine horse, and a good sample of breeding, has won golden opinions at times, but has one bad fault; a tendency to hold his head too high, this renders him liable to a bad fall.

No. 5.---PUFF PASTE.
A description of this horse would be useless—has no chance of winning.

No. 6.---PESTLE AND MORTAR.
A meagre looking horse, it is thought his groom Physics him to much, a very expensive horse to keep; no one thinks that he will win.

WHEN WE TWO PARTED

When we two parted
In silence and tears,
Half broken hearted
To sever the years.
Pale grew thy cheek and cold
Colder thy kiss,
Truly that hour foretold
Sorrow to this.

The dew of the morning
Sunk chill on my brow –
It felt like the warning
Of what I feel now.
Thy vows are all broken,
And light is thy fame,
I hear thy name spoken,
And share in its shame.

They name thee before me,
A knell to mine ear;
A shudder comes o'er me –
Why wert thou so dear?
They know not I knew thee,
Who knew thee too well;
Long, long shall I rue thee,
Too deeply to tell.
In secret we met –
In silence I grieve,
That thy heart could forget,
Thy spirit deceive,
If I should meet thee
After long years,
How should I greet thee?
With silence and tears.

THE 1830s

The name of greatest note whose memory is here preserved is that of Frances Herbert, Viscountess Nelson, Duchess of Brontë, who died in 1831 at her London home, aged 73.

She was brought back to Exmouth and buried in the same grave where her son Joseph Nesbit and four of her grandchildren already lay, at Littleham's cemetery. Queen Victoria gave Lady Nelson away at her marriage to the hero of the Nile and Trafalgar. She was in receipt of an annual amount of £2,000 from the Civil List following the death of her husband at Trafalgar, and this sum reverted to the Crown on her death. Her Ladyship was the daughter of William Herbert Esq. and, at her marriage to her gallant husband in 1787, was the widow of Josiah Nesbit MD, by whom she had several children. She resided in Paris until the memorable conflict there of the 'Three Days', when, in company with her daughter-in-law, she left France for the purpose of making England her permanent home.

On Wednesday 10 August 1831, her Imperial Highness the Grand Duchess Helene, accompanied by Lord and Lady Rolle, crossed from Exmouth to Starcross by the ferry. In the autumn of that year, notice was given that the highway from Lympstone to the Globe Hotel was to be made a turnpike for the collection of tolls.

The usual number of annual Christmas Balls heralded the coming of the New Year 1832, but it passed without any particular event of notice, although in September Lord John Russell arrived to spend the winter with his friend Mr Divett at Bystock. It was in that same month that the steam vessel *Superb* of 400 tons and 120 horse power came from the Isle of Wight to Exmouth before moving on to Torbay and Plymouth on her tour of the South Coast. There was an agent in Exmouth for anyone who wished to sail with her.

In October of the same year the Royal First Devon Yeoman Cavalry assembled at Exmouth under its Colonel, the Rt Hon. Lord Rolle, for its seven days' training and exercises and proved a great attraction. Standards were presented to the Cavalry on Woodbury Common, at Black Hill, followed by a Grand Dinner at the London Inn with a ball at Chapman's, which later became the HQ of the regiment. More than 200 of the fashionable rank of the town were assembled and the band of the regiment attended.

Thursday 16 May 1833 was the official date for the Visitation of the Archdeacon of Exeter. Trewman's *Flying Post* of 25 July 1833 reported:

Exmouth has, we understand, had its share of fashionable visitors during the season. Indeed, the scenery at this delightful watering place alone is such as always must be attractive. The town is very gay and an excellent Band has lately been got up there, to play at stated parties and periods on the Beacon Hill. Among the visitors within these few days, Mr Justice Patterson has been recreating from the fatigue of his judicial duties on the Circuit. The Lord Bishop of the Diocese and his family have taken up their residence in Exmouth. He preached at the new Church in aid of the National School in the town this morning – Sunday 18 August.

The Exmouth Fancy Fair was held in the Temple grounds on 16 October.

Earlier in 1833, Lt General Boye of the Bombay establishment died aged 69; he had served 42 years in India. It was also recorded in January that Lord Lyndhurst had died. He had married the daughter of Charles Brunsdell in March 1819. She was the widow of Lt Col Charles Thomas, formerly of the Regiment of Foot Guards, who had been killed at Waterloo.

In 1834 the country suffered the loss of Mr Justice Holroyd. Although he lived in Berkshire, he had visited Exmouth several times in recent years for the benefit of his health. He had a great reputation as a judge and distinguished himself in his conduct in several important cases in the courts. The year also brought a great number of fashionable people. The Regatta took place on Thursday 25 August, when there was a large assembly to view the aquatic sports. A large number of yachts and boats were on the water, some of them handsomely decorated.

A very unusual visitor arrived in the Bight in October; a Greek felucca. It arrived with a consignment of volonia, which is a species of acorn cob much used in tanning. This vessel was of 300 tons, the sides being pierced for 14 guns. It was very rakish but handsome, and the crew were dressed in national costume.

In December 1835, Ewen's Rooms held the Annual Christmas Ball. It was attended by Turner's Exeter Band, led by Mr Roe who presented many novelties for the occasion. In this year, because of the improvements and the number of houses recently built and still being built, Exmouth increased in size and population. Due to the beauty of its scenery and air, it surpassed other watering places on the Devonshire coast.

In September 1836, the resort was favoured by a visit from the Duke and Duchess of St Albans and a select party dined with Their Graces at Ewen's Rooms. The visitors were very pleased with the Beacon and the beautiful scenery of the town and its district. They were accompanied by the Marchioness of Headford and Lady Mary Taylor.

Above: *New Road, later called Carlton Hill, cut through from the seafront in 1840 to the top of Rolle Road.*

Left: *This building at the top of Bicton Street was at one time Exmouth's Maud Hospital. The old pointed-top door came from the Trinity Chapel (built 1412, demolished in 1820).*

In the following year, Exmouth had the pleasure of receiving Samuel Sebastian Wesley as the organist at the Chapel of the Holy Trinity. He was the son of Samuel Wesley and a Doctor of Music. The accounts for that year show: 'Paid Mr Wesley one year's salary as organist of Exmouth Chapel £10.10s.0d.', but he would not stay. He was the composer of many famous anthems.

In August, Sir T.D. Acland, Bart., arrived at Exmouth from Lisbon with his Lady and family in their splendid yacht *The Lady of St Kilda*.

On Sunday evening 25 February 1838, after strong gales and heavy seas all day, a hurricane arose which caused the spring tide to react with such violence that much damage was done in the town. The sea wall to the new beach bathing houses was completely destroyed and the walk and its platform above the Station House was much damaged. Similarly, much of the Warren was washed away.

The Coronation of Queen Victoria in 1838 was celebrated all over Exmouth. An unprecedented novelty occurred at the Globe Hotel under the patronage of Lady Rolle when the celebrated Hungarian singers, Messrs Lebenstein, Rosen, Calne and Reich gave a grand Morning Concert. They appeared in the national costume of their country and introduced favourite airs from the operas Puritani, Tancredi, Barbiere di Seviglia and

La Dame Blanche. A professor of music presided at the pianoforte.

Between 1830 and 1840, the town of Exmouth grew considerably when several terraces were built as well as new villas in the new roads. A guide to Budleigh Salterton published in the 1840s says of Exmouth:

The town of Exmouth has been from an early period on account of its advantageous situation with regard to Exeter and the surrounding districts, a port of considerable maritime and commercial importance; whilst as a watering place it takes precedence in point of date of all the similar resorts in this part of England. The interior, or old nucleus of the town, has indeed no special attractions for those in search of the picturesque, but the external vicinity is rich in charms that have a power to rivet and delight the most travelled eye. At highwater especially, the prospect is distinguished by a combination of ocean, land and river scenery which we must wander far to find exceeded in variety and splendour. These advantages have judiciously improved by architectural enterprise – the ranges of excellent habitations which line the elevations to the east. [These are described further in the Guide as being 'Ornamental villas'.]

There was, however, a decline in visitors after the end of the Napoleonic Wars, when European holidays and tours were resumed. Exmouth's genteel atmosphere which formerly had been much counted upon, now held less attraction. The numbers arriving were much reduced as other more sheltered resorts, such as Torquay and later Paignton, close neighbours, now became more popular, mainly during the summer. What was Exmouth's future going to hold?

MID 1800s

During the last decade, other Devon resorts had begun to grow as the habit of many people developed to spend time at the seaside. According to the Census reports of 1831 and 1841, Exmouth had grown in population by 1224. Its nearest rival resort was Torquay, which had also grown considerably over the same period. However, Exmouth's population in 1841 was the greater and there was a considerable difference from the little fishing village that it had been at the turn of the century. Possibly the increase was due to the number of visitors who had come to Exmouth and stayed, attracted by the place and by the number of villas that were being built for accommodation.

There were of course other attractions, such as the announcement in July 1840 that a new steam yacht was to operate between Topsham and

Exmouth, making a return trip three times daily and calling at Starcross each trip, which offered a 'great advantage to the public.'

In 1840 the Earl and Countess of Egremont passed the summer at their seat in Devon and the Earl 'went afloat' for the season, his yacht having sailed from Cowes to Exmouth. On 13 August, Ewen's Beacon Hotel announced a Grand Morning Concert to be held on Monday 24 August, the great attraction being the presence of M. Liszt. M. Lavenu had the honour of informing the nobility and gentry that he had succeeded in engaging M. Liszt, who would perform his Grand Galop Chromatique, along with a Grand Duet with Mr Mori. Mlle De Varney, Prima Donna of La Scala, Italian Opera, Paris, and Her Majesty's Theatre, London, sang some of the most popular arias and duets and Miss Louisa Bassino sang some airs and ballads and some most admired compositions. M. Lavenu presided at the piano. The family tickets to admit four cost 21s. and were available, along with single tickets, at Ewen's Beacon Hotel and at Mr Kicks, Exmouth.

In the same year, the death of Comte de Vieme was announced with regret on 31 October. He was one of the French refugees who came over to this country at the time of the French Revolution when the King of France was beheaded in 1793. The Count and Countess had been staying at Bastin's Marine Hotel in Exmouth.

Francis Danby, ARA, came to Exmouth in 1841. He was born in 1793 in Wexford and was a great representative of the historic and poetic school of landscape. He exhibited firstly at the Dublin Academy of Fine Arts in 1812, then came to England in 1820 and contributed to the Royal Academy. In 1823 his reputation was established with his 'Sunset at sea after a storm' which was bought by Sir Thomas Lawrence for 100 guineas, after which he was made an ARA. He travelled extensively, until he arrived in Exmouth. Had he heard of Exmouth's famous sunsets? At first he lived at the top of North Street, until in 1847 he moved to Shell House on the Maer, where he was able to indulge in his hobby of building boats. He died there in 1861 after a short illness and his last painting 'A dewey morning' was completed only days before his death. The present Danby Terrace in the town was named after him.

Among the fashionable visitors at the Beacon Hotel in August 1841 were Lord and Lady Godolphin, Sir John Franks, Captain William Pasley, Lady Montgomery, Revd H. Whitear and family, and several others of some standing. On 2 September the foundation stone of the new sea wall was laid by Mr H. James on behalf of Lord and Lady Rolle, and there was a salute of nine guns. The wall was built to a design by John Smeaton,

the famous nautical engineer. On 8 September there were more arrivals at the Beacon Hotel, including Lady Frances Trail of Park Place, Bath, and James Pattison of London with his family. The Hon. William Moore followed a week later.

On 12 January 1842, Mr Please and John Smeaton arrived at the Royal Beacon Hotel and inspected the work on the sea wall. They declared themselves very pleased with the progress; the wall was due to be completed by midsummer and, it was claimed, when '... this improvement is completed Exmouth will be the most pleasant watering place on the southern coast of Devon.'

In early February a private concert was given at the house of the Prince de Penthieu, to which several of the resident gentlemen and their families were invited. Friends of the Prince were introduced into the Music Room, at the head of which stood the organ, '... a very noble and finely tuned instrument'. Attwater's Quadrille Band attended and Miss Stark from Exeter sang while Mr Jones, the celebrated harpist from Bridgwater, was also present. Sacred music was played during the day, including The Messiah and The Creation. The visitors were delighted and there was warm applause for several of the songs, the best being 'Angels ever bright and fair'. At the event:

Miss Stark did the songs ample justice with sweetness of voice and the harp solos of Mr Jones were also well accepted. The Prince presided at the organ, playing with judgement and beauty. In his solo he was accompanied by the Princess, a very accomplished pianist.

A love of music was springing up in the county. On Sunday evening a public concert was given by Mr Attwater at Ewen's Rooms, with several favourite overtures being played.

In March 1842 the *Flying Post* commented:

Exmouth – this delightful watering place bids fair to become the Brighton of the West of England. The inhabitants have likewise determined on lighting the town with gas, preparations for which will be forthwith commenced. A Water Company has likewise been formed for the purpose of supplying pure water to houses destitute of the same.

In August 1842 Starcross joined with Exmouth for the Regatta and it was very successful; but the rest of the year slipped by without any report about visitors in the town. The sea wall, 1,800 feet long and 22 feet high, was completed with limestone from Babbacombe. Piles 12 feet long had been driven into the beach to secure the foundations, and it contained 70,000 cubic feet of stone, completed at a cost of £20,000, the whole of which

The Cockle Woman.

diversity of pleasant promenades. The cliffs themselves are bedecked with the sylvan luxuriance of nature and a multitude of rare forest and garden shrubs which embellish the terraces and declivities, couch and enjoy the cool and pleasant planetary hour. The walk to Littleham and the row to Starcross and Powderham are alike engaging in their several ramifications. A Band of Music occasionally enlivens the scenery and those who seek the gross but quite as natural sustenance of the body will find the market abundantly stored with fish, poultry, fresh meats and vegetables, etc. Those most careful of ladies, the bathing women, a strange species of amphibia or female Triton of the deep who, when they stuff their flannel petticoats into a capacious pair of trousers for the 'souse', would not put to blush the weird sisters of Macbeth.

On 22 May 1844, the fine schooner *Thames*, one of the London traders from Tuppings Wharf under Captain W. Croft, performed the voyage to Exmouth in 40 hours, from Saturday morning to Sunday evening – a record time.

There were celebrations in Exeter on 1 May when the last section of the Bristol to Exeter Railway was officially opened. This was an event that was to bring many more visitors to Devon. Coaches had been running daily from Exeter to Exmouth for many years and now many more people in the middle classes were linking with the real holidaymakers. Many working-class excursions, too, began to increase the number travelling, although it is likely that many of these just visited Exmouth for the day.

In June there were performances by the African Roseine, who impersonated Othello and Revenge. The entertainments were patronised by Sir George and Lady Collier, Sir Hercules Packenham and Captain Spooner. He went on to Sidmouth the next week.

Bastins Hotel advertised a superb stud of horses and a variety of modern carriages for wedding parties, as well as wagonettes and a drag for excursions. On 1 July 1844 the King of Saxony stayed at the Hotel with the Saxony Minister and others of his suite. It was said that the King was engaged from an early hour making sketches from the window of his drawing-room. He was later rowed to the Saltworks on the Warren. This visit resulted in the name

The Royal Beacon Hotel.

was met by Lord Rolle. Unfortunately he died on 3 April aged 85, but left many enduring memorials of his regard for the town: the plantations and public walks on and below the Beacon, the Chapel of the Holy Trinity and the sea wall to name but a few.

On 11 January 1843, a marriage took place at Littleham Church between Mr Alexander Jameson of Huddersfield in Yorkshire and Eliza, daughter of the late Captain A.E. Spicer of the Twelfth Regiment and Adjutant General of the North Division. In June the S. & S. Equestrian Troop performed at Exmouth. In the following month a letter was printed in the *Flying Post*:

Sir: This delightful watering place, always so noted for the mild temperature of its air and the dryness of its circumjacent soil, is widening its former reputation of being one of the most flourishing retreats from the fervour of the noontide sun and the crowded atmosphere of our cities that can be met within the favour of Devon. Sheltered as its noble villas on the Beacon Heights, at Louisa Terrace and other enticing spots are free from the noxious North and South East winds and the valetudinarian will experience every solace for the feebleness of his pulmonary organs or the treachery of liver. The sands at low tide and the cliffs adjoining afford a

The footpath around Orcombe Point.

of the former Marine Hotel being changed to the Royal Beacon Hotel and advertisements later in the nineteenth century referred to it as Bastin's Royal Beacon Hotel.

On 25 July 1844 at the RFDYC Ball at the Globe Hotel those present included Colonel, Mrs and two Misses Buller, Hon. Lord Courtenay, Lt Col Fulford, Lady and two Misses Lewins, Sir T.B. Duckworth, Bart., T.D. Acland, MP, Captain and Mr T. Garrett and Major Gard.

By 4 December a coach from Exeter to Exmouth was available every day at 8.30a.m. and at 4p.m., awaiting the arrival of the fast trains from London, Oxford, Bath and Bristol. Unfortunately there are no records of any visitors of note coming to Exmouth in the mid 1840s, except the appearance in September 1846 of General Tom Thumb, the internationally famous midget, with his suite, who expected to hold levees in several towns and appeared at a local theatre in Exmouth.

In 1847 it was stated that the steamer *Queen* called off Exmouth every Tuesday on her way to London. The *Senator*, a fine screw steamer under Captain Cavendish, arrived over the Bar on an experimental voyage.

In 1848 about 40 new houses were built in Brunswick Square and a reservoir was also

The sale bill for a house on Mona's Island in 1846.

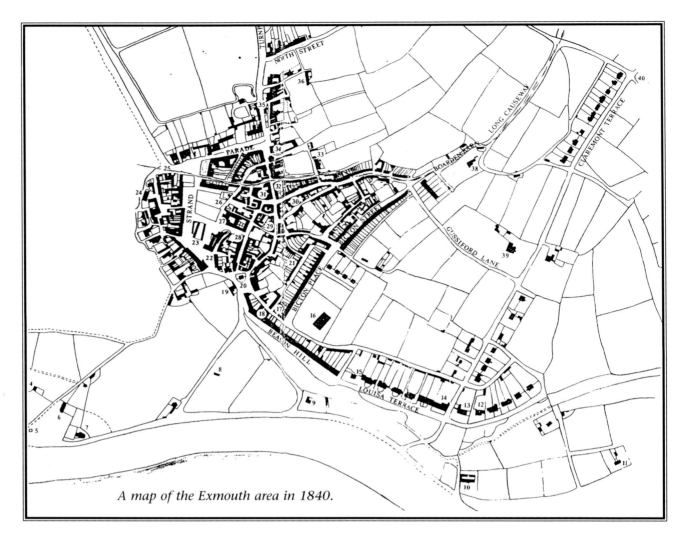

A map of the Exmouth area in 1840.

constructed, to collect the water from the meadows above, which formerly ran to waste down the shoot in North Street and thence into the estuary. Through use of the reservoir, the water supplied many of the houses in the lower part of town.

In February 1849 the sanitary condition of Exmouth was raised at the Woodbury Petty Sessions. A Public Enquiry was held at Bastin's Globe Inn by Thomas Webster Rammell Esq., one of the superintending Inspectors of the General Board of Health. He said that a petition had been presented by the inhabitants of Exmouth in both parishes to the General Board of Health signed by more than ten per cent of the population. It claimed that sewers were badly constructed and highly injurious to the public health. Mr Rammell was going to inspect them and make a report. This comment was passed on 5 July 1849:

... this beautiful marine retreat, in which consider-able improvements have taken place, has received a great accession of fashionable visitors, who are pleased with the general accommodation and facility for sun-bathing and delighted with the magnificent scenery around the town. The town is

in a remarkably healthy state.

The complaints regarding the sewerage system obviously had an effect and the clean-up of the town was successful.

At the end of the first half of the nineteenth century, Trewman's *Flying Post* claimed:

This beautifully situated little seaport town still keeps its position as a place of summer resort for those who are not tied by force of circumstances to large and crowded cities and towns. The first improvements which have of late years been carried out to make this town one of the cleanest and healthiest on the coast has had the desired effect, and has been testified by the number of additional visitors now sojourning here and this with the vigilance of the 'Powers that be', who have brought the lower orders to subjection. The visitor who is fond of a trip on the dark blue sea must acknowledge that our boatmen have made an advance with the times and, pleased with their civility, will more frequently report in their trim little crafts and be borne along upon 'the world of waters'.

LIVING IN STYLE

By 1850 Exmouth had become a very fashionable and well frequented resort. The newest portion of the town was, by this time, composed of well-built houses, supplemented by terraces of good class, some mansions of considerable size and detached villas, pleasantly situated. Many were in the occupation of big and opulent families while numerous furnished houses offered accommodation and invited the visitor 'and seeker of health in a most delightful neighbourhood.' Most of the larger houses in the district were built in the parish of Withycombe; many of them with names and a few of the mansions still survive. During the 1840s as well as the development of 40 houses in Brunswick Square (now renamed as Windsor Square), New Road was cut through from the beach front to the end of Beacon Hill, more recently named as Carlton Hill.

On 17 July 1851, Exmouth invited a cricket team from Lansdown to a match which the Lansdown team won.

On 15 November 1852, Captain Brown of the Ninth Infantry, eldest son of Major General Sir Henry Brown of Bronwylie in Flintshire, was married to Frances Mary Anne, only daughter of Captain Parsons RN and granddaughter of the late F. Adams Esq. of Norton Malreward. The ceremony was conducted by Revd Thomas Rooke at Exmouth. Visitors were busy in Exmouth during the 1850s; there was another marriage on 1 December 1854 at Withycombe Parish Church which was held by Lady Rolle's domestic chaplain. This was the wedding of Theodore Eusebius Galegan Esq., a Madras engineer, and Charlotte Elizabeth, eldest daughter of the late Major A. Foulkes, Madras Artillery.

The Earl and Countess of Devon from Powderham Castle on the opposite side of the river were frequently to be seen enjoying the freedom of the sea breezes at the Beacon and down by the sea wall at the beach for several hours of the day. In the evening on the Beacon, the Band treated the inhabitants as well as the visitors by playing the popular airs of the day.

HRH Prince Alfred visited Exmouth on 8 July 1853. With his suite he had been afloat for some weeks, cruising up the Channel, and visiting Torquay as well as Exmouth. The steam yacht *Black Eagle* brought up just opposite Rodney Steps where the Prince landed at about 5p.m. A pony-chaise drove him along the beach and into the town, no-one realising that he was the Queen's son. He returned at about 6p.m. and re-embarked on the yacht, which immediately put out to sea again. He was the Queen's youngest son and the title of the Duke of Edinburgh was especially created for him. At the time he came to Exmouth he was only nine years old.

In nautical style, the brig HM *Rose*, under Commander Fenwick, arrived at Exmouth to enter boys for the Navy. In July 1855 a vessel arrived from France laden with cider and reports speak favourably of the quality. At around this time, a vessel of 400 tons took emigrants to Australia.

In August 1855 the Regatta and Fête for Archers presented a scene of the liveliest description for two very successful days. Wednesday and Thursday were great gala days for both inhabitants and visitors alike. At the archery contest Mr W. Cole received the visitor's prize.

In 1856 came the death of the Countess de Visme, widow of the Colonel, the Count de Visme of the Coldstream Guards.

In March of the same year a dozen colliers arrived from the North East. More than likely their sailors visited the Inn of that name at the top of Chapel Hill.

On 20 August 1857 at Littleham Church there was another marriage. The service was held by Revd Francis James, DCL, Master of Pembroke College, Oxford and Canon of Gloucester. The marriage was that of the Revd Bartholemew Price, MA, FRS, Fellow and Tutor of Pembroke College, Oxford, and the Sedlerion Professor of Nautical Philosophy, to Ellen, eldest daughter of William Cole-Cole Esq. of Highfield, Exmouth.

The unfortunate death was recorded at Exmouth of Vice-Admiral William Gordon on 3 February 1858. He was aged 74 and was the MP for the County of Aberdeen for over 30 years. Another death occurred in January 1859; that of Daniel Warren Esq. the youngest and last surviving son of Samuel Hayman Warren Esq. of Minehead, the first originator of the Submarine Telegraph. In the same month records reveal the death of Charlotte Sonia, the third and last surviving daughter of the late John Daubeny Esq. of Berkeley Square, Bristol, and sister of the late Lt General Daubeny, CN, Colonel of the Eightieth Foot Regiment. There was, however, a birth recorded in the same month at Exmouth; a girl was born to the wife of Lt Col Howarth of the Military Training Establishment at Bristol.

In September 1859 an Officer of the RNLI visited Exmouth to inspect the new lifeboat. He expressed his entire approval of the excellent order in which he found the boat, its transporting carriage and the boathouse. It was said that there was not a more thoroughly maintained Station than that at Exmouth.

In December 1859, an order from the Secretary of State gave authority for the body of a child buried in the previous August to be exhumed for an inquest to be held at Littleham. The child was the daughter of a Miss Curbert of Cobham who claimed the title of Baroness Maltzell from her first marriage and who came to live at Montpelier Cottage at the end of Bicton Street. The child had died suddenly and the coroner at the time thought an inquiry necessary. The inquest was held at the Globe Hotel on 8 December before R.H. Alexander Esq., the coroner and a jury of 15 respectable tradesmen. In the presence of several representatives it was decided that the death was nothing other than accidental, and a harmless verdict was returned.

In April 1860 there arrived a cargo of French horses belonging to the Hendersons of Exmouth. They were sold at between £25 and £35 each, according to an announcement in the press on 3 April.

On 28 June 1860 was held the marriage of E.A. Seymour Mignon, the third son of the late Mignon Esq. of the Bombay Fusiliers, to Margaret Bridget, second daughter of the late John Charles Campbell, the Commander of the Ninth Foot, and the granddaughter of Richard Daunt Esq. of Lochnar Lowlea, County Cork.

By the end of the 1850s, the new turnpike was facilitating an increase in the number of coach journeys not only around the county but down to Exmouth as well. Obviously, too, the roads into the town were maintained to a higher standard which thus improved Exmouth itself for its visitors.

In 1854 the Trustees of the Exmouth Turnpike Roads had approached sub-contractors, giving them notice that they were ready to consider and receive tenders for the lowering of the hill from the Saddlers Arms in Lympstone up to Courtlands Cross. However, during the 1840s and '50s there had been much activity, and many meetings and discussions concerning proposals for an Exeter, Topsham and Exmouth Railway; proposals that were gaining support from all sections of the community, so much so that work had been started.

By 1860, too, salary earners were usually enjoying two weeks' annual holiday and the trains were beginning to carry them at least to Exeter, which had become affordable for more visitors. The passenger train provided a much more comfortable ride and was in fact a much cheaper form of travel than anything that had gone before.

Elizabeth Jane Brabazon came to Exmouth in the early 1860s, and published her experiences in a book named *Exmouth and its Environs* in 1861. She wrote about her visit in 1860 thus:

At Withycombe, I tasted for the first time the true Devonshire cider, 'home brewed' in a pretty cottage where I had a pleasant rest and learned many small but amazing local particulars. The cider, I said wanted sugar; its vendor said I wanted taste. Withycombe has a Post Office, a few small shops and what they call in London a 'gin palace', very different, however, to the brilliantly lighted gin palaces of the Metropolis. Very different, too, from the picturesque wayside Inn, the Holly Bush, by which the customer passes under a porch of evergreen – as different, my reader, as the Devonshire butter of London, from the pure sweet Devonshire butter of Devon.

In her book she also poses the question:

Where, o'er the beauteous Devon coast
Can anyone yet beauteous boast
And every Summer bring a host
To charming Exmouth.

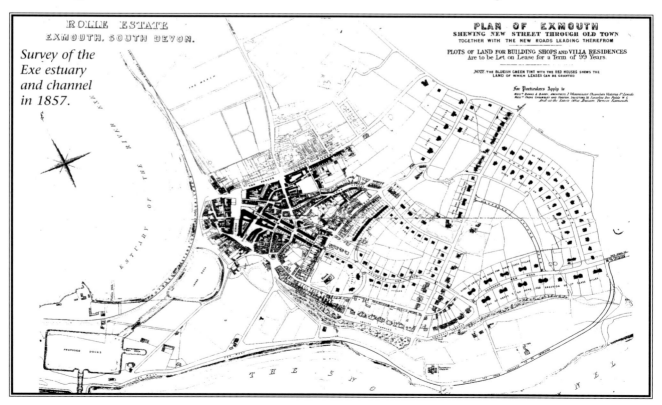

ROLLE ESTATE
EXMOUTH, SOUTH DEVON.

Survey of the Exe estuary and channel in 1857.

PLAN OF EXMOUTH
SHEWING NEW STREET THROUGH OLD TOWN
TOGETHER WITH THE NEW ROADS LEADING THEREFROM

PLOTS OF LAND FOR BUILDING SHOPS AND VILLA RESIDENCES
Are to be Let on Lease for a Term of 99 Years.

BIG TOWN CHANGES

On a Thursday morning in February 1861, the quiet town of Exmouth was shattered by the sudden and unexpected appearance of a Company of Royal Artillery under the command of Captain Ted Croft. From the Topsham Barracks in Exeter came 100 horses and 200 men with four Armstrong guns and ammunition wagons. They entered in complete marching order at noon and halted for several minutes on the Strand where a crowd collected. The troops proceeded over Beacon Hill and the Terraces and down on to the beach where blanks were fired. They left the town after a stay of about one hour.

It was announced on 27 March 1861 that the Exmouth Railway was ready for inspection by the Government Inspector and would open on 1 May that year. The first train was of 11 carriages and took 32 minutes from Exeter to Exmouth (the train was gaily decorated for the occasion) and the directors of the company paraded the streets. A great change in the mode of conveyance for travellers coming to Exmouth was taking place. Now there were to be special trains for all sorts of occasions, including holiday excursions and bathing trips. It certainly improved the method of travel and increased the number of travellers between the two towns, whether day-trippers, weekenders or holiday-makers.

It was soon obvious that expansion was in the minds of those who were making plans for the improvement of the town's mercantile activity. A dock had been discussed to encourage shipping and so, by December 1863, plans were afoot. It was clear that the town both wanted and needed this port. The advantages which Exmouth possessed were great. Nature had provided the area for a dock, and at very little cost it could be made

Hayne's House, 2 The Parade. A sketch of c.1910 – now the Powdermonkey Inn.

suitable for the requirements of an extensive shipping trade. Being brought into direct communication with Exeter by the railway, the goods landed could be despatched in a much more economical manner than previously, and a dock could be built with an entrance in the Channel.

In the early days of 1861 came the death of retired Rear Admiral H.W. Parsons. Shortly after this, on 20 January, Francis Danby, the famous artist, died at Shell House, his home on the Maer, at the age of 68.

In July 1861, a schooner *Albert*, with its master Mr Salt of Fowey, was towed in by the steam tug *Tubal Cain* for a refit, after having been blown on to the shore in front of the York Hotel. At the time the town was full of visitors and lodgings were getting scarce, due no doubt to the increasing use of the new railway.

In the spring of 1862 HRH Prince Arthur had been visiting several of the more interesting places along the coast, particularly in South Devon. He arrived in the Bight off Exmouth on the Royal Yacht *Vivid* on the afternoon of Tuesday 6 May. He went by train on Wednesday morning at 6.50a.m. to Exeter, where he ordered a hamper of Devonshire cider to be sent to Exmouth for the Royal Yacht. In the evening the Royal party returned to Exmouth and was met by a throng of people at the railway station, giving a most enthusiastic demonstration of loyalty.

The increase in the number of visitors since the coming of the railway in the previous year led to a demand for increased accommodation for the public. In addition to the hotels available, Mr Chambers opened a refreshment and boarding house on the Parade. A bed for the night cost 1s., breakfast 1s., dinner with a glass of ale 1s., and tea or supper from 9d. a head.

A Mr George Tupman was soon engaged in drawing up a plan for the Rolle Estate office. This plan not only referred to the dock which had been discussed, but also included another linked dock to be sited further inland. This latter extension was not, however, finally adopted. An Act of Parliament in 1864 enabled the building of a new dock to go ahead with a capital of £60,000. When a new company was formed in 1870, future plans included the purchase of a steamer to be used as a pleasure vessel to entertain Exmouth's visitors. This also required a pier to be built. The acquisition of the steam vessels *Prince*, *Duke* and *Duchess of Devonshire* are mentioned in the previous chapter.

However, much greater plans affecting the town of Exmouth were to be prepared and acted upon. An imposing main street through the town was being envisaged, to be called Rolle Street, which was to continue eastwards as Rolle Road, opening up great vistas of fields to be planned as plots for villas. A new road to the east, previously

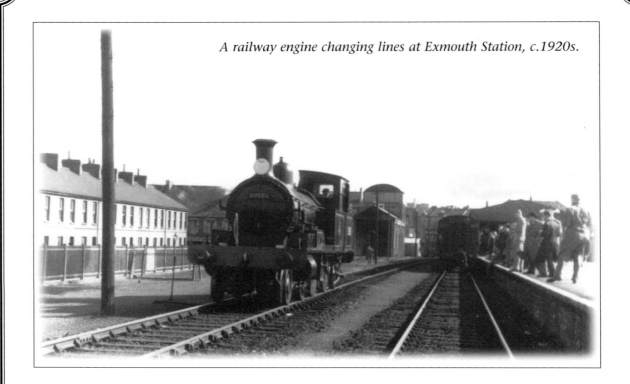

A railway engine changing lines at Exmouth Station, c.1920s.

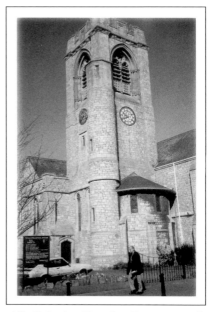

The Tower Street Methodist Church foundation stones were laid in February 1897 and part of the building was ready for use in Whitsun of that year. It was completed by October, the opening service being held on 31 October 1897 by its first Minister, Revd William Keating. The names on the various foundation stones are: H. Avery, F.S. Wilson, W.H. Chapman, Edward Burnell Reeves, J. Ackland, Mrs J.R. Ackland. A booklet to mark the centenary was written by Mr George Pridmore.

All Saint's Church, Exeter Road. Erected on land reclaimed from the estuary in 1812 by Mr W.T. Hull, lord of the manor. The foundation stone was laid on 10 July 1896 by the Bishop of Exeter, Dr Bickeraff. Estimated to take 700 people, it cost £8,000. The tower with its clock was added in 1907.

E.S. Gosling

Carlton Hill, c.1897.

known as Sidmouth Road, would become Salterton Road, with rows of beautiful villas to be erected to the tastes of visitors who came to settle. A new church at Withycombe was also begun and among the guests at the laying of the foundation stone on 21 July 1863 were Lord and Lady Chetwynd with their daughter, General Gamault and his family, Captain Hussey and several priests from churches in the vicinity, all attending despite the bad weather. The stone was laid by Lady Rolle; the architect was Mr Ashworth of Exeter, the builder was Mr Burridge of Exmouth and the site was given by Mr Wood of the Grange.

By August of the same year, Exmouth was full of visitors, more than there had been for many years, including the Lord Chancellor, the Bishop of Adelaide, the Bishop of Lincoln and many others. Even in September it was said that the town had a considerable number of visitors. Can we regard the large number of porpoises observed off the coast and reported on 21 October as visitors as well?

The pier became a centre of entertainment from the early 1860s onwards, being used by pleasure steamers from many of the resorts along the South Coast. At various times it was the home of a fair, a roundabout, a skating rink, a concert hall and even a scooter rink. An early concert party was called the Coronet Entertainers. The entertainment of the visitors took place everywhere; in about 1870 a periodic visit by the Harry Wright Theatre was pitched in the Market Square under a canvas structure. Constable Raikes kept order at a performance of *The Murder of Maria Martin at the Red Barn*, a very popular drama. The stage was lit by naphtha flares.

Returning to the subject of visitors to Exmouth over the years, it was in 1864 that the gunboat *Biter* arrived and landed a new cannon, a 32-pounder, for the use of the Naval Reserve and the Coastguard men. It was placed in the Maer Battery. In September of that year, horse racing took place at Exmouth and the new church at

Withycombe was completed and consecrated in November by the Bishop of Exeter.

In June 1865 a French sloop *Argus* from St Malo attempted to enter the port without a pilot, but was caught on the Pole Sands and again on the Bull Hill sandbank, causing great amusement to the local people. The following month, HM Gunboat *Hind* from Portsmouth arrived, bringing two guns and ammunition for the use of the men of the Royal Naval Reserve who performed their annual training at Exmouth. In the same month, navvies arrived to begin digging out the new dock. There was also the incident of the sailor who dropped into the York Hotel for a meal before catching his train to Portsmouth, but after his departure the publican found that his dog was missing. Hasty action by the police at Salisbury railway station stopped the train and arrested the sailor. He was brought back to Exmouth with the dog, to the delight of the customers of the York, with whom the dog was a great favourite.

There had been the marriage at Littleham Church in June 1865 of Col George de Saumarez of the Indian Army to Louisa D'Arcy, daughter of the Revd Nicholas Walters, MA, Rector of All Saints, Stamford. The wedding was conducted by the Revd Haviland de Saumarez, MA, Rector of St Peter's, Nottingham. James Crackery, writing to the Editor of the *Illustrated Times* said of an event at Exmouth in 1865:

I was strolling along, gazing at the gay scene, and humming – never mind what tune – it directed my steps towards the bathing machines. Judge of my horror when I saw before me the most repulsive form I had ever beheld. The women who wait upon the ladies bathing machines have chosen to assume a costume so bold and repulsive that it is impossible to describe it. I make the attempt. Excuse my agitation – my hand trembles as if I were writing with an aspen. I prefer quills to be minute. A form attired in coarse trousers with something on the head like a cowl approaching. I retreated. By its rounded form and peculiar construction of body, I know it was a female. I concluded it was some mad woman who had put on her husband's clothes by mistake. As I'm a living man she had only a coarse shirt over her shoulders. Alarmed by being chivvied in this manner by the strange female, I fled.

In May 1866 the South Western Railway Company issued a 6d. bathing ticket, which took passengers from Exeter to Exmouth and back. It also offered 1s. excursions, which were available every Saturday, Sunday and Monday.

At Speechley's Beach Hotel, a small family could be accommodated, bringing their own servants, at a very modest cost during the winter months.

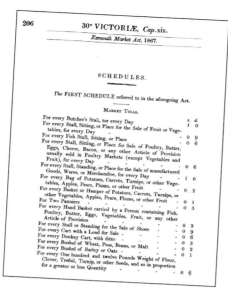

The Market Tolls list of 1867.

This was the only hotel near the sea.

The Trustees of the Rolle Estate made a further announcement in December 1866 to the effect that they intended to erect a new market at Exmouth:

> ... [a] *handsome and commodious structure and in all probability a large Assembly Room or hotel will be built over it, to be an ornament as well as a great utility to the town. The cost will be at least £2,000 with perhaps a fountain or some kind of ornamental structure in the centre.*

Much of this progress in the development of the town and the increase in the number of visitors was due to the train service from Exeter and the cheap excursion fares. The Sunday morning bathing trip was estimated to bring at least 300 visitors each journey!

It should be mentioned that the work of demolition going on during the reconstruction of the town's centre indicated a loss of at least 300 of the old dwellings from the courts and alleys. This included the demolition of the Globe Hotel to make room for the new road, Rolle Street. However, the Imperial Hotel standing in the Temple Fields was built in 1869 and played an important part in the acceptance of the visitors Exmouth was receiving by 1870. Unfortunately in the next century it suffered a disastrous fire and had to be almost completely rebuilt, but it still stands there on the Esplanade as proud as ever.

A crowd of schoolchildren from Crediton held their annual treat in Exmouth in 1869. They played on the beach all day and enjoyed tea and buns to their hearts' content. They all crowded to the station to catch the 9p.m. train home, utterly exhausted!

Thus was set the pattern for the great arrival of countless visitors for the future.

A NEW TOWN

The tremendous changes that began to take place in the 1800s were continuing into the 1870s and gradually creating a new Exmouth, certainly with regard to the new town centre that was arising. There was also a change in the nature of the visitors who came to the town and filled the streets and the seafront.

The new Rolle Street, the docks and most of all the coming of the railway in 1861, had all had a considerable impact on the town. From the top of Carlton Hill (formerly New Street) and going along the road to the east (formerly Budleigh Road), the new map of Exmouth was changing; there were many plots of land destined as sites for mansions or villas on this higher land above Exmouth. Visitors were attracted to the town as they were able to view and choose a site for their new home. This approach to growth succeeded; very soon the builders were busy. Mr and Mrs John Gordon, who were sailing in their yacht towards Maer Bay, were so captivated by the setting that they built themselves a house in which to settle in Exmouth.

The docks were attracting more shipping and the ships brought passengers as well as goods for the town. However, the newest real contributor to the town's visitors and trade was the railway. A train could bring 300 passengers in one journey, and they were coming on day trips as well as on holidays. The business of the coach and horses rapidly diminished, for the train was cheaper and much faster. The types of people coming by train were changing. Many were from the commercial, engineering and professional classes, the salaried section of whom were being granted two weeks' holiday annually. There were certainly fewer from the nobility and gentry who had formerly been the predominant visitors to Exmouth. The realisation that the journey from Exeter and even from distant railway stations took only a comparatively short time attracted people from across the country. More and more houses were built to accommodate them and the population grew.

This increase in visitors by train surprised the hotel and the catering trades. The Exmouth Library kept a list of furnished and unfurnished houses suitable for the needs of genteel families who often brought their own food for the holiday, which in some cases the landlady would cook for them.

The loss of the Globe Hotel during the building of Rolle Street accompanied the loss of many little lanes and courts. As a result many poorer members of the community had to move elsewhere pending the provision of further accommodation. Many went to the outskirts of the town. The Globe Hotel had been a busy centre of the

Paddlers on the beach in 1900.

The chalets on Shelley Beach.

Different types of bathing machines on the beach at Exmouth.

The beach at Sandy Bay.

Exmouth Town Hall, formerly St Bernards House, taken over in 1930.

A £56.5s.0d. share capital certificate for the Devon Dock, Pier and Steamship Company.

Porky Down's shop is still in the Magnolia Centre (formerly Chapel Street), trading in the same building since 1882.

ELECTION.

STATE OF THE POLL.

Stone is "ousted," what a spree,
Benmore could'nt eat his tea ;
"Moder's Ass" said twas'nt he,
　　　O what a lark !

All the morning Stone was there
Seated in the old arm chair,
The poor man looked weighed down with care,
　　But did not say a word.

At length his chum came on the scene,
And scanned the room with an eye so keen ;
Says he " Old Pal " what does it mean ?
　　Why look so very sad ?

" Elephant " looked up in his face,
And felt as though he could embrace,
But whispered, " All my friends are base,
　　They've all deserted me."

Look, what I've done for the Town,
Of public funds spent many a pound,
And now just cast your eyes around,
　　They're laughing up their sleeves.

The wretches! if I had my way
I'd teach them to have naught to say,
Like slaves I'd work them without pay,
　　O for my "Tiger" days!

My poor old Dad, who's dead and gone,
I horsewhipped well at Sal-ter-ton ;
I taught him which was right and wrong,
　　My arm was very strong.

I'd like to serve 'em all the same,
Their haughty spirits I'd soon tame,
To crush the poor, I'm always game,
　　They are not fit to live

My poor dear friend, you must keep cool,
Go home said George, and have some gruel,
Of course I know 'tis very cruel,
　　But what is to be done ?

Election poster from the period 1866–7.

the Great Tree Hotel, renamed the York Hotel after the Duke who brought his mistress to Exmouth in around 1803. Upper Chapel Street became known as High Street, having been rebuilt to provide a wider access to the Beacon. In fact the last quarter of the nineteenth century was the time of greatest activity in the creation of the new Exmouth, especially in the provision of public buildings.

Over the years the number of visitors continued to grow, even into the twentieth century. A place called Sandy Bay was opened to accommodate those visitors who were prepared to simply camp. Tents sprang up on the cliffs above that bay and the beach below became a delight to the children. People still camp in this area, although many now stay in caravans, chalets and bungalows. It is now a big business venture and visitors are brought into town by a regular bus service, where they mix with the town's visitors as they wander around the Strand, go into the indoor market for supplies and generally fill the streets every summer. Exmouth is still a premier holiday resort. Coaches from the home counties and from abroad regularly come to stay in the best hotels on its two miles of seafront. Despite the town's many visitors, each assembly room, each hotel and each public venue for the entertainment of visitors had its own community of local customers, just as the public houses of today have their regulars who form their communities of darts teams, skittles teams and the like. Arthur Sullivan's poem 'Great Haldon' ends with this verse:

> *Where Exe flows forth to meet the sea,*
> *This message hath been granted me*
> *The soul, though fast asleep it lie,*
> *Grows never old, can never die!*

social life of the town, giving the nobility and gentry their balls and assemblies. It was also the terminus for the coach routes from Exeter and Budleigh among other places, and those who stayed chose to move to the London Hotel. To a certain extent the building of the Rolle Hotel covered the loss.

Around the town were various types of private carriages, dog carts, brakes and even sedan chairs readily available, all being under the control of a Mr W. Attwater. He ensured that they were kept in prime condition so that they were always ready for hire to new visitors.

New shops were appearing gradually in the new Rolle Street. At the far end of the Parade was

CHAPTER 6

Ships & Shipbuilding

A new ferry boat, Prince, *built and launched in the Docks.*

The River Exe has a history all of its own and there is little doubt that the use of boats had evolved here long before even the Celts arrived in around 300BC. Before the Romans came to Britain the men of Devon, Cornwall and Brittany were using wooden ships built entirely of oak. Just where the Clyst joins the Exe near Topsham, excavations for the foundations of a railway bridge revealed what was possibly the site of a shipbuilding slipway dating from Roman times.

After AD700 Exmouth was within the Kingdom of Wessex. Alfred the Great is reputed to have built a fleet of warships to his own design, which were twice as long, swifter, steadier and higher than anything that had previously existed. The Bayeux Tapestry includes representations of Saxon ships of this kind in the tenth and eleventh centuries.

In the early-medieval years, the port of Exmouth and others on the South Coast were often asked to provide ships for the king's armies and their expeditions – the Crusades, the wars in Scotland and France – and almost always Exmouth responded. Two of Exmouth's ships of those times were, as previously noted the *Rode Cogg* and the *Cogg Notre Dame*. However, in 1329 both were captured by French pirate ships. By this time, ships were being built on a much bigger scale; in 1363 for example, the *George* (140 tons) of Exmouth belonging to Roger Plente, proved to be too large to discharge at Topsham.

Exmouth must have been building ships at this time (Appendix A names several from the fourteenth century). In 1400 both Exmouth and Lyme Regis were ordered to build one barge each for the king. This is indeed confirmation that Exmouth was able to build seaworthy vessels. The next century or so was a period of evolution in the design of ships. Even before 1520 ships from Exmouth were sailing to Iceland, Greenland and then to Newfoundland, fishing for cod. Is it possible that ships from Devon ports were reaching the New World before Columbus sailed in 1492? By the time of the Spanish Armada in 1588 substantial ocean-going vessels large enough to carry armies of men were being built.

A local man from Withycombe, Richard Whitbourne, was making regular voyages across

Chalets at Shelley Beach with the masts of ships in the docks behind them, c.1900.

A TARPIT FOR SAILS: Mr J. Shapter has tried to save this old pit which was used by the ship-builders for dipping the ship's ropes by nailing this notice to a post on the site:

AN ORIGINAL TARPIT.
THIS BRICK STRUCTURE WAS IN USE
DIPPING ROPES FOR WATERPROOFING IN
SHIPS RIGGING (BEFORE WIRE ROPES) 19th
CENTURY, DEVON. ALSO HERE IS THE
ROPEWALK AND A LIMESTONE WALL
RUNNING BEHIND YOU. LOOK STRAIGHT
AHEAD OF THE TARPIT, THE ROPEWALK IS
EQUAL TO 200 YARDS (CABLE), THAT IS
1/10 OF A NAUTICAL MILE. THE ROPES
WERE MEASURED IN CIRCUMFERENCE FOR
SIZE. ROPES WERE ALL HANDMADE HERE
HENCE "SPINNING A YARN".
FEB. 1996, J. SHAPTER.

Unfortunately this site has since been built upon although an attempt to reproduce a sign has been made.

Cabin Cruiser Manama.

Boat E26 Before We Forget *and men of the Docks.*

the Atlantic in the sixteenth century and his ship, the *Felix*, was probably built in Exmouth. He and other local ships joined Sir Francis Drake's fleet as they came up from Plymouth after the Spanish Fleet in 1588. By 1619 we learn from the Maritime Surveys of Devon and Cornwall that Withycombe parish had two shipwrights, six master mariners and 20 seamen. At that time the neighbouring parish of Woodbury could boast seven ship-wrights, who were probably working at the little port of Lympstone.

It was 1701 before a National Register of Ships was instituted. By then the Port of Exeter included Topsham, Lympstone, Budleigh Salterton, Sidmouth, Beer with Seaton, Starcross and Teignmouth as well as Exmouth. The total registered under this Port of Exeter was approximately 80 per cent of all the Devon and Cornwall ports put together.

In 1744, the Exeter Whale Fishing Company had a ship of 346 tons called *Exeter* fitted out at Lympstone. Meanwhile the *Exmouth* was built in 1756 and there were two or three other whaling ships that went on whaling voyages up to 1787.

In the more modern era of shipbuilding in Exmouth out on the Point, records can be traced, certainly from 1792 onwards, when John and Robert Cunnett, sons of Thomas Cunnett of Honiton, came to Exmouth to work. Robert, after some shipbuilding experience at Sidmouth, was joined by his brother John and started advertising in the *Exeter Flying Post* in December 1792 when John had built a privateer, the *Dolphin*, and Robert finished a 47 foot cutter. In 1794 they built another cutter, the *Friends Goodwill*, which was advertised for sale in February 1795. After this we hear no more of the Cunnetts in Exmouth. Perhaps they emigrated.

Another newcomer to the Point in 1793 was John Hayman, son of Henry and Judith Hayman of Withycombe, who had been baptised there on 23 September 1770. He built a number of ships in the 1790s; see the Appendices for a list of them. Hayman's name is then apparently lost to the records unless he became involved in the building of Lighters, from 1794 onwards, 33 of which were registered with tonnages varying up to 72, all along the Exe. These were the years of the Napoleonic Wars and gun brigs were being built in the Exe estuary over the period 1806 to 1814. They were built to a standard design and we know of one particularly because it was built at Exmouth and riggers from Plymouth came up to bring the necessary stores to complete the rigging. For the most part, however, they were built at Topsham and brought down to Exmouth for rigging and fitting out before sailing to Plymouth or Portsmouth for manning and orders.

During these war years, too, the prize ships taken in battle were often brought into the Exe for repair and conversion.

In 1805 a sloop, the *Weazle*, was copper-bottomed at Exmouth and then in 1810 the newly-formed Exmouth Banking Company leased nine acres of the Point to be used for a repairing yard on the south shore and a shipbuilding yard on the north side. The plan was to build a ware-house, a coal yard and a large three-storey building for use as a sail loft. As noted, that building still stands, and the date 1810 is still visible over its door. To the best of the writer's knowledge, it is still used as a sail loft.

In 1812 the *Sidmouth*, a sloop of 24 tons, was completed at the north Point yard by an unknown shipbuilder and launched. It may be that it was built by Robert Cunnett, who possibly named the sloop after his wife's home town. Either way, the sloop was lost around 1821. There was not a huge amount of activity at this time, following the failure of the Exmouth Bank in 1812.

In 1823 a pleasure yacht, the *Cawsand*, was built of what were said to be '... the very best materials'. Could this perhaps have been one of the early Walters and Wishart ships? More were advertised in the *Exeter Flying Post* in 1828, 1829 and 1830. John Walters teamed up with James Wishart (sometimes spelt Witchart) to build ships from the 1820s onwards. This John Walters was the son of the late-eighteenth-century John Walters who died in 1820 and has a monument to his memory in the church at Littleham. The partnership took over the Point shipyard and remained in business for over 40 years. Following those advertised in the 1820s, came the launch of the second *Exmouth* in 1839, which attracted a crowd of over 3,000 people. This partnership had also erected the Ropewalk in the 1830s, which unfortunately fell into disuse about ten years later. The shipbuilders out on the Point were using the base of the old windmill, which had been demolished in the 1830s after a storm had partially wrecked it. The upper stones were used to build the sail loft. In the remaining part of the base the boat ribs were steamed and bent and sails immersed to be dyed.

John Hayman's name crops up again in 1824 when, with George Hook, he was building boats, possibly fast yachts. They won many prizes in the regattas, which by this time were being held along the coast.

In the second half of the nineteenth century the building of large ships ceased completely. Most of those built after the 1860s were either fishing vessels, yachts or other small vessels for ferrying or pleasure, mainly within the docks or by Dixons at the end of St Andrew's Road.

THE SWAN OF THE EXE

The most amazing vessel seen on the Exe was launched in September 1860. It was the Swan of the Exe *and was described in the* Illustrated London News *of 30 October 1860. It was owned by Captain George Peacock who designed it. He had it fitted out with every luxury to be had afloat. The exterior was painted white, picked out in gold. It was over 17 feet long, and stood 16 feet above the water. It had a double keel and was propelled by two webbed and feathering feet placed between the keels. It was operated by two or four men working hand levers. The progress could be accelerated by two pairs of oars and it could attain 5mph in smooth water. The saloon contained a dining table large enough for ten people and in the table were small oval apertures which opened to the water beneath, thus affording the opportunity of fishing whilst sitting at the table. There was apparatus on board which could prepare and cook the fish so caught. The smells and fumes from the cooking process were able to escape through the neck of the* Swan *and so out through its beak. It was a scale size model of a Bewick Swan.*

In 1907 Thomas Dixon built the Cygnet *as a tender to the famous* Swan of the Exe *built in 1860. The* Cygnet *is now in the Exeter Maritime Museum. The Dixons had been in the shipbuilding trade since about 1760 when Thomas Dixon was active.*

In the 1889 *Directory of Exmouth*, the named boatbuilders were William Bricknell, Thomas Dixon & Sons, John Hook and George Lavis, the son of the Redways' shipwright. In 1893 a Mr Wilson opened a boatyard and he acted as a timber merchant as well.

We know of the following ships built during the period from 1889 to 1919:

Melita – Starcross ferry, built in the docks, 1889.
Melita II – built as a replica to the first of that name, 1894; it became a houseboat in Exmouth.
Sirdar – built 1899 by Lavis, a steam-powered barge, demolished in 1969.
Rowena – built in 1899.
Zulu – built in 1900 by G. Lavis & Co. as a steam ferry.
Starcross – built 1919 as a steam ferry.
Cleetha – also built in 1919 by John Walters' yard.

The Exmouth Sailing Club was founded in 1913, although regattas had been held at Exmouth for many years previously. There were several boatbuilders around the Point prepared to build yachts to order or to repair and fit out anything in that

category. F.J. Horn was a sailmaker, his father was employed by the Redways and his son John Thomas Horn was still based at the Point in 1889. Luther Knight was a sailmaker in the 1860s and his son Luther Martin Knight appears in the 1889 *Directory* in the same trade.

This chapter would not be complete without mentioning smugglers, piracy and shipwrecks. All were commonplace to the inhabitants of Exmouth. There was the notorious smuggler Jack Rattenbury, who mostly worked the coast to the east of Exmouth – Sidmouth and beyond. He fired the imagination of the romantic to emerge as something of a folk hero. He used the Mutter family's turf and wood-cutting operation, with its outlet in Exmouth and as far afield as Exeter, as a 'front' for his activities. That family adopted the situation with alacrity. Sam Mutter, a daring and experienced seaman operated his boat by night, landing cargoes at selected spots along the coast between Exmouth and Seaton and his family worked the distribution network. Mutter's cider shop in Exmouth is thought to have been the nerve centre of the organisation and although Sam Mutter was caught and sent to prison, on his release he returned to his colourful lifestyle. As well as fishing and engaging in the smuggling activities of East Devon, the Mutter family achieved the rare distinction of having a piece of moorland named after them, Mutters Moor near Sidmouth. Rudyard Kipling wrote a very relevant poem:

If you wake at midnight and hear a horse's feet,
Don't go drawing back the blind, or looking in the street,
Them that asks no questions, isn't told a lie,
Watch the wall, my darling, while the gentlemen go by.

Five and twenty ponies,
Trotting through the dark –
Brandy for the Parson
Baccy for the Clerk,
Laces for a lady, letters for a spy,
And watch the wall, my darling, while the Gentlemen go by.

THE REDWAYS

After the 1830s came the era of the two brothers Redway, Richard and Thomas. They were aged 19 and 17 when they arrived at Exmouth in 1843 and took over the Ropewalk. They were born in Bishopsteignton, the sons of John Redway (1787–1848) and his wife Jemima, née Bidder (1792–1871).

The brothers were growing flax at Holcomb near Dawlish, spinning it into twine and travelling

Exmouth Boatmen of 1912. Back row includes: *A. Carder, T. Thompson, Ned Bradford, W. Holman, J.G. Holman;* centre: *H. McCaber, Will Hocking, Bert Hocking, Ned Redman, J. Carder, Ned Bridie, Foggo Carder, Bill Hocking, George Carder, Naddits Pine;* front: *Harry Hocking (Kent), Tom Ferris, Bill Bale Hocking.*

around to sell it. The acquisition of the Ropewalk enabled them to make even bigger twine and rope and so expand their business. They moved into the cottage at the end of the Ropewalk, but almost immediately Richard Redway married Sarah Sharland and the rooms in the cottage were divided between the two brothers. Richard's six children were all born there, but three of them died young. Thomas moved out in 1849 when he married Jeannette Underhill, with whom he had six children. Jeanette died in 1862 and so Thomas remarried in 1865 – this time to Sophia Underhill, possibly the sister of his first wife. They had another five children.

Richard and Thomas soon expanded into the field of shipbuilding, being financed by an Exeter bank. They became a very successful partnership. In the period from 1843 to 1869, they completed about 40 ships of various sizes, the largest being the *Amazon* of 1,100 tons. We can name most of the ships they built in the earliest period and give dates for the later ones (see Appendix G).

In 1853 the Redways were joined by a Mr Bickford to launch a brig called *Empire* for the foreign trade.

The shipyard at Exmouth was on the site of Sharp's boathouse and timber yard. At their peak, the Redways employed 300 workers; 100 were used on the actual building slip and 200 in all the subsidiary trades – rope- and sail-making, black-smiths and fitting shops, block- and spar-making

and a foundry. In addition Richard ran a coal business using imported coal. His sons Edwin and Warwick (the latter recorded much information about his father's business) were both brought up in the business, employed as junior clerks.

In 1869 Richard left Exmouth to take over a shipyard in Dartmouth, where he built a number of 70-ton trawlers for the East Coast owners between 1876 and 1879. But fortune did not favour him there and a fire in 1881 destroyed a lot of machinery as well as a vessel on the stocks. He died a pauper in Dawlish in 1891.

However, before taking leave of Richard we should mention his son Edwin, born in 1848. He married Ellen Rose Hodge, the daughter of John Hodge, a confectioner in Exmouth, and they had four stalwart sons. After some experience with his father, including some voyages on his father's ships, he trained to be a designer of ships himself, first with Scott Russell and then at Dartmouth and Milford Haven. He became a member of the Institute of Naval Architects and in 1884 emigrated with his family to Toronto. There he built the first steel passenger ship on Lake Ontario called *Garden City* and contributed largely to the Canadian shipbuilding industry, assisted by his sons. He died in 1914 after a very busy life.

Thomas Redway continued shipbuilding at Camperdown on John Walters' yard, but he had also developed other interests. The ships he built are listed in Appendix H.

Thomas' son, Thomas Augustine Redway, born in 1855 and known as Augustus, joined his father in the shipbuilding trade and soon began operating a fleet of ships in trading ventures with West Africa. They were ship owners by 1880 with nine vessels – from the small *Cyprus* of 66 tons to the great *Rajah of Sarawak*, 122 feet long, built by the brothers before 1860.

Thomas had diversified into a brickworks, purchasing 20 acres of land below Marpool from Dr Hull. Here he created an extensive production line of bricks which were being used in the various building developments in the town. He then joined A.A. Carter to start building houses. That partnership was responsible for Aylesbury Terrace, Exe View Terrace, Haldon View Terrace on the Exeter Road, Danby Terrace and Belvedere Road. He began to build a swimming pool at the end of Camperdown Road at the Point, but collapsed and died in 1889 before it was completed. Sadly it never reached completion.

Many of the Redway ships were built using second-hand oak and so did not always get top grading at Lloyds. They were almost wholly classed as A1, but for a shorter period of years.

Redway's *Memento* of 1869 and Holman and Sons' *Silurian* built at Topsham in 1870 were about the last of the big sailing ships to be built on the Exe. The first ship described as 'built of iron' was registered at Lloyds in 1836 and from that date the history of the wooden hulls was over. Shipyards which endeavoured to keep to the old 'wooden walls' type of ship were forced to close unless they received a specific order for a ship of timber. Ships were soon being built of iron and steel for the faster voyages to the Far East, which was facilitated by the opening of the Suez Canal in 1869.

WORKERS AT THE REDWAYS' YARDS

Mr Symons operated the Ropewalk. The turntable at the end was turned by a horse.

S. Bowden was the Foreman Shipwright.

George Lavis was the finest shipwright, specialising in stem and stern work.

William Margrie and his son, Fred, worked in the shipyard, but they, with William's wife Sarah, emigrated to Australia. He was said to be good with anything to do with ironwork.

Tom Trim was another good worker; he emigrated to Canada.

Job Edwards worked in all departments and looked after Mrs Redway's cow and pigs.

Mr Horn was Foreman of the Sail Loft and his son F.J. Horn continued in that same trade.

Albert Hayman and John Melhuish were regular workers. The latter's nephew, Albert, helped with the office work.

Jim Bradford and Frank Polson. As a boy, the former turned the wheel at the end of the Ropewalk.

The most interesting man there was perhaps a man known as Tally Jack. He was a Genoese whose real name was Giovanni Basgleoppo. He married a Mrs Bartlett, the mother of Robert Bartlett, who had succeeded Joseph Norrie as Foreman of the Foundry.

Many of the youths of Exmouth were apprenticed at the Yard and had a commencing wage of 1s. per week when the labourers were getting 1s. per day. In the sail loft, the apprentices were taught the basics of reading, writing, spelling and arithmetic. The town was very appreciative of what the Redways did for their youngsters.

The Redways were not, however, the only shipbuilders out at the Point in these years. There had been others. An unknown firm built the ketch *Brothers* of 16 tons in 1840. James Hook began in 1845 with the *Zedora* of 31 tons, followed by the *Surprise* (38 tons) in 1846 and the *Lily of the Exe*, a splendid sloop which was fitted out completely by a Mr Bence. James Hook followed these with *Laura*, a yawl of 22 tons in 1858 and *Black Pioneer*, a 37-ton sloop built in 1862, which was used as a fishing vessel. The builder of the schooner *Eleanor* in 1857 is not recorded, but it belonged to Mr Sheppard, the Exmouth Postmaster of the time. In 1846, John Walters joined with John B. Holman of Topsham to work at the Parsonage Yard there.

CHAPTER 7

The Pubs of Exmouth

It seems opportune with the coming of the new millennium to look back over the last few centuries in order to reflect on how the populace has enjoyed a drink of their favourite brew at their local establishment. In these places, people have traditionally indulged in a good gossip with their neighbours over the politics and problems of the times and passed a very pleasant evening after a hard day's toil.

EARLY PUBS OF EXMOUTH

Names and signs given to a public house (a Victorian term) were mostly of a historical or merely local significance. Some names related to royalty – the King's or Queen's Arms, the Golden or Red Lion or Unicorn. Others perhaps related to the lord of the manor in which the inn stood, by name or Arms. A Globe Inn, a fairly common name, was given to a house which sold principally a port wine from Portugal (whose King Manuel I had adopted a celestial globe as his personal emblem). Another common and no doubt very early method used to signify a drinking place was a bush hung outside, often a holly bush as it was evergreen. Alternatively, signs often related to local trades and occupations and many of medieval origin can be connected with the Church or heraldry. The variety is immense.

The ownership and control of English pubs was mostly in the hands of local people or local breweries. However, in more recent times, breweries have become national concerns in the hands of big financial boards; there is often common management and a tendency to create the same effect within a pub, whether in city, town or even village.

This chapter therefore acts as a record of the history and romance associated with many of the pubs in Exmouth as they have been and how, thankfully, quite a few still remain.

THE ALBION INN

Named no doubt after the street in which it was situated, the name Albion itself came from a fully-rigged, 369-ton ship built in Topsham in 1800 at Boden's Yard and owned by a Mr Hayman. It is probable that he also owned the fields on which the Hill and the Street were built. There was an old lane already there called Boles' Hill which formed one of the old routes into town.

Albion Street was built some time after 1826 and the first licence was granted to the inn just after 1850. John Baker was the licensee in 1857 and he held it until just after 1866. Obviously the newcomers to the houses being built in the area would have been the first customers, keeping John Baker busy for those first ten years.

Below is a list of people who were also licensees, as far as can be traced:

	William Dayman.
1878:	J. Thompson.
1882:	Henry E. Thompson.
1884:	Herman Alfred Sage, for at least seven years.
1897–1902:	George Nelson Wannell.
1910:	James Mitchell.
1910–30:	Henry Helman.
1934:	Mr and Mrs T.W. Sellick.
1948–62:	Mr and Mrs F. Hancock.
1985:	In September of this year, Charles and Jackie Watts took over and within six weeks had transformed the look of the bar, but without losing its local atmosphere or

Albion.

image. A much brighter look resulted and a new fast food kitchen brought further development to the bar.

1995: *Geoffrey A. Matthews with Fred Hancock succeeded to the licence.*

2000: *Keith Barrett and his wife took over, having had experience in the trade.*

It has become known as a good cider pub.

THE ANCHOR INN, LITTLEHAM

9 September 1850:

Whereas a Petition of William Smith of the Anchor Inn, Exmouth in the parish of Littleham, Victualler, previously of Farringdon, Blacksmith and Insolvent Debtor – having been filed in the County Court of Devon at the Castle of Exeter &c. &c... is hereby required to appear in the said Court on 23rd September at 10 o'clock in the forenoon.

No other reference to an Anchor Inn at Littleham has been traced. Moreover there is no reference to a William Smith at the Anchor or Blue Anchor in Tower Street, Exmouth. It must therefore be assumed that this was a separate inn, that existed in 1850 for perhaps a very short time.

THE APOLLO INN

This is a name by which it is said that the Ship Inn in High Street was at first known in the eighteenth century, possibly up to about 1770. No other references to it have been found.

THE BEACH HOTEL, THE POINT

Originally built on the Point as a rest for passengers for the ferry to Starcross (the Ferry Station was moved to the beach there in about 1800), this pub was initially known as the Passage House. The licensees of that house are named up to 1858 when it became known as Attwater's Beach Hotel. Some time later when a Mr Sprague was the licensee, it was reconstructed and named the Beach Hotel, and the road leading to it, formerly just a track across the sands, was then named Beach Road.

It is recorded that in 1856 a bill, sent from the town porter's premises on the Parade charging for eight loads of manure, was delivered to the Beach Family Hotel. That bill also shows a charge for three pints of beer costing 2s.0d., subtracted from the manure cost of 5s.6d. per load.

The names of many of the licensees in the 30 or so years before the pub was moved are:

5 September 1860: *Arthur Brown, late of the Beach Hotel, an insolvent debtor.*

15 October 1862: *The Beach Hotel was up for sale, and was occupied by W. Taylor.*

28 December 1864: *Mr W. Taylor was about to leave Exmouth and the Hotel was to be auctioned on 2 January 1865.*

12 April 1865: *Mr J.R. Blackler opened the Beach Hotel.*

1 August 1865: *A garden was opened having been newly fitted out.*

31 October 1866: *Named Speechley's Beach Hotel, which had accommodation.*

By 1873: *Thomas William Pitts was the owner.*

By the time of this last entry, much development was taking place on the Point: shipbuilding, the construction of the new docks and that of the railway. It was a time when this hotel could have thrived. However, a move was considered in the 1860s and it was some time later that a new Beach Hotel was built on the corner of Alston Terrace at the end of what was then known as Ferry Road (now St Andrew's Road). As such, this house on the beach was closed down.

THE BEACH HOTEL, ALSTON TERRACE

This hotel was built in 1868 and remained on this site for about 30 years whilst all the material being excavated from the construction of the docks was being dumped in the area of what later became Victoria Road. Most of the customers from the Beach Hotel on the Point followed the landlord Thomas Pitts here. One particular customer was called Bimbo Potter and it is said that even when this hotel burnt down, he remained near it, sitting on a nearby bench, calling for his pint!

Beach Hotel, Victoria Rd.

THE BEACH HOTEL, VICTORIA ROAD

Following the fire at the Beach Hotel in Alston Terrace, this new hotel was built in 1895 on the corner of the new Victoria Road with the Pierhead. It was said to be on the site of an old coal dump. It has been described as one of Exmouth's historic public houses, but that must arise from the number of previous pubs with the same name – primarily the one of the Point, previously called the Passage House.

It was not a residential hotel for the first 20 years. It housed collections of photographs of many of the ships built nearby on the Point, and displayed many models and memorabilia of the town's lifeboats and of the men who served in them. Naturally it was the sea-going fraternity of the town who tended to frequent this bar, affectionately known as 'God's Waiting Room'.

The first licensee was J.H. Williams and he was followed by Albert Edward Banfield who stayed until after 1914. By 1919, Henry Meekings had succeeded and he stayed until he died in 1935; his widow Mrs Meekings stayed on for about ten years. After this, her son and his wife (Mr and Mrs F. Meekings) took over. They became the licensees from 1948 until five years later when Mr and Mrs H. Davey followed. It was in 1961 that Neville and Grace Drummond became the landlords. Leonard and Sheila Froment came next and in October 1979 they added a 'Beachcomber Function Room' and were serving a Royal Oak beer from the wood. Ten years later they knocked the lounge and public bar into one, but maintained the name of the hotel and kept on display many of the arte-facts which had been one of the hotel's particular attractions over the years. Now there was a big Victorian-style bar servery with a traditional brass footrail. The public bar was integrated with the Beachcomber Room, serving superb meals.

During Len and Sheila's stay at the hotel, the New Year celebrations brought with them the sound of bagpipes. At that time, too, the *Exmouth Journal* promoted a race along the Esplanade from Orcombe Point to a grand finish at the Beach Hotel. A newly-refurbished Lifeboat Lounge was re-opened on 9 July 1989. The hotel was then a member of the Buccaneer Group.

David and Sheila Russell came as the new licensees from 1995 and were advertising the Lifeboat Bar with its speciality fish dishes. They were still there five years later, running a very successful house.

THE BEACON VAULTS

Standing on Beacon Hill on its approach to the Beacon, this inn, according to the painted inscription over its porch, dates from the year 1774.

Beacon Vaults.

Apparently, it was originally a farmhouse which was converted into an inn. Its wine vaults contain parts of an original building, said to have been the Beacon Farmhouse or perhaps part of the original Sacheverell Hall that once stood on the site.

It became a fashionable meeting-place for the residents of the new houses being built on the Beacon from 1792 onwards. It was popular for games of cards, dancing and social gatherings. It was visited by Lady Byron and her daughter Ada, the Marchioness of Bute and the Countess of Guildford, both daughters of Thomas Coutts, the great London banker, Mr Justice Holroyd, Lady Howard, Lord Ellenborough, Lord Guildford and many others.

Next door to the Vaults, the Assembly Rooms opened in 1817 and became the venue for balls, plays and receptions. A small stage is still visible within the rooms now used for wine storage. It is possible that the two buildings were at one time connected and at the rear a small inn, known for many years as The Hole in the Wall, was also linked. It later became a small public bar at the rear of the Vaults.

In 1873 William Thomas Langford advertised as a wine and spirit merchant when it was rumoured that an underground passage existed. Allegedly the passage was linked with the cliff face below. The tide used to rise to this point, but it is now covered by the Manor Gardens. Excavations following a collapse in the road outside the Vaults in 1945 revealed a very large hole, which could have been part of such a passage. Further evidence was revealed by the presence of a deep brick-lined passage behind the toilet block in the Manor Gardens, leading under the Beacon Hill, which now contains an electricity sub-station. As a result of these findings, it seems reasonable to suggest that the likely existence of the passage means that the Beacon Vaults was at one time linked to the smuggling racket.

The earliest record of licensees in the twentieth century date from 1931 when Mr and Mrs H.E.

Crease were there. They were followed in 1934 by Mr and Mrs H.S. Kerslake until after 1936. After the Second World War, Captain and Mrs Lockley Turner became the licensees until 1953 when Mr and Mrs Blackbourn took over. It was the Blackbourns who acknowledged that the Hole in the Wall behind the Vaults was in fact within their licence. By 1971 John and Beryl Farrell had taken over, but by 1978 Vanda and David were advertising as the landlords. William and Irene M. Gatward succeeded them in 1985. Later that year, on 12 November, an auction was held of unusual items and antiques donated for Bystock Court; the auctioneer was the new landlord and he raised £295 for that cause.

A long advertisement in April 1989 announced that Roy Smith and Angela Tremaine, both Cornish born and with considerable experience in the hotel and catering trades, had taken over and were immediately starting to plan improvements. Two new lounges, one for non-smokers, became available in what has been called the 'Historic Beacon'. However, this couple was replaced by Jerry Keast and Anne Popham from Plymouth in December 1989. Although they only lasted for three years, they claimed to have made the business much more successful. In turn, they were followed in 1992 by Franklyn J. Keast. Yet another change came in 1995 when Stephen Gibbings took over the reins, and then in 1997 came Loretta Williams. In 1999 Stephen D. Whiteman and Diane M. Spence took over.

The Beacon Vaults form an extremely attractive venue and the date above the porch certainly acts as an invitation to enter and see the beautiful beamed ceilings.

THE BICTON INN

Sometimes referred to as the Bicton Hotel, this pub was originally two dwelling houses at the corner of Bicton Street and South Street. They were converted around 1760 into an inn called the Red Lion.

From the records that can be traced, the licensees of the inn have included the Dyer family for a number of years. This included: Henry Dyer, and Mrs Sophia Dyer, presumably Henry's widow, (the Census for this year gives Mrs Dyer's age as 49 and she had three children) and John Henry Dyer, presumably a son of the original Henry. The name for the year 1897 is that of George Salter.

Then there came a change from the Dyers when from 1929 until 1936 Leslie Govier Hearn and his wife May Victoria Gwendoline Hearn were the landlords. Then followed: Mr and Mrs W. Thomas; Mr and Mrs M.A. Ferris; Henry and Myrtle Berry; Ray and Lily T. Turpin – they were the first to place an advertisement for the Bicton

Bicton Inn.

Bistro. (A commentary in 1974 remarked on the friendly atmosphere of the Bicton Bistro, where a vast selection of snacks, salads and grills were served with lunches and dinners.)

Thomas and Janet L. Nichols were the licensees until Thomas died and his widow took over. She was joined by John Slater, but when they left early in 1989 the inn was closed. It was said that it would not be refurbished but would re-open when a new landlord was found. It was not until 1991 that John and Susan H. Elkington were found. However, from 1995 to the time of writing, we find that Allan and Alison Brockbank are in charge and intend to stay.

THE (BLUE) ANCHOR

According to the Rate Book of 1825, this public house and its adjoining Malthouse (the Maltsters Arms), were in Tower Street in the early-nineteenth century and were in the possession of John Pyne from before 1811 until after 1825. Acting as a surety for this John Pyne to the sum of £10 was John Salter, John Pyne himself standing surety for another £10. It was then sold; Henry Newbury took over and stayed until after 1850.

Bartholemew Pickard came in 1851, but by 1859 Charlotte Burgoin was in possession, being granted a spirit licence in that year. On 12 April 1860 the licence was transferred from Mrs Burgoin to Mr W. Summers who, on 16 May 1860, was summoned for allowing gambling in his house. However the case was dismissed after a warning was given.

Thomas Shapter, the new landlord, was taken to the Woodbury Petty Sessions Court on 29 October 1862 for keeping his house open on a Sunday morning, but the case was dismissed. However, on 11 February 1863 he was again taken to Woodbury for harbouring a Police officer whilst he was supposedly on duty on 29 January – he was found in the Taproom of the Anchor playing bagatelle. As a result he was fined 5s.

On 29 January 1864, the licence was transferred

to William Best who stayed until after 1873. It was during his tenancy that trade tokens made of brass in Exeter were issued, being marked 'BEST'S ANCHOR INN, EXMOUTH', with a value of 1½d.

By 1878 a Mr Honeychurch was the landlord, but there is no evidence after that year of an establishment named the Blue Anchor or even just the Anchor being licensed premises. It may be that it was renamed the New Inn, as a public house of that name was burnt down about this time. However, we do know that by 1884 the Criterion existed in Tower Street and was licensed to George Darch; presumably this was the rebuilt New Inn.

THE BREWHOUSE
(POSSIBLY SOUTH BREWTON BREWERY)

Records first mention this house on 3 June 1858. The South Town Brewery, Exmouth, was being offered for sale at auction by the Executors of the will of the late Mrs Radford. The contents of all the furniture included a hogshead copper furnace among other items.

The name appears to be a clue as to where this Brewhouse was sited. It could not have been a predecessor of the Bicton Inn, for on that site there was previously an inn called the Red Lion, which had operated from the middle of the eighteenth century.

THE BREWHOUSE, THE STRAND

The site from which this public house traded is not now identifiable, but it could have been on the corner of the Strand where Lloyds Bank now stands. It traded for the best part of a century, although the earliest date now traceable is 3 September 1773, when it was sold by the owner, Mr Samuel Short. Much later, on 6 June 1844, it was auctioned as a public house, presumably with its licence, but with no name. Two years later, on 7 May 1846, we can read of the bankruptcy of a Mr Richard M. Goodridge. Was this the end of the business?

No further evidence appears to be available, but it is interesting to find that in a directory for 1870 a Railway Hotel was next to Thomas' corner on the Strand. Was this the successor?

THE BUILDERS ARMS

This popular house was on the corner of Union Street and Princes Street. The earliest record traced gives a Mrs Sarah Tozer as the licensee in the early 1870s; she appears in the 1873 *Post Office Directory*. In 1878 she married Frederick Burridge and together they continued running the house until after 1884. His brother-in-law Harry Tozer ran the business for a while, but a Frank Seward had taken over by 1897.

It was during the early 1900s that this house issued trade tokens for 1½d. and there are three of them to be seen in Exmouth Museum.

Edwin George Ferris held the licence from 1897 until after 1910 when John and Maud Carpenter came in 1914. They stayed until after 1930, through all the excitements of the First World War. By 1934 Mr and Mrs F.J. Nicholls were in charge. However, they were not in charge for long, because by 1936 it was Mr and Mrs Britain Stubley. In addition, there was a reference to a W. Hoskin in 1931.

From 1948 until after 1955, Mr and Mrs F.A. Sussenbach were the licensees, followed by Ray and Audrey Watkins by 1961. Harry and Vera R. Hall were in charge by 1972 and were followed by Brian and Jacqueline Collins in 1981. In 1984 came Leonard and Lorraine Stanyer. He was an ex-policeman from Staffordshire and soon settled in, although when he applied for a renewal of the licence, the local Police raised an objection on the grounds that 'he was not a fit person for the trade'. In fact it was during his tenancy that a terrific battle occurred between the Exmouth 'Bikers' and the visiting Exeter 'Bikers'. The bar was the battleground, and the incident resulted in broken glass everywhere, blood stains from alleged stabbings and smashed furniture, windows and bottles. Perhaps it was because of this event that the Builders Arms was closed down and subsequently taken over; after many alterations and extensions it became the Famous Old Barrel.

In June 1986 a big Scooterist Country-wide Rally met at Exmouth. At least four public houses were determined to stay closed; they were the Heavitree Arms, the Queen's Hotel, the Ship Inn and the York, saying that they had had enough trouble in the previous year. Nevertheless, all went very well and there have been other successful visits in later years of up to 2,000 scooterists from all parts of the country who love Exmouth.

THE CHURCH HOUSE INN

This is possibly the early name for what became the Pilot Inn on Chapel Hill. It is thought that the public house was so named because of its proximity to the Holy Trinity Chapel, built in 1412 and demolished in 1824 following the decision to build Holy Trinity Church on Rolle Road.

THE CLARENCE INN

Situated in Meeting Street at its junction with Clarence Street and facing out towards Albion Street, this public house has existed for over 150 years. It is situated in one of the oldest parts of Exmouth and has been traced back as far as 16

The Clarence Inn.

November 1842, when it was reported to be 'now unoccupied'. It was to be sold, together with the dwelling house next door, which had been in the occupation of Mr Harvey, a bookbinder and stationer. The date of the sale was to be 27 November 1842.

After the sale, a William Taverner moved in on 2 May 1843. The next licensee to be traced was Emanuel Vine on 6 October 1864. He also occupied premises in Meeting Place as a beer retailer under the name of 'Alma'. We know that there was also a maltster and brewery business in nearby Meadow Street. Were they all under the control of Emanuel Vine? However, by 23 June 1869 it was the representatives of Emanuel Vine, deceased, who were in possession.

According to later street directories, the succeeding licensees included:

1878:	*Henry Cross, followed by Charles Baker.*
1891–7:	*Charles Robert Salter until after 1923.*
1930:	*James and Elizabeth Stradling.*
1934:	*Mr and Mrs T. Addis, succeeded by Mr and Mrs T. Maxwell.*
1950:	*Mr and Mrs B.K. Smith.*
1961:	*Bertram and Marjorie E. Oldham.*
1971:	*Frederick and Marjorie Oldham, possibly the son taking his father's place.*

In February 1943, the licensee was on his allotment on Albion Hill when six FW190 German planes attacked the town. He was killed and a gas holder nearby was set on fire.

In the summer of 1989 a new landlord, Brian Johnson, took over with his wife Stella. He created a new Stable Room Bar as a new venue for functions. This room was aptly named, for it was indeed formerly a stable and the older locals and customers could remember the sound of horses' hooves there. Brian Johnson, however, gave way

to Dennis and Janet Harding, and in 1984 they were succeeded by Tom Payne. He was a former Metropolitan Police officer who, with his daughter Kathleen, carried out a number of changes for the better. In 1987 the Exmouth Licensees Association was formed and met regularly at the Clarence Inn. Its influence created a reduction in the number of violent incidents in pubs, as reported a year later. The Hardings left in 1992 after an active life in the trade.

Brian and Lilian Hawkins were there in 1998, but they gave way to Mark A. Knapman. However, Graham Wortz took over in April that year. According to the *Exmouth Herald* of 21 January 2000, the doors of the Clarence Inn were closed as a result of a lack of custom. There was a brief period during which the pub was re-opened but when the shutters went down again it was put up for sale by the Heavitree Brewery. An advertisement claimed the building was suitable for conversion into two or three cottages. What an end to this historic site!

In the latter half of the year 2000 it was occupied as a private home, but unaltered in the bar. The lifting of a floorboard, however, revealed an anchor and part of a boat. Was there a nautical connection at one time?

THE CLINTON ARMS, MAER LANE

Situated on a prominent corner site in Littleham village, which was previously occupied by a New Inn, this house has been named, no doubt, after the Clinton family, lords of the manor of Littleham.

It began under this name in the late 1960s and the licensees named in the 1971 Voters List were Ernest and Joyce Bidmead, who remained until after 1985. They were followed by Anthony J. and Anne C. Gummery, who were still there after 1992. However, by 1997 Simon E. and Sonia A. Allchurch had taken over and were running a very popular house.

The Clinton Arms.

THE COUNTRY HOUSE INN, WITHYCOMBE

Situated at the eastern end of Withycombe village, this pub was probably just a cider house until 1887, selling cider at 2½d. per quart and cider-vinegar at 1½d. per pint. The inn's own cider press was in a large shed by the road, near where the present front door stands. The cider was then made by a Charles Snow. During the late-nineteenth century, the landlord was Mr George Beavis. He was certainly present from 1873 onwards when he was described as a blacksmith as well as a beer retailer.

After a couple of changes of landlords, we come to Matthew Mark Stark and Miss Mary Anne Thomas, who were licensees from 1929 to 1934. In 1936 Mr and Mrs C.P. McLean took over, possibly remaining throughout the Second World War and until 1954. The licence must have stayed in the family, for in 1961 Arthur and Maud McLean were acting as the landlords. William Norris was in charge in 1973; R.G. Leonard by 1978 and Henry and Joan Horn by 1984. (To celebrate the New Year in January 1985, all the ladies in the Darts team dressed as men.) By 1988, Jonathan and Marylin Channing had taken over, staying until 1999 when Jonathan was too ill to carry on, and they were succeeded by Rob and Trudie Seabrook.

Advertisements always said the inn sold 'a real good pint of real good ale'. A previous landlord was the proud owner of two large Newfoundland dogs, fine specimens of their breed. He also acquired a racehorse called Fandango Boy and he syndicated the ownership among all his regular customers. With the jockey Peter Scudamore, they won 11 races and were placed 8 times. There was a field at the rear of the property in those days, on which are now built a number of houses. Despite this, there is still enough room for a lovely garden with an aviary, a barbecue area and tables and chairs for the family, accessible over a bridge from the inn. In fact animals have always been associated with the Country House Inn, probably because of the rear garden through which the Bradham stream flows. It has been known for goats to be grazed on the edge of the stream – and for rather large rabbits to chase them!

In the year 2000 Superleague Darts, a country-wide league, returned to Exmouth and a new team became based at the Country House Inn.

The inn itself is now a very well appointed house with plenty of space around the attractive bar, where meals may be ordered to be served in a dining room. In this room all the walls were once decorated with Walt Disney characters and a collection of wood carvings by Guy Salf.

In August the Withycombe Regatta is held, when there are bric-a-brac stalls, a bouncy castle, a boat race and pony rides. Ferret racing is the local speciality, as is the duck race. A prize draw is also held – all in support of the charity Hospiscare. It is always a great success; in the millennium year 2000 over £1,700 was raised.

THE CRANFORD HOTEL

This was a rather fine building standing on the junction of Salterton Road and Littleham Road. At one time a small inn, the Halfway House stood here, either actually on the same site or slightly to the rear, although the original establishment is believed to have stood on the line of a Saxon trackway or boundary. Excavations were undertaken in the hope of confirming this possibility, but archaeologists did not achieve a positive result.

The earliest record of the Cranford Hotel itself was in 1929 when the licensees were William and Maybelle Pearce. By 1932 Mr and Mrs H. Seward were in charge and by 1939, Gordon Gilbert and his wife were there. They no doubt stayed throughout the Second World War. In 1948 they were succeeded by Wing Cdr and Mrs J.V. Edwards.

The Country House Inn.

The Cranford Hotel.

By 1961 Charles and Rachel E. Frank were the landlords, though the next year shows that Anthony and Barbara Mawn were there, also only for a short period – by 1971 Francis and Deborah R. Betts had taken over.

By 1974 a full licence had been obtained and lots of improvements had been made (including the installation of a Swedish solarium). In the promotion of the hotel, it was claimed that it was only a mile from the seafront and the main shopping area.

In 1992 there was a serious fire and the premises were completely burnt down. This disaster led to planning permission being sought for the construction of 66 flats on the site. Permission was granted and the landowners at that time were Messrs McCarthy and Stone.

THE CRITERION INN

This rather small house was situated on the corner of Tower Street with the small alley called Criterion Place. It was probably the last of four inns that had existed on the site. The names of those discovered there are: The Blue Anchor (or just The Anchor); the Maltsters; and the New Inn which burnt down and was probably rebuilt as the Criterion. Please look at the first three under their names.

The Criterion Inn.

The licensees known to be at the Criterion were:

1884:   *George Darch.*
1891:   *Mr Soper.*
1897:   *Henry Cross.*
1902:   *Francis Thomas Dyer.*
1906:   *George Gray.*

It is not known at what date the inn finally closed down.

THE DEER LEAP

Beneath the twentieth-century façade of this house on the Esplanade lies one of the oldest buildings in Exmouth; a Bath House. Here in the 1790s two local doctors established their hot and cold, salt, fresh-water and mineral water bathing facilities for the nobility and for others who flocked to Exmouth to be cured of every manner of ailment. It was re-opened in 1842 by Thomas Burridge who established an underground pipe out to the sea. During excavations in the road outside in the late-twentieth century, the pipework to the sea was uncovered.

The present building dates from 1871 and became a very popular venue. In 1893, a hot sea-water bath cost 2s.6d. and a cold sea-water bath just 1s. This bath business lasted into the early-1900s (up to the 1930s it was still the bath house on the Esplanade).

When converted in 1960 it became a very popular outdoor venue for a drink and a meal. In 1974 a sign proclaimed: 'Welcome to the Whitbread House'. The licensees traced include William G. Tumilty (1961) and Raymond and Iris Harvey (1971).

From the late 1970s and through the 1980s, the Deer Leap used an anchor logo in its advertisements on which the words 'Admiral's Discotheque' appeared, with a rope above saying 'Happiest sounds around'. The DJs at that time

The Deer Leap.

were Dick and Stuart. However, the increase in the pub's popularity brought some trouble, for on Christmas Eve 1983 there was fighting in the grounds between large groups of youths. The case came before the Exeter Crown Court on 15 September 1984; one man was sent to prison and fines of between £200 and £250 were imposed on others.

Stephen White took over the premises in 1984 and was still there in 1989 when it was reported that a series of improvements had been put in place: a new food bar, an upstairs restaurant and copper-topped tables in the main bar. Customers were simply invited to 'drop in'. Unfortunately the advertisement in the *Exmouth Journal* in 1989 was headed 'The Dear Leap'. It is unlikely that trade dropped as a result of this mis-spelling.

In 1990 Tim Buckle was the manager for Whitbreads when live traditional jazz was played by a six-piece band on Sundays. Next, in 1994, Andrew and Doreen Bawm took over, succeeded in 1996 by David and Esther Ramsay, and followed by Stephen and Diane Bond.

Still the holiday visitors crowd the outer tables and chairs on Exmouth's sunny days.

THE DOLPHIN INN

This inn has quite a history; it certainly dates from the eighteenth century, for in 1778 James Foster was the landlord. It stood at the Cross, the very centre of the town. Two fairs were held each year in the nearby market-place; one in April and one in October. This was the relic of an ancient medieval right still held by the lord of the manor at Littleham from the time when Sir Thomas Dennys bought the manor in 1539.

The name Dolphin possibly came from the protection vessel of that name which patrolled the waters in the early-eighteenth century. It was perpetuated when a local shipbuilder, John Connett, built another *Dolphin* in 1793. The pub was often called the Dolphin Brewery up to about 1930.

In March 1787, John, the son of George Zorn of the Exeter Inn in Chapel Street, established a stage coach to run from the Bristol Inn in Exeter to the Dolphin in Exmouth every Tuesday, Thursday and Sunday, leaving at 8a.m. and returning the same evening.

On 10 January 1795 Mrs Honor Dane, the wife of the landlord James Dane, died. On New Year's Day in the same year, the Exmouth Volunteers assembled at the Dolphin under Captain Lovering and Lt Hobbs.

In May 1801, the landlord James Dane put the newly decorated inn up to let. It then consisted of two parlours, a kitchen, a bar on the ground floor, a large dining room (almost 24 feet by 15 feet) and

The Dolphin Inn.

five good bedrooms on the second floor. There were three other bedrooms and a large garret along with a courtelage of a brewhouse, plus outhouses and stabling for ten horses. It was said to be newly built as an inn and that there was only one other beside it in Exmouth!

A Mr Reed was there in 1802 until Mr Ewens on 22 July that year put it up for sale again with its cellars and a brewhouse. Apparently Mr Silas Allen then acquired the inn, for it was he who after 17 years sold it on 21 October 1819 to Thomas Ewens. Acting as surety for Silas Allen was Samuel Salter for the sum of £10 and Allen himself also stood for another £10. There was apparently a retail spirit cellar attached to the inn, the licensee of which was Orlando Lockyer. He gave surety for £10 as well as Samuel Salter's further £10 for this spirit cellar.

An early rate book for 1825 was discovered during a salvage drive during the Second World War and it listed the Dolphin as being held by Philip Ducarrel. The only other inns listed in that rate book were the Jolly Sailor, the Volunteer, the Globe and the York.

Another James Foster held the Dolphin from 1831 until after 1844 despite efforts to sell it in 1831, 1834 and 1844. Certain events during his tenancy should be noted.

On 7 August 1837, there was an early rising for the voters for Sir J.Y. Buller. They sat down at 7a.m. to a capital breakfast laid for 60 respectable freeholders. The landlord had devoted the previous day to decorating his large room with various flags, banners and ensigns with loyal and appropriate inscriptions tastefully entwined with flowers. A parade of the town followed which proceeded towards Exeter.

On 1 January 1838 the Union Society Benefit Club, after a procession to the church, brought 80 members to dine at the Dolphin where the land-lord, James Foster, placed on the tables a most substantial dinner which was much commended. Captain Scott, RN, presided and there were many loyal toasts. The remnants of that dinner were distributed amongst the poor and on Monday 31 December the poor were given 1 cwt. of meat; the landlord was called a true and loyal Conservative.

The Brethren of the Sun Lodge dined together on St John's Day on 7 January 1840 at Foster's Dolphin Inn, where there was a plentiful supply of game and venison presented by Lord Rolle.

The Inn appears on an 1840 map of the town. On 2 July the following year the laying of the foundation stone of the new sea wall took place. A huge procession was marshalled in a field near the turnpike gate, the present site of the library, and a public dinner was later held at the Dolphin, attended by about 100 tradespeople of the town. In fact the inn was the centre of many public dinners, meetings, auctions, public functions and celebrations because of its very central position at the Cross. Lord Rolle's birthday on 18 October was a particular reason to celebrate every year. Then there were the meetings of the Freemasons (Sun Lodge), the Oddfellows and several other societies and groups in the town. The Exmouth Rifle Corps was regularly inspected in the commodious covered accommodation that the inn offered. Appeals against the Tithe Apportionment were heard also, certainly from 1840 onwards.

A separate maltster or brewer was often employed for that part of the inn and we have the names of two from this time: John Wolsford in 1832 and Mr Mitchell in 1851.

James Courtenay held the licence after 1840, but he died on 27 June 1849 after a long illness and his widow, Elizabeth Courtenay, took over for a period until Thomas Otten Burton succeeded in 1850. He paid his rates of 3s.1½d. in 1855, then on 2 October 1856, he left the pub, in order to return home to Bude in Cornwall.

A rowing match took place on Monday 23 September 1851. Mr Spencer and a young man in his employment named James Tupman, were rowing against Mr Burton of the Dolphin Inn and a Mr Upright of Exeter for stakes of £1. The course was from the Great Tree to the Pier at Starcross and back, approximately four miles. Spencer and Tupman won by 12 minutes.

The Dolphin was then advertised to let on 22 January 1857. It was to be made available from the following Midsummer. Burton was still listed as the licensee, but in 1859 he or his manager was found guilty of keeping a disorderly house and for remaining open after 11a.m. on Sundays.

By 1873, Henry Hawkins was at the Dolphin. The landlords for the latter part of the nineteenth century appear to have been James Farmer in 1878; Charles Hawking appears as a manager in the Census of 1881; Tom Rogers in 1884; John Pimm in 1891 and Edward Bradford in 1897.

Henry Atkins is listed for 1902 and 1906, but George Young is there for 1910, followed by George Wills in 1914; George Isaac in 1923 and John Bickle or Bicknell in 1931 until 1936. Then with the Second World War came tragedy. The premises were bombed in January 1941 and completely destroyed together with an area of the Cross, the market-place and a maze of little courts and alleys. Up until then this had been a quaint, untouched part of Old Exmouth.

This was one of the inns of Exmouth that used trade tokens in the 1820s. They were of a white metal with a milled edge and the name 'Dolphin Inn' appeared on the obverse with a figure '6' on the reverse and the letter 'F' which could have been the initial of the landlord of the time, e.g. James Foster was there in the 1930s.

Over the years this inn had been an extremely popular venue. On Saturday nights the customers and their friends from other local pubs would gather outside after closing time had been called and all join in singing the popular songs of the day before gradually drifting off home after their very enjoyable evening out.

THE EXETER INN

This inn was formerly the New Inn in Chapel Street near the Chapel of St Margaret's and adjacent to Mr Broom's Quay and the Pratteshyde, from where the ferry boats left for Starcross. It became the Exeter Inn when William Morris was the licensee.

From 14 September 1770 it was advertised that from the grounds of William Morris was stolen a dark bay mare, 15hh, and a reward of half a guinea was offered for its recovery. On the death of William Morris, his widow Sarah assumed the tenancy and boasted of a fresh assortment of fine wines, a neat post-chaise, able horses and careful drivers. Obviously a regular stagecoach to Exeter had been established, hence the change of name of the inn.

On 29 March 1787, John, the son of George Zorn, an Attorney-at-Law, who had kept the Exeter Inn for many years, established a new stagecoach to run from the Bristol Inn in Exeter through Topsham and Lympstone to this house, as well as to the Dolphin Inn.

On 29 April 1802 the inn was advertised to be sold under a lease of two lives on the messuage and tenement. It came up for sale again on 26 May 1803, at that time held by William Thomas Hull, still on lease for two lives. It then had a large coach-house and stabling for 15 horses. At one end of the building was a thatched roof over three good rooms, occupied by Mr J. Haynes for seven years from 25 December 1812. Apparently it was not a very profitable inn for it proved difficult to sell or even let. It was advertised on 18 October 1826: 'To be let for a year or a term of years with immediate possession at a moderate rent'. Then Mr Abraham Staple, a builder of Exmouth, became the proprietor. Another advertisement of 22 May 1827 stated that it was formerly occupied by Mr Silas Allen – he had of course come here from the Dolphin Inn in 1819.

Auctions were held on 16 August 1827 when the inn was occupied by a Mr Baker and again on 1 May 1828 and 21 October 1828, when it was unoccupied and offered for the residue of a term for three lives. However, it was still empty in 1830. Mr W. Holway held it up to 1850 when it was again empty for a while, before William Dalgliesh, aged 29, took over in 1851. In 1852 Mr Robert Taverner was licensee; his wife died there on 26 September 1852 and he married a Miss Granger from London on 16 January 1853.

In the 1855 Rate Book the inn was described as being in Bond Street. Obviously some small development had taken place, and it was rated for 11s.½d., still to Robert Taverner. He continued until 1857 at least, but by 1866 John Heard was the licensee. Little more is heard of the Exeter Inn after that as the building had become a shop. The Pencavel building which appeared next door was probably built over the site of what had been the coach-houses.

THE EXMOUTH ARMS, FORMERLY THE EXMOUTH INN

This inn, a Whitbread house, stands on the corner of Exeter Road with Sheppard's Row leading to Exmouth Museum. The earliest mention of a licence here seems to be in 1856 when Joseph Russell was the landlord, although it is claimed that the inn has been in existence since 1800.

Following a Police report of 5 February 1857, Joseph Russell was summoned for not allowing PC Horn to come into his house in the discharge of

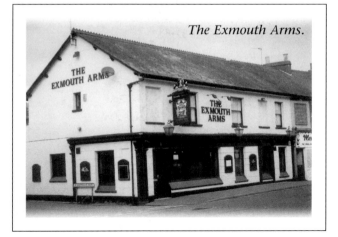

The Exmouth Arms.

his duties. He was fined £2 plus expenses, but he continued as a publican.

On the 27 October 1862, however, the business was put up for sale by auction at the Globe Hotel on the Strand. It was then described as having two parlours, three bedrooms, a kitchen, Bar Taproom, wash-house yard, brewhouse, stable and cellar. It was not sold at the time, for Joseph Russell was still there four years later. It was around this time that trade tokens were used, in the hope of increasing trade.

In 1887 the city brewery, which later became part of the Whitbread Group, bought the premises and John Podbury became the licensee from 1878 until after 1891. It was the regular meeting place of the First Rifle Volunteers. John seems to have died around 1896, for in 1897 Mrs Emma Podbury was the landlady. She remained there for many years, certainly until William Calloway came in 1914. He was followed by Albert Earnshaw in 1923, but his widow had taken over by 1929. Soon after, Mr and Mrs R. Holmes were in charge until 1936 at least and most probably continued throughout the war years.

For several years after 1948 the pub was run by Mr and Mrs H. Hitchcock; in 1953 the business was taken over by Mr and Mrs D.M. Mastick and by 1961 it was run by John and Teresa Tenby. It was in 1963 that the name of the house was changed from the 'Exmouth Inn' to the 'Exmouth Arms', but these were not the Arms of the town but those of Lord Exmouth. The next change of landlord was in 1971 when Ernest and Cynthia G. Mann took over. They were followed in the late 1970s by Leonard and Kathleen Rogers, who had arrived from the Dolphin in Exeter and stayed for almost 20 years. They were helped by their son, also called Leonard, and during their stay at the Exmouth Arms many alterations were carried out.

In addition to the alterations carried out during the 1980s, work was also completed to provide a children's room and a roof garden, which could be used as a beer garden as well. Len Rogers, the son of Leonard and Kathleen, was running the business in 2000, though Graham Wortz held it for a long time before going to the Clarence Inn.

It became a very active pub in the sports line and was a popular venue for many sportsmen of the town. Three football teams used it as their headquarters in addition to the pub's own football, pool and darts teams.

THE FARMHOUSE INN

This was the first public house to be created on the Brixington estate, at Churchill Road, following its development in the 1950s and '60s. It was a converted farmhouse attached to a 93-acre farm occupied by Gregory Jackson. It was first licensed

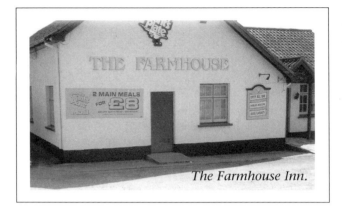

The Farmhouse Inn.

as an inn in 1968, and the first licensees were David and Barbara Gutteridge. They stayed for a number of years and established a regular clientele. In their advertisements they used a lovely old sketch of the farmhouse as it had once been.

However, by 1980 Alan Jones and his wife Lorraine had taken over. Lorraine was chosen as Exmouth's Carnival Queen for 1984. They stayed until after 1990, and advertised regularly in the *Exmouth Journal*, using the same logo of the sketch. After an extension and various other changes had affected the look of the place, the sketch of the old farmhouse was dropped and another sketch of a milk churn and a wagon wheel was used instead.

There was always music and entertainment in the house, usually by the Farmhouse Folk and Johnny Hutton from 1979 onwards, though Tony Osborne and the Three Brass Monkeys became a regular feature from 1985.

Alistair and Lynne Robertson were running the pub by 1990, and were followed by Rita and Frank Burns. However, they moved out in 1995 to take on the revamped Park Hotel in Exeter Road. Leslie C. Richards, who was landlord by 1997, brought about many changes to the appearance of the building, although many of its original features were retained.

An old bread oven and an old fireplace that had long ago been installed in the building had been saved and are on display in another part of the bar. At the time of writing there were two bars, a family room and a function room seating 180 with a water-wheel lounge and a skittle alley. The house holds a reputation, too, for good food. The welcoming landlords are Richard and Dawn Ousley.

THE FIRST AND LAST HOUSE (NO. 1)

The original business on this site at the top of Fore Street on the left-hand side was known as the Town's End House which later became the Smith's Cider Shop. It later took the name of the First and Last House for very obvious reasons; it was the first

such house on the way into the town and also the last as you left. The main route into the centre in the town's early days was via Gypsy Lane and Marpool Hill to come down Long Causeway and Boarden Barn into Fore Street.

It was never listed as an inn at first and was rather a quaint thatched house where cider was sold and possibly dating from the early-seventeenth century. It is likely that it continued as such until it was rebuilt in the 1920s.

Known licensees over the years have included:

1830–38:	James Hayward.
1857:	Charles Smith.
1878:	Edward Hoskin.
1884–97:	Henry Hussey.
1902–23:	Francis Charles Horn.
1926:	Mr and Mrs A.F.H. Pratley.
1948:	E.G. Holman.

There is a well-known painting of the inn in 1900, now in the town's library. During this period of tenancy the landlord's brother, Ben Horn, played for Exmouth Rugby Club. He died in 1962. After 1957 the inn was closed and the licence and name was transferred to the Kimberley Hotel, further down the road and on the other side.

THE FIRST AND LAST HOUSE (NO.2)

The old First and Last had been demolished when the licence was transferred further down the street to this property which had traded as the Kimberley Hotel.

By 1961, the licensee was Beatrice Holman, followed by Edgar G. and Vera E. Holman. By 1971 Frederick J. and Irma H. George had taken over. Throughout the 1980s and into the 1990s, Gerald J. and Margarita V. Wall were running the house, but by 1998 it was run by John F. Minall. In 1999, Gary Bell was behind the bar with Derek Francis.

First and Last (2).

A Customs and Excise raid in March 2000 in the search for contraband tobacco failed to find anything. In June of the same year a rather unusual evening took place: Laser Karaoke.

In the autumn of 2000 Mrs Vera Holman died, aged 90, having served this inn for very many years.

THE FORRESTERS ARMS, CHAPEL STREET

This was a small and friendly inn on the corner of Chapel Street and Market Street. Dating from the mid-nineteenth century, it may have been frequented earlier as a cider house. It was demolished when the Magnolia Centre was created in the 1970s.

The licensees known to have worked at the Forresters Arms include:

1873:	James Lesley.
1878:	William Coombes.
1884:	Edwin George Ferris, until after 1897.
1902:	Tom Rogers.
1906:	Charles Henry Tucker.
1914:	Alfred Bulley.
1919:	William Pope, followed by Frank Pope until after 1930.
1936:	Mr and Mrs F.J. Nicholls, who were probably present throughout the Second World War.
1948:	Mr and Mrs R. Eddy.
1950–71:	Mr and Mrs Greenway.

THE GEORGE INN

Situated in George Street from which it obviously took its name, the George Inn existed solely, as far as has been traced, in the nineteenth century. The earliest reference to this public house is in 1830, when the licensee was Charles Maypee. In 1850 it was described as a beerhouse with the same Charles Maypee still in charge, but on 9 June 1859, the licence was transferred from James Wishart to Richard Bayley.

A further transfer of the licence occurred on 24 December 1862, from Mrs Emily Best (formerly Williams) to William Best. Clearly her new husband, who was a shipowner in Exmouth, had taken over. However, only just over a year later, on 27 January 1864, he transferred the licence to Tryphena Tooze of Exmouth.

Two years afterwards, William Crowther was the landlord and by 1873 Samuel Milton had succeeded, during whose tenancy the inn was probably closed down. Nothing is traceable after this date.

THE GLOBE (FACING THE STRAND)

For many years the Globe Inn was the most famous and popular hotel in the town. It was the centre of the social scene and community life. It was said to have been originally standing in Wellington Place before 1700 and was the venue for the monthly Petty Sessional Court and the annual Manor Court, which was held on the first Thursday in November. The Founder's Feast of Drakes Charity was also held annually at the Globe. Old play bills reveal that the corner on which the hotel stood was referred to as Theatre Street, where the various travelling companies produced their plays. This was also the area where trading stalls were set up by hawkers and travelling salesmen.

Stagecoaches ran from London to Exeter as early as 1678 and the Globe was the terminus of the Exeter and Salterton coaches. By 1790 the Mail, presumably a carrier service, left the Globe at 7a.m., six days a week. Another coach, the Defiance, went between the Globe and the London hotels, leaving daily at 9.30a.m. and departing from Exeter for the return journey at 4p.m. This coach was run by a local firm, Russell's Coaches. From 1836, a steam packet ship ran from Exmouth to London weekly and in 1858 a steamboat, the *Royal Princess*, ran three times a month to the Channel Islands. This was an eight-hour journey.

The Globe stood facing the Strand, which at that time was the coastline, as the tide came to within a few yards of its gardens. These gardens faced the northern half of what became known as the Square, and later the Strand Gardens. There was sufficient room for grazing horses, a bowling green and gardens for leisure. All this was available for the guests and stood between the Clink and part of what later became the old Market Place. There was one drawback; an open yard nearby, belonging to a Robert Bird, was a receptacle for every type of rubbish.

As noted the name of this famous hostelry, the Globe, appears in many a town or village. It was the symbol adopted by King Manuel of Portugal and by the merchants of that country. It became popular as an inn sign after the marriage of England's Charles II and the Portuguese Princess Catherine of Braganza in 1662 and the treaty with Portugal.

Records dating from 1748 show that the Globe was mistakenly called the New Inn. In 1770 Robert Wood was the proprietor and the whole premises were refurbished, and an extension was added. It was then described as being 'in an elegant manner' with a new Assembly Room and a new bowling green opened by subscription on Saturday 26 May 1770. A public breakfast was served every Thursday and a card assembly organized every Monday. Robert Wood charged his guests 10s.6d. per week for full board. He gave way to Mr Bastin in 1778, who did not stay long.

On 17 February 1780, the Fleet's success against Spain under Admiral Rodney was celebrated on the Parade as well as on the long plain in front of the Globe. On 27 October in the same year the Globe Inn was offered to let for a term. At this time the premises consisted of four parlours, a coffee room, large dining room, eight bed chambers, a large enclosed stable yard, coach-houses and sheds for carriages as well as a garden with a small field. The furniture was to be taken at its valuation, and applicants were told to contact Mrs Wood. All of this begs the question – had Mr Wood died?

Mr William Pomeroy came from the Golden Lion Inn to take over the Globe in 1783. He had been Exmouth's first Postmaster. However, the lavish balls he put on brought him to bankruptcy in 1798, despite a good Assembly in the previous year. Admittedly there had been a rather high tide in February 1792, which brought flooding up as far as the Globe's garden hedge. Endeavouring to recoup some of his losses, he turned to the open road as a highwayman, but was soon captured trying to rob a passing carriage when a passenger was able to identify him. As a result of his bankruptcy, the Globe Inn was put up for sale by private tender in June 1798.

The Revd Richard Polwhele in his *History of Devonshire* of 1797 described the Globe as having a good Assembly Room.

Around this time, Mr Orlando Lockyer junr arrived and announced that he had entered the inn and begged '... to inform the nobility, gentry and others' on 5 January 1799. He was not there for long; in May 1800, Thomas Chapman, butler to Archdeacon Moore for 28 years, took over. By 1802, Thomas Chapman had fitted the inn to cater more successfully for the summer season. He remained as landlord up until 1822 when he died. His widow Grace Chapman (who was said to have been a rather large lady) took over, having the surety of Richard Palfrey and J. Force to the sum of £20. During her period of tenancy there were many celebrations, in particular the Jubilee of King George III in 1809, Nelson's victories at sea and that of Wellington at Waterloo in 1815, when '... the tyrant conquered on the plains of Waterloo'. There was a call for subscriptions for the benefit of the families of the brave men killed and for the wounded sufferers of the British Army under the command of the illustrious Wellington.

While Grace Chapman was still the licensee, the 1826 Christmas Ball was cancelled '... on account of the lamentable death of the Duke of York'. However, by March 1831 there was an announcement:

To be let by tender for a term of seven years with early possession, that old established, commodious and highly respectable Family and Posting House called the Globe Hotel, with the Coach Houses, Stabling, Garden and Premises thereto belonging, situated in the most eligible part of the above highly esteemed watering place [Exmouth]... Apply to Mrs Chapman at the Globe Hotel.

Also in 1831 Parliament's permission was sought to change the route of the road from Burnt House in Lympstone to the Globe in Exmouth, making it a toll road with toll houses. The toll house at the top of the hill near the road to A la Ronde still survives; it is privately occupied.

By September 1832 it was announced that the Exmouth Christmas Ball at the Globe Hotel would be under the distinguished patronage of Lady Rolle. Unfortunately she was unable to be present on the day, but Lord and Lady William Somerset and family, Sir J.B.Y. and Lady Butler and a large party from Bicton House did attend. The music was advertised as the best of Exeter. There were many of these events during the 1830s.

On 27 November 1835 it was announced that the Globe Hotel was to be sold by tender:

... not having been sold at the Auction last week. It is now in the occupation of a very responsible tenant for a term of ten years from Ladyday 1834 at a low rent of £102 payable quarterly, clear of taxes. Sealed tenders are invited.

By 1838 Henry Bastin had taken over, to be joined by his brother Benjamin soon afterwards. They had also owned Wellington House and by 1844 were running the Marine Hotel on the Beacon. However, they continued at the Globe for many years, the Bastin name being known through the 1850s and on into the 1860s. In about 1840 the Globe Inn was described as having:

... Ball and Assembly Rooms, with retiring and card rooms of ample dimensions where the gentry held it to be a pleasurable duty to meet in public and set forth examples of courtesy and manners – all the existing fashion and beauty of the place.

The Property and Income Tax Commissioners met at the Globe on Monday 23 January 1843. They sat for nine hours, but had to resume on the following day to finish business; the Surveyor and the Assistant Clerk also had to remain. The following month Mr J.P. Anderson, Professor of Rhetoric, held lectures on Thursday and Friday, 15 and 16 February at 2s. per lecture or 3s.6d. for two. He only charged 1s. for the evening lecture.

On 2 September 1845 a meeting at the Globe was convened by the inhabitants of the town to receive a deputation of the Exeter, Topsham and Exmouth Railway. The Mayor of Exeter on behalf of the proprietors of the railway detailed the expected advantages of a cheap and easy communication between Exeter and Exmouth. More details followed with various questions and observations from the inhabitants. Resolutions followed and were recorded.

On 1 May 1861, the opening of the Exeter and Exmouth Railway was celebrated and after the formal ceremony at the station, attended by the Exeter, Exmouth and Teignmouth Artillery Corps, as well as the Coastguard and Naval Reserve under the command of Captain Hawkins, everyone gathered in a square in front of the Globe Hotel. The hotel was crowded and a testimonial was presented to Mr Walter Aylesbury who had contributed much to the promotion of the railway. At 3p.m. between 150 and 200 people sat down to a sumptuous banquet provided by the host, Mr Bastin.

On 21 March 1862 a son was born to the wife of Mr Benjamin Bastin. The Globe Hotel had to be demolished in 1867 to make way for the development of the new Rolle Street, which was not completed until 1875. This was a sad loss to the town. There are pictures in the Exmouth Reference Library of the Globe in the 1860s.

THE GOLDEN LION

From what information seems to be available, this pub appears to have been in existence only during the latter half of the eighteenth century, and then just for a few years. Where it was situated has never been indicated.

We know that on 12 March 1779 a sale took place at the inn and that on 11 June in the same year it was described as the house of Mr Pomeroy (who was the butler to the Ducarrel family at the Manor House on Chapel Hill). It was then known as the Golden Lion. Also in 1779, a Survey was held there on 31 December.

On 4 May 1781 a public auction was advertised to be held there on 16 May. Then on 18 May the place was described as 'Mr Pomeroy's Golden Lion.' However, we know that William Pomeroy moved to the Globe Inn, so it is possible that his move from these premises brought an end to this comparatively short period of trading.

THE GREAT TREE INN

This eighteenth-century inn was described as a long, low thatched building near Manchester Quay, where the tide came in close and not far from where Manchester House was built in 1795.

It had been so named because the Great Tree stood outside and marked the boundary between the parishes of Littleham, in which the inn stood, and Withycombe Raleigh. Pictures of the Great Tree Inn show that the River Exe was very close.

In 1761 the inn was under the control of a Captain Mitchell, but no further records appear to exist of any other landlords. It is possible that from around 1780 onwards the inn served as a stopover for the passengers of the Starcross ferry whilst it was using Manchester Quay. The name of the inn was changed to the York Hotel because Manchester House had become a 'grace and favour house' of the Duke of York. The full story of the change and the reasons for it are told under the history of the York Hotel itself.

THE GROVE

Situated at the western end of the Esplanade, this late-Victorian house was built in the grounds of Templetown Lodge. It is likely that initially it was called Templetown Cottage. The design is based along the lines of a Bavarian house with its steep pitched roofs and black timbered frames. It was occupied in the early years of the twentieth century by Mr and Mrs H. Avery. By the time of the outbreak of the Second World War it had become the Grove Hotel, with Major J.P. Moon as the proprietor. After the war, still a hotel, the Grove was being managed by Mr S.H. Elphinstone and then by 1952 it was owned by Mr and Mrs S.T. Weller.

The property changed hands once or twice in the 1960s and was renamed Eymard House, but in 1988 the Anderson family bought it, carried out much renovation and alteration and took up the old name again; it became The Grove. The licensees were Steve and Stephanie Doble. It became a good house for food, and with the layout of the front gardens with tables and chairs it attracted many customers.

There was a period during which a varying

The Grove.

selection of real ales were available, attracting their specialist customers. The Dobles were still running the inn in 2000. They placed a double-page advertisement in the *Exmouth Journal* telling of its newly-created upstairs dining room, which then featured a display of drawings of local river and estuary views by Paul Butler. The bar downstairs had been described as having a traditional timber décor and furniture.

THE HALF-WAY HOUSE
(FORMERLY BURT'S)

This was a picturesque, thatched little house on the Salterton Road at Littleham Cross. It appeared in the 1856 *Devonshire Directory*. Before that, on 13 March 1851 at the Devon Lent Assizes, John Bast was prosecuted in an assault and robbery case at the Half-Way House.

It is not certain whether the Half-Way House became the Cranford Hotel or the Cranford was built slightly in front of the original; general opinion favours the latter theory. It seems that when the Cranford Hotel was built in the 1920s, its car park covered the Half-Way House.

THE HEAVITREE ARMS

This inn was the successor to the North Country Sailor which had traded for over 150 years at the top of Chapel Hill and on the corner of High Street, before the name was changed around 1890.

William George Manley was the first tenant trading under this name. In 1893 a trade token was issued for the Heavitree Arms under the name of J. Rook. He continued until 1902 when John Woods took over and held the licence until after the end of the First World War. Another member of the Woods family, Hugo Sandford Wood, became the landlord in 1923 and he was followed by Edward Metcalf from 1926 until 1930. Then a Mr W. Letten came in until 1936 when, during his

The Heavitree Arms.

tenancy, two adjacent properties were purchased: Dodds Dairy and Ferris' Crab Shop. After this much of the pub was rebuilt, so that a fine outdoor section for family groups was provided, and the interior was modernised, although the original underground cellars still remain.

By 1939 William Patrick McCarthy became landlord and presumably stayed throughout the Second World War. Mr and Mrs E.R. Hillier came in 1953 after a short period during which R.T. Gough held the inn. The Hilliers stayed for ten years and were followed by Guy and Ethel Goodman. Gerald and Mary Bolton were there by 1971, but the Voters List for 1981–2 shows that Leslie and Moira Holland were in charge. They were still landlords as late as 1995 – they were among the longest serving landlords in Exmouth at the time.

Although it is still one of the most popular places in town where customers can sit out in the sun, there have been complaints about the noise. These were registered with the East Devon District Council Licensing Committee in April 2000. After a hearing, with the joint licensees present, Mrs Sara Diane Ross was granted a renewal on condition that a rear door to the premises was kept closed to reduce the level of noise.

(It is worth mentioning that in researching the history of this public house, the author was loaned a history of the Heavitree Arms and its former North Country Sailor Inn, with the kind permission of Miss E. Burridge. This family had in the past been associated with not only this pub but the Builders Arms as well. The Burridges were also builders of several of Exmouth's churches and fine houses.)

THE HOLE IN THE WALL

This seems to have been a small inn or just a bar at the rear of the Beacon Vaults. There is no trace of a separate licence at any time for this house. In fact in 1953 it was recorded as being integral to the Beacon Vaults. There was certainly a separate bar and entrance and it attracted a different clientele that gave the bar its individual identity.

THE HOLLY TREE INN

Situated in the centre of Withycombe village, this was originally a brewhouse, where the Stocker family originally brewed their own beers. One of the early names for the brewhouse was The Bush or The Holly Bush, but it is unknown when the bush became a tree; an event that led to the name change. A rumour claims the establishment was an alehouse by 1670. However, there is a reference in 1757 to a meet at Mrs Mason's public house in the parish of Withycombe Raleigh during the reign of George II.

The Holly Tree Inn.

THE JOLLY SAILOR

This inn was situated in Fore Street from the late-eighteenth century onwards. It was reported that on 13 December 1792 the Loyal Assembly of British Rats and reputable tradesmen met here. Meetings each evening were chaired by Captain W.W. After drinking to 'King and Constitution' many other patriotic toasts were given and songs were sung into the early hours.

On 26 December 1805 a Survey was held at the Jolly Sailor for a number of premises in the town to be sold on 15 January 1806. Then on 2 August 1823 it was announced that the Jolly Sailor Inn on Fore Street was to be sold by auction. At that time under the occupation of Mrs Thomasina Tillman, the property was held for two lives under Lord Rolle. Mrs Tillman was the widow of Thomas Tillman, the previous tenants and standing surety for her at this time were Thomas Linscott and J. Cridge together in the sum of £20. Mrs Tillman married again in 1822, this time to a Thomas Goodsir, and by June had decided to leave the trade at the Jolly Sailor. Consequently, business there was suspended for a while. It seems logical to assume that if just two years were remaining on a 99-year lease, the lease was originally granted in 1724.

It was put up for sale on 18 June 1822 and a Mr Martin became the landlord. However, it was reported that he had died just seven years later. There seems to be no record of any subsequent trading, so the inn was probably closed down then.

The earliest reference to it as the Holly Tree Inn related to an auction held there on 22 February 1849. It next appears in the 1836 *Devonshire Directory* when the licensee was Henry Barnes with his wife Sarah; both were aged 43 and they had a son of 20, another Henry. This licensee was charged on 4 June 1857 with keeping his house open after 3p.m. on a Sunday afternoon. He was fined 5s. plus expenses – 16s. in all. He was in trouble again in 1860 and was charged by Mr Carter, the Overseer of the Poor, with failing to contribute to the maintenance of his mother, who was elderly. The Bench made an order for 2s. per week. Other sundry events are recorded in the 1860s, the house being in the hub of village life. The Riot Act was read on 27 November 1867 to a mob outside the inn, following the Bread Riots which took place throughout Exmouth at this time.

Then in 1868 the pub was taken down completely and rebuilt. It should be noted that in 1887 the beer was sold at 4½d. per pint, which included an ounce of tobacco! The next licensee was Richard Windover. There then seems to be a gap in the records for the rest of the nineteenth century; the next entry is dated 1911 when Mr Stocker was the licensee. He and his wife stayed there until after 1934, for a period of over 20 years.

Other landlords recorded include: Mr and Mrs C.H. West, staying for over ten years from 1950, and Aubrey E. and Maureen Watkins, who were there in 1981–2. In the 1990s the building was largely refurbished, being converted from the two or three individual bars into one large open area. It now also displays a Spitfire propeller.

The premises themselves are owned by the Inn Partnership, and by 2000 the licensees were Chris and Maria Bridle, having been there for about five years. There is evidence that it is a popular meeting place for the local football club with all its supporters.

THE KIMBERLEY HOTEL

Situated in Church Street, this house has, since 1957, been called the First and Last Inn.

It appears to have been in existence from the late-nineteenth century when a Mr Treville was the licensee. He was succeeded in 1902 by Henry Havill who came from the Customs House on the Quay in Exeter. He issued a brass token marked with the maker's name of Seage and Sons and valued at 3d.

It was Havill who continued to hold the licence as a brewer until 1923 when he moved to the Old Coach and Horse Inn in Exeter. By 1929 Thomas and Lilian Lee were the landlords, but between 1931 and 1936 Mr and Mrs L.A. Emms were in charge. By 1948 it was Mr and Mrs T. Sellick who had taken over, and another change saw Mr and Mrs T.J. Shepherd becoming licensees. In 1957 the change was made to the First and Last.

Why the original name, Kimberley, was used is not known. It may be that it had some link with the diamond mine in South Africa of that name, which was well known in England.

THE KING'S ARMS

This inn was in Lower Fore Street near the Cross. The earliest records were of a report on 19 April 1827 that thieves had broken into the public house kept by Mrs Elizabeth Crudge and carried away £9 in silver and other change, some silver tablespoons, the public licence itself and some spirits. Standing surety for her at this time to the sum of £10 was John Crudge, possibly her husband, but she also had to stand surety for £10.

The house was put up for sale on 19 November 1829, the tenant at that time being David Lewis. He probably failed to sell, for it was reported that his wife, aged 37, had died there in December 1834. It was up for sale again on 18 June 1839:

The King's Arms – Near the Cross – the premises now in the occupation of John Potter, tenant at will, being famed for good beer and great custom. It is a Free House.

The 1851 Census shows the occupier as John Toby with his wife Mary and a daughter of 14. Joseph Fletcher then became the landlord. He was served in September 1857 by a maltster named Emanuel Vine (see Clarence Inn) with deliveries of malt. Fletcher had been paying Vine in instalments when he could. On nine occasions he had made payments for which he had not been given a receipt. Vine then sued Fletcher for the money. Fortunately, Fletcher was able to provide witnesses to the payments and so Vine was fined a total of £90 – in other words, £10 for each queried payment.

Fletcher stayed at the pub until later that year when a Mrs Snow moved in. The next change appears to have been on 11 June 1862 when the licence was transferred from the late Mrs Snow to Thomas Searle Harding. By 1873 though, a *Post Office Directory* shows that a Richard Smith was holding the King's Arms, and that seems to have been the last record of this inn.

LEE'S ALEHOUSE

This 'well-accustomed' public house was primarily a dwelling house that held a licence for many years. It was situated behind the Cliff's End House (now the Park Hotel) and had every convenience for the business. On 14 February 1777 it was advertised to be let on the following Lady Day, but no further records have been found.

A store at the rear of the Park Hotel has the appearance of having been at some time a small house, which may have been Lee's Alehouse.

LENNARD'S BAR

Originally a grocer's shop known as East India House, these premises needed very little alteration to convert them into a free public house in the late 1960s. The first licensee was R.L. Lennard and the house simply took his name. He had previously been with Clark's Shoe Factory, so the trade was completely new to him and his wife Mabel. He was responsible for the design of the bar and dining areas, and he made the appearance identical to a pub they had visited in Strasbourg.

There was an emphasis on grills and snacks and success followed; after he died in the 1980s, his widow continued working before their son Bruce joined her. There were great celebrations to welcome him into the trade with his mother. In September 1984 Lennard's Bar was the venue for the Super League Darts Tournament for that year; Bruce and his staff welcomed the teams and their supporters to what had by then become known as Exmouth's most popular free house.

When Mabel Lennard died, Bruce continued the business himself into the 1990s, although his wife Nichola left. However, Bruce was married again in 1997, to Gillian King, and they ran the pub together for another two years. Then in late 1999 the Lennards retired and the bar was sold. The house was renamed Molloys and that sign went up in early 2000. There now appears to be an Irish connection.

THE LONDON INN / HOTEL

Built in 1800 in Bond Street, an extension of Chapel Street at the bottom of Albion Hill, this very fine building soon became known as a coaching inn. From here Messrs Chapman and Reed introduced a service from Exmouth to Exeter at a single fare of 3s.6d. or a same-day return of 5s. At the time of its building there were found on the site some ancient fish hooks, oyster shells, pottery from old cooking pots, clay pipe stems and, most surprisingly, the timber frame of a thirteenth-century house.

John Gifford was the first landlord, having taken over on 21 November 1805. Three years later he was making it clear that he intended to continue in the business; he kept a good larder, the best of liqueurs, well-aired beds, stall stabling, lock-up coach-houses, neat post chaises, good horses and careful drivers!

The open area in front of the building was known as London Square and was used for rallies and public meetings. The Town Crier used the canopy as a vantage point from which to hail the populace.

A dance academy run by Mr Diot commenced at the London Hotel from Monday 30 January 1809 at 12 noon. From 7 March 1815, the hotel was also used by Dr Lambert of the Exeter Dispensary to meet patients on Tuesdays.

Peace with France was celebrated in 1815 and a procession of 500 children dressed as shepherds and shepherdesses paraded through the town led by Britannia's carriage, drawn by four horses abreast. This procession marched from the Beacon to Marpool Hill where 'a profession of wines, cider, ale and cakes were in readiness' before returning then to the Point where, near the windmill, an immense dinner had been prepared by the Globe and London Inns.

After four years of illness, John Gifford died. In the following year, on 27 May 1819, the inn was put up for sale, after a period during which the widow was the host. However, no sale resulted, and Mrs Sarah Gifford had to renew the licence on 27 January 1820. In the following years she continued as a most capable hostess and numerous events were celebrated. However, on 31 May 1831 it was reported that she had in her possession nine gallons and two quarts of rum over and above the quantity entered in the proper officers' books. The case against her was heard on 12 July 1831, when the quantity of rum claimed was forfeited.

In February 1835 a dinner at Gifford's London Hotel was held to celebrate the triumph of Conservative principles with the return of Sir John Buller as MP.

In May 1843, Sarah's son William Clifford married a Miss Chapman of North Street, Exmouth. By 1850, Sarah Gifford was 83 and her other son John was 53. He became the landlord after her death, expressing his gratitude for the liberal support given to him by his late mother who had been the licensee for over 30 years.

Ten years later, in March 1862, Walter Gifford from Teignmouth, perhaps another son of Sarah, succeeded to the hotel, but he was soon in trouble. He was summoned for keeping his house open after hours on Sunday 18 May and was fined 2s. plus costs of 10s. He then announced that he had taken over the refreshment room at the new railway station.

Throughout the years, the London Hotel was a favourite venue for the many and varied events being held in the town: dinners, celebrations and society meetings. However, on 29 January 1863 it was put up for sale:

All that valuable desirable public commercial and Posting House known as the London Inn – successful for the past 30 years – sold because of the death of the owner.

Succeeding owners had continued to run a very successful and thriving business.

In 1873 another Walter Gifford took the licence, perhaps the son of the previous Walter, and in 1878 Henry Hawkins was in charge. In 1884 John Everett Poole was in situ, but by 1897 William John Thomas had taken over. The inn was sold in 1902 to John Richard Newberry but in 1906 J.E. Poole was running it for the second time. He stayed into the 1920s by which time Thomas and William Pearce were the licensees. By 1936, Mr and Mrs D.S. Purnell were the licensees and they advertised that they would meet any train as a way of welcoming their guests. At the beginning of the Second World War, Mr H. Kemp was in charge; Mr and Mrs F.D.R. Baker came in 1948, followed by Mr and Mrs E.A. Marshall in 1953. Mrs G.W. Abell ran the hotel in the late 1950s. Peter M. Haslock was in charge until 1962, but the last landlady was Mrs D. Rose.

Warned that the premises might be demolished because of a development project, the brewery transferred the licence to one of their Directors, John B. Coulson. The plan for a major reconstruction was prepared, but Devon County Council warned that there could be plans for the compulsory acquisition of the premises, and in 1964 the hotel was completely demolished (although the name can still be seen in the London Inn car park at the rear). After demolition the site was absorbed in the widening of that end of Chapel Street, which became Bond Street and the foot of Albion Street. It was a great loss to the town for it was a fine building.

THE MALTSTERS ARMS

This public house was situated in Tower Street in the early 1800s. The licensee at that time was Emanuel Vine and he stayed for a number of years. According to records, he was there from 1830 to 1850, but he was fined on 12 July 1849 for having three pint cups deficient of measure and unstamped. He was fined 5s. with 6s. expenses.

See the entries for the Blue Anchor, the Anchor, the New Inn and the Criterion for consideration as to how each in turn traded from what seem to have been the same premises in Tower Street.

MUTTER'S CIDER SHOP

Situated at the corner of Hamilton Road and the Salterton Road, Mutter's Cider Shop was held by Abraham and Sam Mutter and in former times was said to be a place where much contraband changed hands. It was thought to have been the nerve centre of the Jack Rattenbury smuggling operation in the Exmouth area. Sam Mutter, a daring and experienced seaman, operated his boat by night, landing cargoes at selected spots along the coast between Exmouth and Seaton, whilst his family worked the distribution racket. Runs came up from the coast through the Maer and Limekiln Lane. It is also said that if Mrs Mutter was the only one in the shop, it meant that Sam and Abraham were away on a 'run'. However Sam was caught in 1843, convicted and imprisoned, but he soon bounced back into his colourful lifestyle once he was released.

In 1866 when Mrs Mary Mutter was also a beer retailer, which continued until 1873, the Mutter family had the rare distinction of having a county moor named after them. Mutters Moor is near Sidmouth and no doubt the little village called Mutterton was also named after them.

THE NEW INN, CHAPEL STREET

In 1724 this inn was said to be next to the Chapel of St Margaret's. It possibly acted as a resting place for passengers for the nearby ferry to Starcross, which started from Pratteshyde. Polwhele, the historian, noted in 1791 that by the 1724 description he understood this resting place to be the Globe Inn, but this theory seems unlikely.

It was in about 1770 that the name changed to that of the Exeter Inn, but no further record has been traced in terms of the licensees.

THE NEW INN, LITTLEHAM

Erected in 1903, the New Inn's first landlord was Ted Addis. He came here when the Strand Hotel, next to Miller's Garage on the Strand, was closed and the licence transferred. Coincidentally the branch line of the Exmouth to Littleham railway also reached here in 1903. Ted Addis stayed until 1930 giving a fine service to the locals.

Later licensees were another Mr and Mrs Addis, who had taken over by 1934 and stayed until after 1939. It is possible that they stayed through the war years as well. In 1950 a Mr and Mrs W.J. Norris became the licensees and they stayed until after 1962. It was in the late 1960s that the name of the inn was changed to the Clinton Arms.

THE NEW INN, TOWER STREET

There are anomalies surrounding the dates of this inn in Tower Street, where there were also three other public houses. Based on the dates of known licensees, they seem to be:

The Anchor or Blue Anchor:	*c.1811 to 1830.*
The Maltsters:	*1830 to 1850.*
The New Inn:	*1850 until it burnt down.*
The Criterion:	*1880 to 1902.*

THE NEW INN, SOUTH TOWN

The New Inn certainly traded as such from the early-nineteenth century until 1866, when it is said to have become the Bicton Inn. However, this contrasts with the information about the Red Lion. Known licensees are: Ann Taverner, John Taverner, Mr Radford and William Podbury.

THE NORTH COUNTRY SAILOR

This is an early name for what is now known as the Heavitree Arms. It dates from the early-eighteenth century, being well known by 1758 when Richard Parker took over as licensee. It was then a brick- and stone-faced building with a thatched roof projecting into what was then known as Chapel Street and is now High Street. This inn's name refers mainly to the men who frequented it; sailors from the colliers bringing coal from the north-east coalfields of Durham and Yorkshire. At that time Exmouth was the port from which the hinterland of South Devon was supplied with coal.

It was probably just a beerhouse at first and before 1758 it was said to be mainly in the possession of the Langford and Huxley families. The sea was fairly close then, covering the present Manor Gardens and reaching to the foot of Beacon Cliff. The coal boats were often beached and unloaded at low tide into horse-drawn carts on the beach beside them. There were no docks until a century later.

A report in Flindell's *Western Luminary* of 11 January 1810 gave the prices of coal in a barrel as 24s. for Sunderland coal and the same per quarter of Newcastle coal. By May 1815, the price had dropped to 18s.6d. per quarter as 11 colliers had arrived in Exmouth at the same time and competition was fierce.

Richard Parker, mentioned above, died in 1770 and his widow Mary Parker carried on until 1772, when her daughter Elizabeth took over. Elizabeth continued until 1794 when another relative, Hannah Parker, came in. She was named in the *Licensed Victuallers Recognisances* of 1797 when she sold out to Robert Palfrey, a cabinet maker who went on to hold the licence for about 30 years until his death on 10 January 1827 at the age of 72. He was described then as 'a truly honest man'. His widow, Sarah Palfrey, carried on until 1830 when the inn passed to William Mildren. At this time, Mr J. Force and Richard Palfrey (no doubt related to Robert) stood surety in the sum of £20 for Robert. The same two gentlemen were also standing surety for George Chapman of the Globe Inn.

The next proprietor was William Blake who came in 1830, but he died in 1845 and his widow, Tamsin Blake, continued. She was still there in 1857, but went bankrupt in 1863 and died in December 1864 aged 67. There seems to have been a period with no licensee in possession and so the inn remained closed. It was nine years later, in 1873, that William Brewer became the licensee and he was succeeded by Folliott Burridge, who had been given the licence as a wedding present. He soon lost it again through keeping open late at night. The Burridge family were builders of Exmouth houses and churches.

It was at this stage, in view of the loss of the licence, that the Heavitree Brewery stepped in, changed the name and put in a manager. The story therefore continues under the name of the Heavitree Arms.

THE OLD COUNTRY HOUSE INN, LITTLEHAM

This public house was situated on Westdown Lane, Littleham, and was once described as 'another local' in the village. It seems that other locals in the village were the New Inn which became the Clinton Arms, and possibly the Plough, which was next to the churchyard.

The earliest known record of a licensee at this inn referred to Mr and Mrs C.P. McClean. They retired in 1931 and Mr and Mrs W.P. Pascoe took over. They stayed until 1936. There is a gap in the records until 1948 when Frederick and Mary Stenner came in. It was 1973 before Barry Wakefield succeeded. By 1979 the James family were there, but it is questionable as to whether it was still an inn at this point. The Voters Lists from then on seem to imply that it was privately occupied.

THE PARK HOTEL

This was originally a Georgian mansion built in 1777 and known then as Cliff End House. It was literally standing on a small cliff overlooking the River Exe estuary. The Embankment, built by Mr Hull in 1812 out on the river edge, was some distance to the west and the development which followed, consisting of a number of houses between the Park Hotel and the river, became what is now known as the Colony. The creation of the coast road before it became a toll road, now known as the Exeter Road, was an even more important development.

The Park Hotel.

The house was first occupied by Charles Gifford, the brother of Lord Gifford, the Master of the Rolls, who died there on 4 February 1855, aged 80. In 1887 the house was taken over by a Roman Catholic priest, Father Grainger, and an upstairs room was converted into a chapel where, for the first time in 350 years, Mass was said in Exmouth. In 1891 the house was renamed 'The Lawn' and was taken over in the 1930s by the Exeter brewers Carr and Quick. It was then named the Park Hotel, presumably in recognition of Phear Park nearby. Mr C.J. Clarke was the manager and the weekly terms were 6 guineas.

In 1948, Mr and Mrs F. Lucas were the managers, followed by Mr and Mrs Stanley H. Smith in 1953. It seems that it opened as a public house in 1950 when Mr and Mrs H. Lee were there, but that would obviously have been for a short period between the Lucases and the Smiths.

Tracing the licensees in more recent years has been easier. In 1961 Mr and Mrs Alfred Hughes took over and in 1979 Carnival Week, the biggest giggle was the sponsored Pram Push with over 26 teams taking part. Each team of three adults, one of whom was in the pram, had to visit 11 Exmouth pubs and drink half a pint of ale in every one. First prize was for the fastest team and there was another for the team collecting the largest sum of sponsored cash. The route was from the Park Hotel to the Exmouth Arms via the Clarence, Volunteer, South Western Hotel, Lennard's Bar, Pilot, Heavitree Arms, Beacon Vaults, Imperial Hotel and Deer Leap.

The next licensees were Brian and Lilian Hawkins in 1981, who stayed until after 1985. Then in January of that year there was fighting in the bar and the house had to be closed down. By 1991 Philip W. Hall and Nicola Grubb were there, followed by Rita and Frank Burns in 1995, coming from the Farmhouse. Unfortunately a year or two later Rita died from a brain tumour. She was very much loved and excellent at her job. Then Dennis and Frances Brown were appointed, during which period Mrs Rowsell, their most efficient cook, retired.

In 1999 Mark Hardy and his sister Nicki took over. The hotel gained the title of 'Pub of the Year' for 2000 and hosts various events and entertainments throughout each week. Buddy Holley, who for many years was the DJ at the Cranford Hotel, has become the Park's DJ. In fact he held a Cranford Reunion night at the Park in July 2000. There is a large car park and a garden, which is suitable for children. The Park Hotel also has a website to facilitate bookings.

Behind the Park Hotel there was another dwelling house which at one time was known as Lee's Alehouse and on 14 February 1777 was let with the Park itself. Is it still a part of the Park's property?

THE PASSAGE HOUSE INN, THE POINT

When the Starcross ferry terminal was moved from its original site at Pratteshyde to Manchester Quay and then out on to the beach at the Point, where a ferry house was erected, this inn was built to serve waiting passengers. It provided accommodation as well as food and drink, and became popular with the workmen at the shipyards.

Following the very high spring tides on 1 February 1815, both the Passage House Inn and Sprague's Ferry House had to be vacated and the rear wall of the ferry house simply collapsed. Again in January 1817, the inn was flooded and the house was destroyed by the fury of the waves. A more substantial house was built in early 1817, the landlord then being Thomas Elson; he also happened to be the ferryman. He held the inn's licence until he died in 1827 at the grand old age of 96 years.

In 1830, John Treble ran the inn and he was followed by Mr W. Howe, who died six years later on 18 May 1836. He had previously been the gamekeeper to the late Earl of Devon at Powderham Castle across the river. Edward Howe, possibly the son, took over in 1838, his daughter having married a Mr H.J. Pyne in the previous December. During this period a raised footpath had been built to the preventive station nearby; it was about half a mile long and was completed by March 1836.

In March 1843, the body of a boy was picked up on Exmouth beach and lodged at this inn pending identification. In August of the same year, a fatal accident occurred when three passengers crossing on a boat from the Warren were thrown into the water by rough seas and a young servant girl was drowned. A man and a woman on the boat were saved and taken to the Passage House Inn. In January 1857, the body of a man named Little was found floating in the tide and another appeared a day later. Both were taken to the Passage House Inn to await a Coroner's inquest. Then in June of the same year, a man aged 20 from Tavistock was also found and the inquest verdict was 'accidentally drowned'.

In February 1850 John Treble transferred the licence to John Gard, but in the April of the same year, George Gard took over from John. George Gard had been fined in September 1856 for keeping his house open during Divine Service.

John Harris had become the landlord by 1857, then on 15 July 1858 he put the contents of the Passage House Inn up for sale. It was at this point that the name was changed to the Beach Hotel. There was a period, however, when it was known by both names.

THE PILOT INN

This inn stands at the top of Tower Street on the corner with Chapel Hill. It was known at one time as the Church House Inn at the top of Vicarage Hill. This name and address was linked with Holy Trinity Chapel almost directly opposite, which had been built in 1412 and demolished in 1827 when Trinity Church was built at the top of Rolle Road to accommodate the increase in the population of the town.

For a period the inn was also known as the Pilot Boat Inn, but the 'boat' part was dropped many years ago. Until the chapel opposite was demolished, the vicar of Littleham tried in vain to get the inn closed altogether because of the rowdy behaviour of its customers.

The earliest record of a licensee dates from 1830 when Robert Snell was the landlord for many years. However, on 12 July 1849, he was summoned by Mr Southcott, the Inspector of Weights and Measures, for having pint and half pint cups deficient of measure and unstamped. He was fined 10s. with 6s. expenses. He stayed until 1850; his application for the renewal of his licence on 29 May was refused as the vicar of Littleham presented a petition signed by many who complained of the pub's patrons' disorderly conduct. Some neighbours were even against the inn being on that site. It was common knowledge, too, that Robert Snell had a drunken wife, and so he was given notice to quit. The property itself was actually owned by a Mr Phillips.

It was George Leach who succeeded, but his wife unfortunately died in March 1852, aged only 35, a much-respected lady. It was reported on 14 October 1851 that a rather drunken man called Mealy went into the pub; the landlord attempted to remove him from the premises and Mealy's ear was almost cut off. A surgeon stitched it back on and George Leach was charged with assault, but the case was dismissed after several witnesses had been heard.

The Pilot Inn.

The Pilot Inn with its museum section.

On 18 May 1852, a new landlord, Mr Beavis, held his opening dinner. A local Rate Book for 1855 showed that a George Ellett was charged 8s.9d. for the inn, and he also seems to have had a brewery on the premises. He was a partner in the firm Ellett and Matthews, ship-brokers, and Chairman of the Ratepayers' Committee. In political circles he had the nickname of 'Mary Anne'. In 1870 Joseph Casley took over the inn. During that period of occupancy there was a meeting of local shipowners on 31 October 1866 with the merchants and pilots of the Port of Exeter.

It was after 1878 that a successor to Joseph Casley arrived; William Axon, who stayed until after 1884, appearing on the National Census Report of 1881. He must have died soon after, for his widow was there until after 1891. Then in 1897 the unusually-named Fortunatus Perriam became the landlord, staying until 1906. A famous relative, Nancy Perriam, had lived and died in the cottage next door to the inn, passing away at the age of 96 in 1865.

William James Axon, probably a relative of the previous William, took over in 1914, staying until after 1929, when Charles William and Jane Elizabeth Baker arrived. Charles Baker stayed for at least 20 years.

For many years, the inn's sign was a portrait of 'Dido' Bradford, a much-respected skipper of the pilot boat in which he served for many years with distinction. That sign has now been retired to the Lifeboat House on the Esplanade.

A landlord called B.G. Baylis was at the Pilot during the 1940s and by 1950 Mr and Mrs O.F. Rous were the licensees, followed by E. Huth in 1953. By 1961, Edward and Ellen Steer came, to be followed by Ronald and Jean Fiddaman in 1971. They stayed for some years, certainly until after 1985. In late August 1981, five pubs took part in a darts marathon, in aid of the Royal Devon and Exeter Kidney Unit Appeal. The pubs were led by the Pilot and followed by the Country House in Withycombe, the Swan at Lympstone, The

London and South Western at Topsham and the First and Last in Exeter. The event took place over the course of a week.

In fact the Fiddamans stayed until December 1986 when Rodney G. and Wendy Blackmore came from Watchet, but after three years they made way for David and Lynda Mone from Par in Cornwall. In 1999 Paul and Rachel Taylor arrived. In November of the same year it was said that the Pilot was the only inn sign to portray the Arms of Trinity House, due to its long standing association with pilots.

The inn now has two bars. The window boxes have won a prize in the Britain in Bloom competition. For many years this inn has displayed to its customers a fine collection of memorabilia relating to the profession of the pilots.

THE PLOUGH INN, LITTLEHAM

This house stood beside the churchyard in Littleham and had been a very old thatched building. The 1881 Census gave the occupier as Emanuel Ponsford, aged 49, with his wife Elizabeth. It was known locally as Ponsford's Cider Shop. The landlord was a well-known character and his house was a great meeting-place for the locals.

Cider was then 1½d. for the first pint and 1d. per pint thereafter. Many customers would order their 2 quarts on arrival and it was said that the bell-ringers from the church would drink off their quart without taking breath. One customer, 'Butcher' Dagworthy, rode his pony up the steps and right into the bar.

However, in 1906 on the death of Mr Ponsford, the Plough Inn closed; it was demolished by 1913 and the site used to extend the churchyard. The Plough was owned by Mr G. Burridge and his licence ended in 1907. There was an outcry at the time that the living had to make room for the dead! The front wall of the Plough was propped up in 1890 because of its dangerous state. After the demolition

The Plough.

there remained a brick pier with the hook for tethering horses.

Coincidentally a Jack Burridge, who had been born in the Plough Inn, died in the early days of 1996, aged 95; he was laid to rest in that part of Littleham Churchyard which had been the garden of the inn. Such an old building, so close to the church and the churchyard, must have had a very early history and it is a pity that nothing of it can now be traced.

THE PRINCE OF WALES INN (1)

This inn was sited in Chapel Street, though in which part it is not known. The only reference to it that has been traced was dated 24 October 1866, when Alexander Goss Luke was the licensee, and an inquest was held there on a blind man who had been brought into the inn.

The Prince of Wales (2) refers to a new pub in Brixington.

THE QUEEN'S HOTEL

Situated on the first corner of Victoria Road at the rear of Lloyd's Bank, this hotel was one of the last buildings to be erected on the road, having been started in 1897. It is a very decorative building, at the rear of which Tommy Lockyer, the donkey specialist, used to keep his animals, which were used for pulling invalid and special wheeled carriages.

This hotel opened for business when the nearby Railway Hotel was demolished – the Railway Hotel transferred its licence to the Queen's. The earliest known landlord was Henry Stephenson Coles in 1903, who stayed until after 1919. During his tenancy a famous drinking party was held there in 1903, which was headed by Bert Bridle and his friends. The event was captured in a photograph, which can now be seen in Exmouth's Reference Library.

The Queen's Hotel.

By 1923, Henry Meekings was the landlord and he did not stay long, for John and Mabel Harris were in by 1929. In 1948 Mr and Mrs C.M. Nelson were running the hotel and they stayed until after 1953, possibly until James and Freda Parkinson arrived in 1981 (although it is possible that in between James and Evelyn Leisk spent some time there in the 1960s).

The New Year's Fancy Dress Party in December 1978 was a great success, with music from the Glad Band. By 1981 the Queen's had become an Antarctic pub with a completely reconstructed lounge, new bench seats in what was formerly the snug and a completely new toilet block. It served a wide range of Whitbread beers and the landlord, Basil Parkinson, was the Chairman of the Exeter and District LVA. He was helped by his daughter Susan and her husband Paul Bishop, who added some of the attractive finishing touches to the new bar.

In 1985 the hotel was running a football team and this was when Paul and Susan Bishop were in charge. By 1991, Pauline Ward and Paul and Susan Bishop were there, but later that same year, Pauline Ward with Kevin Wint were holding the licence. By 1999, it had been renamed the Pitchers and a century of history as the Queen's had come to an end.

THE RAILWAY INN

This public house stood on the Strand on the junction with Victoria Road and with Thomas' on the other side. At that time Thomas' was the predecessor to Hancock and Wheeler's ironmongery shop, outside which hung the huge kettle. This inn may have been the successor to the Brewhouse on the Strand, though there appears to be an overlapping in the dates. The inn was located next to Underhill's shoe shop, which later became the Post Office and later still Lloyd's Bank. Litten's fruit and vegetable shop was demolished to make way for the entry of Victoria Road into the Strand in 1897, when Thomas Waters was the landlord of the inn. The licence was at that time transferred to the Queen's Hotel in Victoria Road.

There are records of licensees here at the Brewhouse long before the railway itself came into the town in 1861. Under the name of the Railway Inn, however, we have James Pound in 1839, William J. Fouracre in 1857, John Dove Dixon from 1865 until after 1870, and we find his widow Mrs Louise Dixon there from 1873. By 1878 James Henry Clode is named and he remained until after the 1881 Census Report. By 1884 Samuel Williams had arrived, followed by Thomas Waters (mentioned above) when it was known as Waters' Railway Hotel in

Strand Court. It was he who transferred the Railway Inn's licence to the Queen's Hotel in 1897, by which time the railway was more established.

However, an alternative record suggests that James Melhuish was licensee in 1834 and he was followed by Mr Neave, who on 17 September 1846 put the business up for sale because he was about to leave the trade. Another James Pound with his wife Joanna came in 1850 and then it was William J. Fouracre by 1857. It is difficult to determine which is correct.

THE RED LION

This public house stood in South Street at its corner with Bicton Street and appears to date from the period 1760 to 1790, although there are no surviving records of the licensees of those days. We only know that Henry Bastin had the tenancy from 1850, for on 15 June 1864 he was fined £3 plus expenses for selling beer on Sunday morning, 4 June. He was certainly there in 1862 when he issued a brass trade token. Then in 1866 it became the Bicton Inn.

THE ROYAL OAK

This inn was situated on the newly-built Exeter Road at the time when that side was being developed; it then had a rear exit into New Street.

The first licensee was Joseph Russell in 1878 and he was also named in the 1881 Census Report with his wife Jane (52) and daughter (29). At that time he was 56 years of age, but seems to have died soon afterwards, as Jane, the widow, was named in 1884 as the licensee. She stayed for quite a long time, at least until 1910, when she was over 80 years old but still in charge, and probably up to 1914. By 1923 Walter Ebdon Ramsey was the landlord, to be followed by Edgar Norton in 1929. He stayed until 1932.

By 1934 Mr H.T. Bradford was landlord, staying until about 1950. He was also trading as H.J. Bradford and Sons from this address. Later licensees were Mr and Mrs H.L. Morrish from 1953, Cyril and Nancy Warren from 1961 and John and Winifred Barnes from 1971. Then from 1976 to 1983, Jeffrey and Rosemary Jenkins held the licence. He left to join the local bus company and was succeeded by Graham and Pamela Day, who were there from 1984 until 1989 when Alistair R. and Caroline Rose arrived to stay until 1990.

Then there were changes. The inn was renamed the Town Crier and traded as such for over three years before being taken over again, this time to become O'Malleys.

THE SHIP INN

The Ship is one of the oldest inns in Exmouth, dating from the early 1700s if not before, when it was known as the Apollo. There is a possibility that part of the building dates from medieval times. It was frequented in its early days by the local fishermen. The pub witnessed many boisterous and noisy times echoing from the room nicknamed 'the Clink' because of the bars across its window. Saturday nights were particularly rowdy, after the men had come ashore with big catches of herring or mackerel. A peep into the front lobby today reveals the very attractive old stained glass window depicting a ship.

This inn stands in the High Street, formerly known as Chapel Street, when it had a view of the old Holy Trinity Chapel. The earliest record of licensees seems to date from 1823 when Elizabeth Harris is named. Standing surety for her at that time was herself in the sum of £10 and Samuel Fair, also for £10. She was followed by William Metherall, who stayed for almost 50 years. He is recorded in many reports of 1830, 1850, 1857 and 1878. On 24 September 1880, James Salter took over the lease and he is mentioned in the 1881 Census Report and was still there in 1902.

A description of the inn in 1880 tells of a yard, brewhouse, offices and outbuildings as well as the inn itself – and all for a rent of £60 per year. The property was owned by Mr W. Linscott and leased to the licensees. Obviously the property had already been leased for almost 50 years to William Metherell who had given up during the last lease before it expired, leaving Mr Salter to take the unexpired period. The new lease was due in 1886 when he (Salter) renewed it and stayed on at the new rent of £46 per year in equal quarterly instalments but on 14 September 1905 the rent was increased to £60 p.a. when the new 14-year lease was signed. By 1911, William had died and his widow, Mrs Fanny Linscott, was named in the lease to Geoff Henry and John Francis Vallance, though still at the annual rent of £60, this time for the limited period of 13 years. By 1914 John T. Arberry was the licensee, and there followed: Alfred Henry Hunt in 1923, Thomas Vickery

The Ship Inn.

in 1930, E. Sprague in 1931, Mr and Mrs S.S. Whitaker in 1934 and S. Whitton from 1936–39.

After the Second World War the licensees were Mr and Mrs T.C. Burnhill in 1948, Mr and Mrs L.H. Boyce by 1950, and Ernest and Reba Adams in 1961; Francesca (Frank) and Stephen Ferrari were certainly there in 1971. They also provided bed and breakfast, but Frank went to the Royal Oak in Exeter Road and that left Stephen and his wife as the licensees. In the New Year of 1985, the customers had great celebrations; they all dressed up as pirates for a very exciting evening. By April 1989, however, Roger and Enid Coombes, who had come from Weymouth, were the licensees. They advertised real ale and a good menu was available in an upstairs dining room. They were followed by Christopher and Enid Coombes in 1991; they completely refurbished the inn. In 1992 the *Exmouth Herald Seaside Edition* informed the public that the licensees, then Richard and Mary Derbyshire, were able to provide a very wide range of meals. Paul A. Collins came in 1998, following Pamela Millard who only the year before had come from the Town Crier. By 2000, Paul M. Ward and Lesley J. Catherall were available to welcome all customers to what is described as a typical Devenish pub. Just recently the title of this Inn has been glamourised by the addition of the word 'famous' in front of its name.

Smith's Cider Shop

It was recorded on 10 August 1746 that the property left by John Stafford included Town's End House, which became Smith's Cider Shop, at the top of Fore Street. This property next became the First and Last House and throughout this period it was a pretty small thatched house which seems to have changed its name around 1830.

The South Western Hotel

Now known as No.1 The Parade, this hotel is at the western end of that street. It was at one time adjacent to the original railway station; its opening dates back to almost immediately after the arrival of the first train in 1861. Apparently two former houses on the site were converted into the hotel to meet the expected business.

The first landlord was Mr Rockett, who with his daughter Sarah Jane had to appear in Court on 24 October 1861 as witnesses to a theft. The next name of note was that of Edward Arnold, whose son Ted Arnold, born in 1878, became a famous cricketer and was described as the Factotum and Gentleman of the Cricket Club. All the hotels of that day had to provide stabling for horses and those for this hotel were at the rear. There were however a large number of stables in what became Miller's Garage and is now the indoor market.

The 1881 Census Report shows Edward Arnold and his wife Eliza, with four children and two servants at the hotel; however, by 1884 a Mr Ryder Durant was licensee. He stayed for about ten years until Frank Blackmore came, who stayed for a further ten years until another Durant followed – Frank this time – from 1906. From 1914 to 1923, Frank William Brown was the hotelier, followed by Kenneth W. Duly who was there by 1939. He stayed until at least 1948, then we know that Mr and Mrs E. Lethbridge moved in during 1950, though by 1955 Mrs Lethbridge had been left on her own. In 1961 she gave way to Ralph and Jessie Christmas, and by 1971 it was Albert and Mabel Ford.

All through this period there had been a close connection with the South Western Railway, through its station and stationmaster next door, and many artifacts and pictures were on display in the bars of the hotel. When Tom Power and his wife Jean came in the early 1970s, he managed to acquire more of these artifacts and he even hung railway lamps from the ceilings. Then, when the Exmouth Museum opened in 1985, it was not long before a special display of railway memorabilia was set up, all lent by Tom Power. The exhibition was organised by the curator of the museum. A number of those artifacts remained at the museum; gifted by Tom after he had retired. He and his wife had held the licence of the South Western Hotel for over 20 years and when he retired, he was missed very much. Being Irish, he always stressed the Irish whiskey selection and his Guinness was always a fine drink. In 1987 he had joined the Exmouth LVA and was soon made its Chairman. He now lives with his son at Exton.

There followed a major change of layout before the House reopened about a year later as the Strand, the second of that name.

The Strand Inn (1)

This hotel stood next to Miller's Garage on the Strand (now the indoor market), when Miller's was mainly a large stabling house for all the neighbouring horses. The hotel seems to have opened in 1878 when Sidney Carpenter became its licensee; he also appears in the 1881 Census Report, aged 32, with his sister Susan, both of them coming to Exmouth from Plymouth. After Carpenter came John Mann in 1880, but unfortunately he was drowned in a boating accident.

At about this time, the hotel issued tokens which came from Exeter, being made by a firm called E. Seege. By 1886–7, Mrs Susan Sydenham Carpenter had taken over because her husband had died, but she did not stay long, because Frederick Carter was there from 1889 until 1906.

Finally Henry Kenwood ran the hotel from 1906 until it was closed in 1925, no doubt until the period of the licence had expired, when it was transferred to the New Inn at Littleham.

The Swan Inn
(Also Known as The White Swan)

This inn is said to have been in Church Street and in 1778 it was licensed to Mr R. Clode. No more is known about it during the eighteenth century.

On Sunday 5 November 1820 a coroner's inquest was held at the inn on Ewen Griffiths, the mate of the schooner *Geres* from Liverpool.

It was reported on 9 July 1822 that Miss Jane Perriam, the daughter of Mrs Perriam of the Swan Inn, was married at Littleham Church to Mr Robert Hooper, a branch pilot at Exmouth. Then on 6 February there was an announcement in the local press that Mrs Jane Perriam had died, widow of the late William Perriam, who had recently kept the Swan Inn. Around the same time, John Crudge stood surety for her in the sum of £10, she also having stood surety for a similar amount.

In 1823, John Hayne the licensee, died and his widow Elizabeth Hayne, continued to hold the tenancy from 1830 until 1838. The inn was sold on 30 May 1839. In the intervening period, Mr P. Clode had been a tenant. The inn appeared on a map of the town in 1840, but was probably closed down soon afterwards.

Town's End House

This public house stood at the top of Fore Street where the road from Exeter came to the top of Marpool Hill and then turned down into Long Causeway and Boarden Barn to reach Fore Street. It traded in the early years of the eighteenth century, maybe from even earlier; it was possibly one of the earliest alehouses in Exmouth. No records of licensees have been traced.

In August 1746, it became Smith's Cider Shop and later the First and Last House.

The Victoria Inn

This inn was at No. 8 New Street and No. 9 New North Road; it had an entrance in both streets. It was also extremely close to the rear end of the Royal Oak Inn (now O'Malleys) in Exeter Road. There was a billiards room upstairs with a sloping glass roof.

It is not known when this pub opened, but there was a steady development of the whole area west of Exeter Road from about 1800 onwards, following the building of the huge bank on which the railway now runs. It was built by Mr Hull of Phear Park in about 1812, to reclaim many acres of

the 'Ooze', as it was called for many years. New Street was the next street to Shepherd's Row where stables and cottages had been built by 1789.

Records of the licensees can only be traced from about 1884. It was a cider house in its early days, and was supplied from Newton Abbot. John Stone was licensee from 1884 until 1902, and in 1906 Henry Ernest Wiltshire took over. In 1910, William Henry Mitchell was there and from 1923 to 1939 it was licensed to Mr and Mrs T.W. Sellick who had previously run the Kimberley. They were followed by Reginald and Vera Smith in 1960. Soon afterwards it became Langdon House, the home of Age Concern, the charity for the elderly. There is now a completely new building on the site.

The Volunteer Inn

In its final days this inn was a very fine building with long windows looking out on Chapel Street. It was sited on the corner with Margaret Street and opposite St Margaret's Chapel, built in 1329. This chapel was long since disused and changed in use until it was finally demolished.

The Volunteer was founded in the late-eighteenth century, probably relating to the period when volunteers for the Napoleonic War were urgently wanted. Originally the inn's sign had an Army theme, but when it was repainted the landlord was an ex-Navy man so the new sign took on a Naval theme. It may now be seen in the Lifeboat House on the Esplanade.

An early record shows Philip Nowell as the licensee in 1823, and standing surety for him for the sum of £20 were William Salter and Robert Morey. The latter also stood surety for £10 for the retail spirit cellar attached to the inn, in the name of Ann Grace, who also was standing for £10. In the 1825 Rate Book, the name of the person running the inn was Joseph Copp. From 1830 William Norris took over and he was followed by Mr Orchard, who died on 25 May 1836. Then came Mr Phillips, but when he died on 17 March 1843, aged 78, another William Norris, presumably the son of the former William Norris, took over. The inn is marked

The Volunteer Inn.

on the 1840 map of the town. In 1844 Oddfellows Lodges were meeting at the inn and in the 1851 Census Report, William Norris appears with his wife Mary and their four children. A picture of the inn was taken in 1840, which can now be seen in the town's library.

On 3 July 1851, William Norris was charged by the police for staying open beyond legal hours. He was fined 13s., including expenses. The licensee by 1857 was Robert Williams, who was also charged on 4 June with various offences against the police and with permitting drinking after hours. By 9 June 1859 he had transferred the licence to James Carter who stayed there for many years, certainly up to 1878, and he also appears in the 1881 Census. However, he must have died soon after, for in 1884 his widow took over. She was still there until 1902 when Frank Seward succeeded. In 1910 Alfred Skinner was the landlord and by 1923 it was Frederick Astley. He was followed by the Summers family; Sydney in 1929 and Sydney H.A. Summers in 1939.

By 1948 Mrs D.M. Jewell held the licence and she was followed by Mr and Mrs A.R. Whiteman in 1953. It was Valiant H. and Betty Bond who had succeeded by 1961, and in 1971 John and Phyllis Morin came, followed by Robert and Freda Hines. In 1979 the site of the Chapel of St Margaret's was levelled after an archaeological investigation and then the Volunteer was permitted to set out its tables and chairs as a beer garden. From 1981 until 1984, Elsie and Eileen Scott kept the licence and then, with the development of the Magnolia Centre, the inn was demolished. For a while the site was home to a Dewhurst's butcher's shop, before it was converted into a charity shop. Much of the town regarded these changes as unnecessary and it was considered a great loss to the town of a lively little pub of some architectural merit.

The White Hart Inn

This inn was on Lower Fore Street and was later rebuilt as the local Employment Exchange.

The earliest reference to it as the White Hart seems to be in about 1830, although the Jolly Sailor had been put up for sale in 1822. It is possible that the reversal of names had already taken place. The landlord of the White Hart was John Toby until at least 1850. He was followed by Mr George Street and his wife Sarah in June 1855 and when he died, Sarah took over for around two years. Henry Pellew was the next landlord, but as a result of a fire next door in August 1860 considerable damage was done to the inn. Furniture had to be removed and a roof was partly stripped to restrict the spread of the fire. Poor Henry died on 15 March 1863 aged 57. After repairs were completed, James Carter took over and is believed to have stayed until 1873, when William Henry Lee succeeded. In 1878, Mr W. Dagworthy was there, but he only stayed three years. Richard Smith was in charge from 1881 and with temporary help from Mrs Harriet Smith in 1884, he continued until 1898 when the house was taken down and a public dispensary erected on the site. This took the place of the service begun in 1868 at Manchester House by Dr R. Richardson of Cranford. The site was later secured for the changes set out in the first paragraph above.

The York Inn

The York Inn or Hotel, formerly the Great Tree Inn, is now a busy free house at the start of Imperial Road and is possibly one of the oldest pubs in Exmouth. The earliest reference found is of a beer-house in 1742. There is also a 1761 drawing of the Great Tree Inn, so called because of its situation opposite that tree. The name change must have taken place after 1800 when the lovely plaster ceiling in the upper part of the main bar was created. That area has been known as various things, including the snug and the breakfast room in its hotel days. It can still be seen today.

The inn was once described as 'a quaint thatched house' and the Great Tree standing in the middle of the road outside marked the end of the boundary between Withycombe Raleigh and Littleham parishes. That boundary is now extended through the row of trees across the road by the car park out to the river's edge. In those times the river itself came to within 20 feet of the front door, and Manchester House, built in 1795, had its own quay.

It was in about 1804 that Mary Anne Clarke, mistress of the Duke of York and the second son of King George III, Ernest Augustus (1763–1823), came to live in Manchester House just around the corner. This is according to Daphne du Maurier's biography of Mary Anne, who was in fact her great-great-grandmother. That biography is a pleasure to read.

Known as the York Hotel from the early 1800s, this house has continued to trade and serve its regulars. The records show that in a Rate Book of 1825 it was listed as the York and frequently used for such activities as auctions.

On 23 May 1825 Silas Allen returned his best thanks to the nobility and gentry and his friends for their support:

... he had made considerable improvements in his establishment and... laid in a choice stock of

The York Inn.

genuine wines and spirits, home brewed beer, London Porter and cider, together with an excellent larder, good beds and every other requisite. The House is fronting the sea and commands one of the most delightful and picturesque views in the kingdom. Prime old Port at 3s.6d. a bottle. Good stabling, neat post chaise, good car and gig with excellent horses and careful drivers.

In the first days of 1827, it was put up for sale by private contract, being described on 6 March 1827 as:

The York Hotel – in the occupation of Mr Silas Allen – the dwelling house and premises facing the River Exe are held for the residue of a possessionary term of 99 years determinable on the death of one life aged about 27 years and for a reversionary term of 99 years to be determinable on the decease of another life aged about 29 years. There is a pew in the New Chapel of Exmouth which is attached and will be sold with the premises.

Apparently there was no sale by private contract, for on 31 March 1827 it was to be sold by auction on the premises at 3p.m. At the auction the description was:

... a sale of valuable household goods, furniture, a stock of beer, brandy, utensils, horses, chaise, gig, carts and other effects including a coal lighter (probably lying on the river nearby), large and small empty casks, the property of Mr Silas Allen. To be sold without reserve by Thomas Crudge, the auctioneer.

William Copp was the landlord from 1830 to 1838 and then the records are quiet for about 20 years until we come across the following: on 15 September 1859, John Lee of the York

Hotel went to the King's Arms at Ottery and Mr Tancock took over. However, less than a year later, on 12 April 1860, he passed the licence to William Summers. On 24 June 1863, when Richard Smerdon was the landlord, he was summoned by Sarah Crockett (daughter of the landlord of the South Western Hotel on the other side of the road) for assaulting her. Apparently he threw a bucket of water over her and consequently was fined 5s.

Edward Smerdon, the landlord, died on 18 September 1866, aged 55, and his widow, Mrs Maria Smerdon, continued the trade. She held the licence until 1884. In the 1881 Census she was said to be 45 years of age, with one servant. By 1897, the licence was held by George Perriam, who continued until after 1910.

The late-Victorian rebuilding of the inn, which can still be seen, was very attractively done in a variety of differently coloured bricks, and since the arrival of the railway 40 years earlier, the road outside had been called Station Parade. Since the station was moved further away, it is now addressed as the start of Imperial Road.

Later tenants have included:

1923:   *J. William Dawes.*
1930:   *Sydney Dawes, possibly a son of J.W. Dawes.*
1931:   *S. Robinson.*
1934:   *Mr and Mrs H.E. Crease who stayed until after 1939.*
1948:   *Mr and Mrs A.F. Bird.*
1953:   *Mr and Mrs F.C. Rawlings.*
1961:   *Frederick C. and Winifred H. Rawlings (perhaps related to F.C. Rawlings). They were still listed as living there in 1974.*
Before 1981:   *Nigel B. and Caroline L. Taylor, in whose time the cost of bed and breakfast was just £8.*

Roger Taylor then succeeded, but after more than 13 years the brewery wanted to introduce substantial rent increases, so he closed up and the brewery itself took over, with Peter H. and Doreen Cutler holding the licence. By 1992 the present licensees, Messrs E.G.H., S.J. and E.E. Drinkall, had taken over what had become rather a run-down hotel which had been boarded up. The premises were fully refurbished and soon became a very popular venue and free house. Later a new function room was added. This made it an excellent inn that catered for a vast number of celebrations.

The fine plaster ceiling to which reference has already been made, can still be seen, having lasted for almost 200 years.

MODERN PUBS

There are now a number of newer public houses in Exmouth. These include establishments that are new names for older houses and others which are completely new businesses. The former will already have been described to some extent in this chapter, under their old names and cross-referenced. However, all those pubs mentioned below have yet to create their own history, to gain their customers, build their business and maintain their regulars.

These new pubs will of course enjoy the rivalry of Exmouth's old established pubs, but times do change and so do people's habits and customs. Will the older houses meet the challenge and update their methods in order to maintain their popularity amongst locals and holiday-makers alike?

Best wishes to them all! No doubt they will contribute to Exmouth's history and be noted in the records of the future. In summary, the new pubs at the time of writing are:

The Amazon (a new pub but now taken over and renamed as the Prince of Wales).
The Bank (a new building in the heart of town).
CJ's (originally a wine bar, but now a pub).
The Famous Old Barrel (almost a rebuild of what was the Builders' Arms).
Molloys (in the Strand on the site of Lennard's Bar).
O'Malleys (on the Exeter Road and formerly the Town Crier).
Pitchers (was the Queen's Hotel in Victoria Road).
The Powder Monkey (a new building).
The Prince of Wales (previously the Amazon).
The Strand (2) (originally the South Western).
Remedies Bar (completely new pub, established in what used to be a chemist's shop).
The Town Crier (formerly the Royal Oak).

THE AMAZON INN

This was a new public house on the corner of Dinan Way and Prince of Wales Drive in the Brixington estate. Built in May 1986, it was potentially a rival to the Farmhouse Inn, but seemed to cater for a different clientele. It was a Devenish pub and was opened by the Devenish Group's Managing Director, Bill Ludlow.

The accommodation consists of a large bar, an attractive lounge, and a skittle alley for two teams, as well as space for euchre and darts. A wide variety of food is served, and the family room also has a paved patio outside. Roy and Ann Hartshorne were the first landlords and a warm welcome was extended to all. They were followed by Neil and Elise Gatehouse.

The name 'Amazon' comes from the barque of that name, the largest ship (1,100 tons) built in Exmouth by the Redway brothers in 1867. The nautical theme is echoed throughout the pub, with prints of sailing vessels and a ship's bell on which to call 'time'.

A change in 1992 brought Robert and Wendy Logan, but only a year later Bryant and Julia Matthews followed. They stayed until 1995, when Stephen and Tracey H. Taylor took over. By these fairly frequent changes it would appear that business was not particularly good. David and Beverley Howard (née Payne) were the licensees at the time when the pub was acquired by the Inn Partnership, who renamed it the Prince of Wales in 1998. The first licensees operating under this name were Tony R. Smith and Debora J. Carrow.

THE BANK

This rather unusually shaped brick building stands at No. 5 St Andrew's Road, between the Manor Cottage Club and the Exmouth Banqueting Suite, and below Samantha's Night Club. It started life as a wine bar in the mid 1980s and became a public house a few years later. Many of its furnishings came from what was a nearby bowling alley. The main bar is a wood and steel construction and it took many men to lift it into place.

From around 1994, Richard Middleton became the landlord, to be joined by Nikki Griffin some time later. At the time of writing they are still there, so they must be making a success of it. The food offered at the pub is of a high standard and the venue certainly has regular customers.

CJ's BAR

This public house is sited at 9A The Strand in what was formerly the wine and aperitif bar for Clapp's Restaurant on the first floor. It is managed by Chi Fan Jim and Ching Wai Jim, whose initials give the clue to its name. They have held the licence since 1996.

CJ's bar.

Molloys.

THE FAMOUS OLD BARREL

Popular with the rock and loud music fraternity, this pub is located at No. 4 Princes Street, where formerly stood the Builders Arms, which was closed in 1988.

The Devenish and Weymouth Brewery expanded this building into a nearby property that it had already purchased, in order to attain more storage space. The premises were then altered and redecorated and opened to the public on 8 June 1989.

The first licensee was Gillian E. Kennard, followed shortly after by Stephen Flood and Terry Wheatley. There was a mention of Michael Burt and Laura Cash in between, but by 2000, the licensees named on the door were Emma Josephine Sandford and Terry Wheatley.

It has become quite famous for its rock music atmosphere and the collections of memorabilia from the 1960s and '70s hung on the walls.

The Famous Old Barrel.

MOLLOYS

The successor to Lennard's Bar, this pub's change of name occurred at the end of 2000. An advertisement on 1 June 2000 mentioned the special service available from Saturday to Saturday, 12 noon to 3p.m., and specifically referred to the bar

at the rear called 'The Shed'. It was said that there was room for over 100 customers in that bar and it carried a Public Entertainment Licence.

The pub sign went up when the licensee moved in. He was Richard M. Molloy, after whom the inn was obviously named. The décor in the main is timber based.

The landlord at the time of writing is Doug Rayment, who organised a Charity Pram Parade to raise money for the Breast Cancer Care Charity, held on Bank Holiday Monday 27 August. The teams were in fancy dress and prizes were awarded for the best dressed participant and the first pram to complete the course around a number of Exmouth's pubs. That effort was very successful, and raised over £1,480 for the charity, which was handed over by Sheila Delgram and Liz Bruford.

PITCHERS

Formerly the Queen's Hotel, this pub was altered in 1999 to meet the present description of being both a bar and diner. In February 2000 it was unfortunately the focus of an unusual call-out of the Tactical Air Group from Exeter. There was a disturbance at the pub, which resulted in a number of injuries.

The licensees at the time of writing are William G. and June Perkin and they enjoy good customer relations with the regular clientele. They have yet to become an attraction to the holiday-makers, but no doubt this will come with time.

O'MALLEY'S INN

This pub succeeded the Town Crier at 31 Exeter Road and it is still affectionately referred to as the Royal Oak, its original name. The accommodation is spartan but spacious, with a timber character and décor. In 1998 John Kane became the first licensee, with Ian D. Kerr taking over in the following year. He left a year later in June 2000.

This pub was held under a Management Lease from Greenalls, who owned the premises, but then

O'Malley's.

The Powder Monkey side entrance in Crudge's Lane.

it closed for a period. In July 2000 a couple from Helston in Cornwall, David and Diane Burgess, applied to take over. Although they did not have an inn previously, Mrs Burgess' family had licensing experience and a relative helped them open O'Malley's again after its somewhat troubled past.

Apparently the ownership of the premises had changed from Greenalls to the Scottish and Newcastle Breweries, who were prepared to grant a five-year franchise to the Burgesses. A possession order was granted on 25 July 2000. Meanwhile David Burgess junr had joined his parents to work as chef in the pub. Once the pub was up and running again, it has become popular for the regular entertainment and live music held there.

THE POWDER MONKEY

This is a new public house on a new site, opened on 4 October 2000. The name refers to the men and women in the Navy whose efforts in battle

The Powder Monkey.

brought the gunpowder to the guns and who often helped to fill the shells themselves. Exmouth's Nancy Perriam was one who served with Nelson's fleet and is remembered in the use of the name now. At the opening of the pub, Peggy Eyres, Nancy's great-great-niece, cut the ribbon in the presence of other descendants as well as a Guard of Honour of the Royal Navy and the White Ensign Association.

Plans for the development of the pub were announced in January. It was located on the site of a house in a ruinous state (once known as Hayne House) that would need a lot of expenditure for its rebuilding and refurbishing. A local businessman, Eddie Drinkall of the York Inn, had invited a national chain, J.D. Wetherspoon, to take an interest in the scheme and as a result work was soon under way. Much had to be done to improve the premises, including creating a large bar area over what was originally a garden.

Pam Cowan, the Manager of the Powder Monkey, welcomes all her customers to the new pub and trusts that it will make a mark in Exmouth and attract a regular clientele. Indeed the number of regulars has increased, although some of them refer to it as the 'Powder Puff'.

THE PRINCE OF WALES (2)

This pub was the successor to the Amazon, formerly on this site. In 1998 Tony R. Smith and Debora J. Carron took on the new Prince of Wales, called after the adjacent road of that name. In March 1999 they gave way to Nora James with her daughter-in-law Coz Masters, assisted by Kevin James.

It is an active centre for the local football, darts and pool teams, with an ample car park. It is certainly worth a visit.

THE STRAND (2)

Formerly the South Western Public House at No. 1 The Parade, this house was taken over in the mid 1990s when Tom Power and his wife Jean retired. The premises were completely refurbished and became one long bar instead of the previous two.

The licensees Philip and Elizabeth Bruford were replaced by Gareth and Dawn Williamson in 1999. An advertisement on 1 June 2000 states that it is open all day with a menu offering a variety of meals.

This pub is frequented by a fairly young clientele and proves to be very popular with them.

The Strand.

REMEDIES BAR

The choice of a chemist's shop as the site of a public house was a surprise to many in Exmouth. This was formerly the shop of Messrs Holman and Hunt who had been running the business for many years at No. 38 The Strand. Little alteration was necessary to the exterior and the influence of the chemist may be clearly seen in the interior.

The first licensee was Timothy Fagan with a

Remedies Bar.

colleague, but in 2000 he suddenly disappeared, apparently to go abroad, and the brewery's Area Manager had to take over.

It appeared that the police had not been satisfied about a noise problem and a Noise Abatement Notice which was served on 29 April 2000 had not been complied with. The problem was caused by a love of rather loud music when visiting bands attracted many customers, sometimes as many as 200 at any one time.

At the time of writing a permanent manager has not been found so the Area Manager, Andrew Davey, holds the licence.

THE TOWN CRIER

This pub was opened in 1987 on the premises of what was previously the Royal Oak at No. 31 Exeter Road. The opening was celebrated with an assembly of Town Criers from other towns and villages in the area, resplendent in their colourful coats and bonnets. The only previous record of a Town Crier in Exmouth was in September 1838 when the 'Public Cryer' assured the public that a great display of fireworks would take place on Beacon Hill. In actual fact, there was only a tar barrel blazing away!

This was a Devenish Brewery House and the first licensee was Frank Ferrari and his wife Margaret. The house had an attractive interior with a lounge and low-timbered ceiling supported by pillars as an extra architectural feature, following the line of the building.

It offered a fine range of draught beers including the Newquay Steam range of bitters and stout. For food the speciality was home-made pizza. However, towards the end of 1999, there were changes, not only to the décor, but also the name and the ownership. It was purchased by Greenalls and renamed O'Malleys.

The opening of Dotton's Waterworks in 1911.

A wedding in 1913.

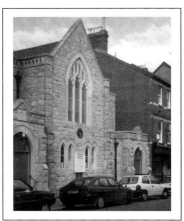

The Baptist Chapel, built in 1900 in Victoria Road.

Exeter Road Board Schools (now the Public Library) was erected from 1875–7, intended to provide education for 100 children, but soon the numbers were up to 200.

CHAPTER 8

Twentieth-Century Exmouth

King Edward VII came to the throne at the age of 60 and only reigned for nine years. He was succeeded by his son, King George V, whose Silver Jubilee celebrations were held in 1935. He died in 1936, when his eldest son, who had been the Prince of Wales for so long, succeeded and became King Edward VIII. He was king for only a very short time, for he abdicated in December the same year and his brother King George VI then took over the monarchy, which position he served well, being loved by all. It was a period of great changes and many events and this chapter covers the years up to the outbreak of the Second World War in September 1939.

A war was already in progress in South Africa when the twentieth century began. A numerous company of men had already left Exmouth to serve in the Baden Powell Police, the City Imperial Volunteers and the Devonshire Regiment. It was a remote war and news of the troops' progress was somewhat sporadic. Particularly remembered were the three battles: the relief of Mafeking, Ladysmith and Kimberley. Celebrations took the form of torchlight processions and to celebrate the winning of Kimberley, a huge bonfire was lit on the seafront by Temple Steps. A local celebrity, Mr W.J. Gorfin, dressed up as General French and made a speech – at least he tried to, but the crowd lit the bonfire! For Mafeking night, several loads of timber brought from Bicton were burnt on the seafront and the bonfire could be seen from all the towns around the bay.

Captain Alexander Bryce of Bystock House came home and was met by a carriage and horses, but half the crowd harnessed themselves to the carriage to tow him home through the streets in triumph, being met with cakes and ale for all. Other Exmothians returning from South Africa were Sergeants J. Snow and W. Lockyer.

In Exmouth the century began with a tremendous catch of approximately half a million herrings which realised 40s. per thousand, with buyers coming from as far as Plymouth to share in the harvest. Events such as this meant more to the people of Exmouth than all the events up-country; indeed the Boer War of 1899–1902 had hardly affected East Devon.

The town itself had begun to spread northwards and eastwards over Beacon Hill, along the Salterton Road and Douglas Avenue, with avenues of well-built villas. The population of the town naturally increased as its reputation as a resort spread. There were 385 artisans' houses in terraces available.

In August 1902 the town celebrated the Coronation of the new king. By this time Exmouth School had 500 pupils and was very popular. In the same year, excavation work took place on the streets to lay and connect the new town sewer to an outlet that ran to the sea near the docks. The foundation stone of the new cottage hospital was laid on a site purchased by Lady Rolle. The formal opening of the completed cottage hospital took place in June 1903, with Lady Gertrude Rolle officiating. The old Maud Hospital building had been sold.

In January 1903, Samuel Hutton, an engineer and surveyor, was appointed to Exmouth as its Water Engineer. He began to carry out many important works in the town, improving the Beach Gardens and the sea wall. On 1 June came an important development in the town with the linking of the branch line to Budleigh Salterton and thence to Ottery St Mary. However, it suffered the Beeching axe in due course and was closed in 1967 after serving the East Devon community for 60 years.

In November 1903 a new lifeboat arrived, which carried the same name as the old one, *Joseph Somes*. It was stored in a new lifeboat house on the site of the old one. A popular cutter appearing in the regattas of these years was the *Busty*, built by E.C. Clatworthy and skippered by Tom Horn with Bill Thompson as crew.

It was in 1906 that Bystock House was destroyed by fire and General Booth of the Salvation Army visited the town. There was also much public agitation over people's right to erect stalls on the foreshore to sell refreshments. It came to a head when a Mrs Hunt refused to move a tea hut from the beach, despite an order to do so. She was arrested for Contempt of Court and sent to prison on 29 June 1906. Great action and reaction by everyone followed and the matter was even the subject of debate in Parliament. Mrs Hunt was released on 19 July and returned to Exmouth amid great acclaim. It is said that the Exmouth Town

Aerial view of the Point and the docks, 1971.

Band met her at the local railway station. One of the results of this stand by Mrs Hunt was a general relaxation of the local bye-laws. During this period there were also public appeals for the removal of the unsightly bathing machines.

In June 1906 the Trinity Buoy Depot was built on land reclaimed from the foreshore by the tipping of rubbish, sand and soil. It was considered an admirable improvement of the area at the western end of the Point.

In the following year, the Sailors Rest was rebuilt in St Andrew's Road; the previous building was considered too close to the noise and bustle of the docks, and it was converted into a children's home. In the same year, a timber ship coming from Norway, called the *Tehwija*, was caught in a south-westerly gale off Teignmouth. With considerable difficulty the Teignmouth Lifeboat rescued the crew of eight while she was caught fast on the Pole Sands. The force of the waves, however, moved her and she ended up at Orcombe Point with her deck timber scattered all over the beach. It became a harvest for all the local beachcombers. Her main steering wheel is now on view in Exmouth Museum. The Charity for Shipwrecked Fishermen and Mariners had been founded in the previous year, its first Secretary being Mr G. Tupman.

The Australian convict ship the *Success* was to be seen in the docks at this time. She was a three-masted barque, originally a tea clipper built in Burma. The ship was restored as a convict vessel for exhibition purposes to illustrate the conditions under which convicts were once transported to Botany Bay. This was the year 1908, when the Pencarwick School was closed after a very successful period during which many famous people passed through its classes.

One of the dock's walls collapsed in 1910, following a severe storm in December. In 1911, a Bronze-Age sword was discovered on the Pole Sands and sent to the British Museum. A replica can be seen in Exmouth Museum. This was the year of the succession of King George V and a Coronation Dinner was held in his honour.

The completion of the installation of an electricity works in 1913 brought a supply for which the town had long been waiting. In December that year, three pilots, George Thompson, Samuel Pym and William Holman with a boatman, Henry Blackler, all of Exmouth, claimed £300 for salvage services from the owner of the schooner *Rose* when the tug *Queen of the Exe* hauled her off the Maer Rocks and into the safety of the Bight.

The *Exmouth Journal* at this time carried many advertisements relating to Christmas in the shops of the town. Harry Law's shop in Chapel Street had a seal from Newfoundland in its shop window; F. Ferris, the fish merchant, also in Chapel Street, was offering fresh fish, crabs and lobsters every day '... caught by my own boat – no connection with any other Ferris in the town'. His shop was later at the top of Tower Street, opposite the Pilot Inn and next door to Dodd's Dairy which later became part of the Heavitree Arms.

At this time, too, HM Training ship *Exmouth II* was described as:

... one of the happy ships of the Navy, being the sea-going tender of HMS Exmouth I *which is a fore-and-aft rigged three-masted steam and sailing vessel. The lads are taught all the branches of seamanship, stoking, mechanical engineering, wireless telegraphy and signalling.*

THE FIRST WORLD WAR

In August 1914 came the newspaper headlines 'European War' and 'Amazing German Aggression', for on the night of Tuesday 8 August England declared war against Germany. It soon became an international affair, for the conflict spread to many other countries as they each took sides. The Bank Holiday was spent quietly – people were beginning to realise how seriously the recent events were to affect their everyday lives.

Exmouth's popular paddle steamer *Duke of Devonshire* was requisitioned by the Admiralty, renamed HMS *Duke III* and converted into a minesweeper. She was sent to Mesopotamia under her own steam to carry out her duties and Exmouth was not to see her again until after the cessation of hostilities. Her sister ship the *Duchess of Devonshire* was taken on charter by P. and A. Campbell to maintain a service across the Bristol Channel between Weston-super-Mare and Cardiff.

Many of the younger men who had crewed the lifeboat went away on war service and it was an elderly crew who attended to emergency calls during the war. German ships in British harbours were seized; German spies were arrested; and then came the call for volunteers for all the Armed Services, including the Red Cross. The Exmouth Miniature Rifle Club as a body volunteered to teach the townspeople to use firearms. Lord Clinton inaugurated a Devon Patriotic Fund and a voluntary Coast-watch Corps was raised under the direction of the War Office. By September came the call of 'Buy British' produce and there were meetings and calls for contributions to the Fund. In November there was a general appeal against apathy as pictures of some men of Exmouth who had been killed in the first battles appeared in the *Exmouth Journal*.

Approximately 1,000 Territorials were billeted to Exmouth for training, although they used Woodbury Common as their training ground. Eight Regimental Police were drafted in and orders came to screen all windows looking seaward.

In early December 1914, a trawler in distress off Exmouth was saved by another trawler fishing nearby and towed into Brixham. At the same time, refugees from Belgium arrived in the town and were cared for. In the following February, 1915, the Devon Dock and Pier Company held its Annual General Meeting and declared a two per cent dividend, having come creditably out of a difficult year. Their ships had all been taken for war service and they were receiving a rent for them; their launches were all laid up except for the Starcross ferry boat, so some revenue was being received by the Company.

In April 1915 there was a proposal that a memorial be subscribed for in each parish. Progress on the building of the sea wall was satisfactory and it now ran from the site of the old Naval Reserve Battery to the Coastguard Station. It helped to prevent a lot of erosion on the sand-hills. It was hoped to later incorporate a Marine Drive. It is perhaps surprising to us now that in the midst of the war there seemed to be time to think of the town's future development. The war, however, continued to alarm people by its progress – or rather the lack of progress. More pictures of lost Exmouth men appeared from time to time in the local newspapers, with the reports of the fighting in France and elsewhere.

Known by many as the 'Father of the British Navy', Mr Charles Lacey, who had reached the age of 100 in November 1914, died on 9 May 1915. He had drawn his Naval pension longer than anyone.

The war was not regarded as headline news in the *Exmouth Journal* on 1 January 1916. Instead, the headlines referred to the passing of the Christmas holiday and the soldiers' concerts in the town, although it was reported that vegetables were being collected for the Fleet amid thanks from Admiral Jellicoe. After their training period in Exmouth, the Devon and Cornwall Territorials left for the Front. The Red Cross was busy and there was a Belgian Bazaar. A whole page of the newspaper told the story of the war on the Front, with news of the Exmothians who had been lucky enough to get home for Christmas. Air raids by German aircraft had occurred on the Kent coast and in East Anglia. Many letters from the Front were quoted in the newspaper.

The Annual General Meeting of the Exe Board of Conservatores said that during the year 1915 a record was achieved for the number of salmon caught in the River Exe, the total amounting to about 24 tons. Holiday-makers were still coming to Exmouth in great numbers, but by this time there were over 600 names on Exmouth's Roll of Honour, proving what sacrifices the townsfolk were making. There appeared in the *Exmouth Journal* a picture of the five brothers of the Trim family, all coming from Fore Street and all serving in the Forces. According to a report in the Exeter paper, much of the Warren had been washed away in September 1916.

In 1917 many more men were wanted at the Front and appeals were being made for more volunteers. At the Annual General Meeting of the National Lifeboat Institution, the crew of the Exmouth Lifeboat were voted an extra grant because of their age and for the valiant service they gave when the steamship *St Paul* came ashore the previous year. The dividend recommended by the Devon Dock, Pier and Steamship Company for

Donkey rides on the beach.

their 1916 year of trading was for both the Ordinary and the Preference shares. Trade itself was stagnant but the revenue came mainly from the piers at Paignton and Teignmouth along with rents from the steamers *Duke of Devonshire*, *King Edward* and *Zulu*, a launch. At the Docks Engineering Works, staff had been busy in the month of March, repairing and sharpening lawn mowers!

The newspapers were carrying appeals to eat less bread and meat; more men were wanted at the Front; and Tribunals were often held. There was a shortage of paper, so readers were advised to order their *Exmouth Journal* in advance. Additionally there were fewer copies and they were smaller – it was reduced to only four pages and news from the Front was often omitted because of the serious situation out there. The paper mainly contained lists of casualties of Exmouth people, along with accounts of concerts and other fund-raising activities, plus advertisements which then filled the paper. Stress was being laid on producing food at home. Rewards were also offered for the killing of shags and cormorants of 1s. each, to save on the number of fish being eaten.

The bathing huts on the Maer Sands were still being used in the summer, let for the 1917 season, and in June, Bronco Bill's 'Wild West Exhibition' came to Exmouth and set up on Carter's field in the Exeter Road. The Troupe called the 'Bric-a-Bracs' was still entertaining at the Pier Pavilion.

At the same time, F. Ferris still offered his fresh fish, lobsters and crab, but fishermen received a blow in September when a Prohibition Order came covering the area from Portland Bill to Bardsey Island in North Wales, stating that the laying of nets, crab or other pots, trawling, drifting or anchoring by day or by night were forbidden. In October that Order was printed in much greater detail. This marked the year of greatest strain in Exmouth and district. Surely things could only improve from this point on.

In the January of 1918 a proposal to form a Company of Cadets was put forward, adopted and

soon carried out, just as the pantomime *Cinderella* was being performed at the Public Hall. A 'Save and Hasten Victory' appeal was launched in the town, and even old boots, the larger sizes particularly, were requested in order to give to wounded soldiers.

February 1918 saw the award of a Military medal to Bombardier N. Gorfin being reported, while April brought the news that a meat-rationing scheme was to come into force. In October an 'After the War' article was published which brought the possibility of an end to the war much nearer; there was better news from the Western Front and a final rally called for the Huns' overthrow.

The *Exmouth Journal* of 19 October began a 'Feed the Guns' week and then in November at last there was the wonderful news of the Armistice. There was great relief all round in Exmouth. Ferris was able once more to advertise fresh fish daily '... from our own boats'.

Exmouth people then collaborated to place a tank on the Esplanade in 1919 as a reminder of the Great War. The date 19 July 1919 was chosen as a Special Day for Exmouth's Peace celebrations and in November a memorial window was dedicated in Withycombe Church.

A PERIOD OF PEACE

By 1920 the paddle steamers *Duke of Devonshire* and *Duchess of Devonshire* had returned to their owners at Exmouth and were prepared to render service for passenger trips to Weymouth and Plymouth as they had done before the war. Other trips to the places in between were also resumed. The building of Marine Drive, an extension of Queen's Drive, was completed at a cost of £3,650. Motor charabancs became available for public hire and the Starcross ferry boats began providing trips up the River Exe, which became very popular.

The following year, 1921, was said to be the biggest salmon season of all time. Literally thousands were caught in the river and many were handled by the Exmouth firm of W.R. Redway & Sons. The docks were using a recently built and fully equipped foundry to carry out major repairs. This business was later sold to the Point Ironworks and even at the end of the twentieth century was still operational on the same premises.

In 1922, John Walters' yard launched its latest ship, the *Cleetha*. The wholesale fish business run for so many years by the Redway family with its export market for crabs, crayfish, lobsters and mullet to France, had ceased because of the French import tariff. The lobsters, crabs and even herrings were instead regularly exported to New Zealand as well as to buyers in Ireland, Scotland, Cornwall and Billingsgate. People from several other towns in the West Country came to Exmouth regularly to purchase whole catches, particularly after the record harvests of the year 1900 and of 1919, when the catch of a single boat during the course of one night fetched £293.

In 1924 a monster conger eel 6 feet long and weighing over 35lbs was caught off Exmouth by a Mr Hill. It was also reported at the same time that a High Street grocer had a shop on the Warren, rowing across to it every morning. At that time quite large bungalows were located there, which helped to develop the area into a popular part of the town for holidays. The Exe Sailing Club with its Club House at the docks was founded in this year and soon had a thriving membership.

About this time there was great concern over the removal of sand from the foreshore, not only by the heavy seas, but also for building purposes. This affected the area between the clock tower and the dock entrance. It seems that over 8,000 loads had been removed in a period of about 18 months.

By 1925, the steamers *Duke* and *Duchess* were facing some competition from the firm Cozens of Weymouth, who brought their ship *Alexandra* to operate from Torquay.

It appears that by 1925 there were four cinemas operating very successfully in the town.

Exmouth's new railway station was built in 1926 with a very imposing façade, but alas it was demolished in around 1980, when a new combined bus and railway station complex was built, together with a new road to the area. It was in this year, too, that the Madeira Rowing Club was founded on the Maer. In November of the same year, the submarine R4 ran aground on the Pole Sands, being reported by a large Flying Boat which circled the area. Later a destroyer and a large Trinity House vessel arrived and the submarine was floated off at a subsequent high tide.

In 1927, Cozens of Weymouth withdrew his vessel from Torquay back to Weymouth due to a reduction in business. The General Strike of 1926 had been one of the causes of the fall in business, and that unpleasant situation also generally affected the leisure and pleasure industry as well as causing unemployment everywhere. The Devonshire Association held its Annual General Meeting in Exmouth that year and in its exhibition of local artifacts there was displayed a Phoenix vessel which had been found at Marpool among the flints and arrowheads from the neighbourhood.

By 1928, the hospital, which was originally built in Claremont Grove in 1903, had been remodelled. The present Health Centre on the site was added much later. A Devon Omnibus timetable published at the time, covering the Exeter and Torquay districts, gives the price of a one-day return ticket from Exeter to Exmouth as 1s.8d. The timetable also contains some advertisements for Exmouth: Clapp's Café at No. 2 Rolle Street, and Emery's Café at No. 2 The Parade.

Following a severe storm in 1929, Exmouth beach was a scene of devastation. The whole of the seafront was littered with the wreckage of beach huts and other detritus. The sea had surged over the Esplanade and much of the town had been flooded.

Crowded beaches at Exmouth, c.1960.

The new bowling green on the Esplanade, c.1910.

The interior of the railway station.

Gardens and Madeira Walk, Exmouth, from an old postcard sent in 1939.

E.S. Gosling

The fine 1926 railway station.

An early form of motor transport.

Throughout the 1920s there were several pleasure steamers using the Pier and the docks. One in particular was the *Black Joke* owned by Commander Adams; she was a beautiful vessel. At this time an unusual sight was that of cattle being taken out to the Shilhay Sandbank and feeding there.

In 1930, the Chairman of Exmouth Town Council accepted for safe-keeping a Centenary Vellum awarded by the RNLI.

It was around this time that a character could be found in the town called 'Pony' Moore, who took his horse and cart around the Exmouth streets selling locally-caught fish. Also in this period the grand house, Marley, was demolished.

'Talkies' came to the town at the Kings Cinema – later called the Grand and after that, the Royal Cinema. About this time, too, the estuary fore-shore near Powderham Castle was made into a bird sanctuary, one of the first in the country to be so designated. The estuary had eelgrass growing on the Cockle Sands, which supported Brent geese from Arctic Russia and many other waterfowl.

It was said that at the turn of the century there had been no 'colony' and no railway to Budleigh Salterton. By 1931, however, there was an evening train service from Queen Street Station, for 6d. return to Exmouth and 8d. to Budleigh Salterton. However, there was a national slump at this time and in Exmouth alone there were over 500 men out of work. Despite this, a new Pavilion was built in 1932, which is still a very popular venue today.

The *Duke of Devonshire* steamer was sold to P. and A. Campbell at Weymouth, and after running pleasure trips to and from various ports along the South Coast, it returned to Weymouth in 1938, having in the meantime been renamed *Consul*.

An open-air swimming pool was built on the seafront near the lifeboat house and it was used for swimming galas and water polo. It was redesigned in 1987 and opened the following year.

A major redevelopment occurred in the docks in the years 1932–3 when the Renwick Group, who leased part of the docks, built a coal wharf on the north side which, with transport cranes of 3-ton and 4-ton capacity, provided a fully mechanised coal quay. The timber yard and its warehouses expanded at the same time. Further extensions to the town's sewerage system were made during this period and the infilling of the area on the river side of Imperial Road began in 1932, becoming known as the King George V Pleasure Grounds by 1935.

A new lifeboat was in place by 1933. It was self-righting and fitted with a 35hp engine. She was named *Catherine Harriet Eaton*, the first motorised lifeboat in the port. The paddle-steamer *Duchess of Devonshire* was sold to the South Devon and West Bay Steamship Company that year. Surprisingly, she was brought back into service at

Exmouth in 1934, but under new owners. Before long, however, she was stranded on Sidmouth beach when her stern anchor failed to hold. She came broadside to the beach and all efforts to refloat her failed. She came to an ignominious end by being broken up there. Some of her remains were visible on Sidmouth beach for some years afterwards.

In 1933 the dock gates had been removed and the dock became tidal. A comparison of the trade in the docks in 1934 with that of ten years previous revealed that trade levels had trebled. The tonnage being discharged exceeded that of Exeter, the principal cargoes being of coal, timber, fertiliser, cider and potatoes.

In 1933 also, one of England's finest batsmen, L.C.H. Palairet, was buried in Littleham's churchyard.

In the following year, a new destroyer with the name *Exmouth* was launched, but she was lost in the Second World War in 1940. Also, the Dock Company acquired the *Tamar Queen*, originally a Naval pinnace. She was fitted with new engines and used on the Starcross ferry route. She kept that ferry running during the war, when the regular ferry boat was taken on war duty in 1939.

The Silver Jubilee of King George V was celebrated with street parties throughout the town, and in the same year, 1935, the townspeople also presented a silver Challenge Cup to the men of HMS *Exmouth*.

In the early part of the year 1938, storms lashed the seafront, smashing scores of beach huts and damaging the sea wall. The lifeboat was called out on two occasions to rescue yachts in difficulties.

By 1939, Exmouth had an automatic Telephone Exchange. Within months, the Second World War had begun.

E.S. Gosling

The George and Sarah Strachan *lifeboat going to a call out of Exmouth, c.1960.*

THE SECOND WORLD WAR & AFTERMATH

Everybody heard the broadcast on the morning of Sunday 3 September 1939, when England declared war on Germany. Very soon after this, the Army took over the beach and removed everything there – including the beach huts and kiosks. Barbed wire entanglements were placed along the length of it. Steel barriers were erected below the high-tide mark, gun emplacements were built at Foxholes, and machine gun pillboxes were placed at intervals along the front, all as defence against invasion by the enemy from the sea.

Tragedy very soon struck Exmouth when four local men lost their lives at sea when the aircraft carrier *Courageous* was sunk by an enemy submarine not far out in the Atlantic. The survivors were brought into Plymouth.

It was necessary for Exmouth to consider potential defence for the town and an Air Raid Precaution Centre was established in what is now the library, with a look-out tower above Orcombe Point. Bulletins were regularly posted in the windows of the *Exmouth Chronicle* newspaper building. All the Home Front organisations were numbered and in their turn given action stations – the ARP, Fire Guard, Local Defence Volunteers (later to be called the Home Guard after a broadcast in May 1940), and soon 27,000 gas masks had been issued to the local populace. With

an increase in the St John Ambulance personnel and the formation of a Rescue Squad, Exmouth was quite soon fully manned, covering every contingency. It is worth noting that when the Home Guard was disbanded in late 1944 it numbered over 800!

All members of the defence branches went into rigorous training, exercising on the cliffs, climbing, drilling, doing night duties and plane-spotting and picket duty in the remote areas such as the Common, where enemy troops might land. By July 1940, 22 air-raid shelters had been provided for the townsfolk. The town had also been called upon to accept a number of evacuees from London, one of whom, Denis Cozens, wrote about his experiences in Exmouth.

The town soon found itself in the front line of enemy air attack, directed against the coastal towns and their shipping. Sniping and the dropping of bombs resulted in many local casualties and a great number of the town's buildings suffered damage. Many of the old and favourite buildings were destroyed – the Dolphin Hotel in the Cross area was bombed out completely, disappearing under a pile of rubble.

Initially in 1940 sporadic raids by enemy planes were dropping bombs until it was realised that they were using the river as a guide. As a result, a confidential letter of 10 June 1940 arrived with instructions to remove the buoys marking the entrance to the river. It came from the Secretary to the Commander-in-Chief, Western

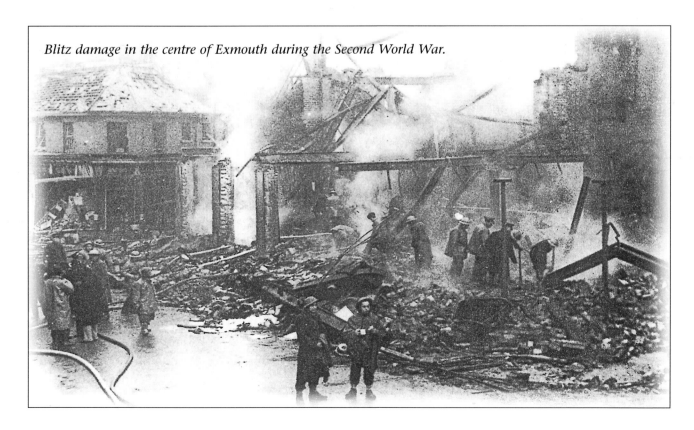

Blitz damage in the centre of Exmouth during the Second World War.

Approaches at Mount Wise, Devonport. The sound of approaching aircraft coming from the south was often to be heard and an alert was regularly sounded. People took shelter, bombs were dropped and the action was recorded. A map of the aerial action was built up and such maps still exist. However, most of the raiders that passed over the West of England were in fact heading for targets further afield; many were aiming for places such as Liverpool and chose this less direct route in order to avoid the heavy concentrations of defences that were in place up through the middle of the country. The alerts continued all through the night until the aircraft returned and the 'all clear' sounded.

However, in January 1942 there was a direct attack on Exmouth itself, when the Dolphin was demolished (as mentioned above). In addition, Walton's Stores, the Gas Company and various other buildings were badly damaged, while Wilson's and Otton's Stores were completely destroyed. Eleven people were killed and two others died later. Many parts of the town suffered in further raids and up until September of that year, nine more people were killed and another fifteen injured. The town was machine-gunned in the following February and the driver of a train at Starcross was killed by gunfire. Holy Trinity Church was damaged as well on that occasion, as was Beacon Congregational Church. When the gas holder was hit in the February raid, the flames soared high above the town. In the same month, bombs landed in Bicton Place and people ran out on Chapel Hill in time to see that particular enemy aircraft pass immediately overhead; five people were killed.

Writing in March 1992, Mr G.T. Battens recalled seeing a lone aircraft. He also remembers being called to Exeter to assist after the town's period of severe bombing. Exmouth's St Andrews Church was also damaged in that 1942 raid. There was another severe raid in February 1943, when 25 people were killed and 40 injured. It was in this year that the Exmouth Sea Cadets were formed – initially membership stood at 6 officers and 50 cadets. In December 1943, the SS *South Coaster* ran aground on the Pole Sands and 13 men were rescued by the lifeboat under its new coxswain Reginald Searle.

The Blitz on Exeter occurred in May 1942, and planes were continually heard overhead. The Observer Post was machine-gunned, but was not severely damaged. There were many of these 'Tip and Run' incidents during 1942 and 1943 in the daytime, in-and-out visits which Exmothians had cause to remember. Nevertheless the public demonstrated terrific bravery and strength, enduring the raids with patience. Eventually the daylight raids were deemed ineffective and were called off.

In late 1943, the build-up of forces along the South-West coast to prepare for the imminent invasion of Europe brought the E Company of the 70th Battalion, Queen's Royal Regiment, to Exmouth. They were billeted in Tower Street Church Hall and the Company's Headquarters were in a row of shops with offices upstairs. The men frequented the Pilot Inn, but were allowed to drink beer in half pint measures.

Then came the American contingent of troops. It was almost an 'occupation' and they were billeted in preparation for the forthcoming invasion. The Ivy Division of American troops was stationed in Exmouth. Although the GIs were in the area in order to train, they nevertheless showed much interest in the English girls; indeed there is a record of a wedding on 15 April 1944, when Anna Emma Hall married PFC Ernest Paul Hall of Welles View, Kansas. No doubt there were other such weddings. The Americans exercised over Orcombe Point, using the cliffs particularly. They trained in full battle-order and General Eisenhower came to Exmouth to see his troops perform.

The number of troops stationed in the area was gradually increased as plans were cemented for the D-Day invasion. When it did arrive, the whole area of Exmouth seemed to have been suddenly deserted; all the ships had gone, taking all the troops that had trained in the area. Exmouth's

EXMOUTH'S WAR EFFORT

Fund-raising campaign	Target set	Target reached
War Weapons Week	£100,000	£208,000
Warship Week	£120,000	£132,650
Wings for Victory	£120,000	£181,650
Salute the Soldier	£150,000	£154,000
Thanksgiving Week	£100,000	£106,340

Fireguard volunteers of the Second World War.

E.S. Gosling

Exmouth Boys' Brigade outside Tower Street Church, c.1955.

A gun dome, now on the seafront near the Octagon Café.

Royal National Lifeboat Institution – Exmouth and Budleigh Salterton Branch. The Station Officer is Brian Cole and he was kind enough to permit a number of photographs to be sent, from which the author has selected this one to be shown here. This picture shows our crew. Back row includes, left to right: ?, John Walpole, Terry Mears, Spud Rousell, Reg Mogeridge; middle: Peter Harris, Glenn Smith, John Williams, Mark Mellish, Brian Rounsell, Bernard Bradford, Ron Lavis; front: Peter Heney, Martin Handoll, Brian Harding, Tom Chandler, Roy Richards. Photograph taken at the Exe Sailing Club in 1973 at the retirement of second coxswain Mark Mellish.

paddle-steamer the *Duke of Devonshire* also played her part in the D-Day landings. The *Exmouth Journal* of 9 June 1944 reported the event of D-Day when G.T. Phillips of Littleham was in the 2nd Division and he landed on Gold Beach, Normandy at 7a.m. He said that the big guns of the Royal Navy opened up at 5a.m. 'like hell let loose'. Charles Fenwick of Scott Drive, Exmouth was a member of the Air Sea Rescue Service at that time. A special commemorative D-Day was held on 5 June 1994, 50 years after the original event, at Holy Trinity Church, Exmouth when a commemorative plaque was unveiled.

A visitor to Exmouth on 17 June 1944 was Lt General Sir Gifford Le Q. Martel KBE, CB, DSO, MC.

The members of Exmouth's Anglo-Russia Council held a Russia Day on Thursday 22 June 1944, the Chairman being F.N. Beckhart of No. 2, The Beacon.

In December 1944, the lifeboat assisted a destroyer to give aid to a Dutch coaster carrying 11 survivors picked up in the Channel. A tug arrived and towed the boat to safety.

Before leaving the subject of the Second World War, there are a few notes that should be recorded. The standard rate of Income Tax for the War Years was 10s. in the pound. The local people of the town were often asked to support their Forces in various ways, and they more than exceeded the targets set.

Everybody celebrated VE Day (8 May 1945) and VJ Day (16 August 1945). The bonfire for VE Day took place on the King George V playing fields. Street parties were held to celebrate the victory all over the country, including Exmouth; the long tables were set out in the streets and both days were blessed with fine weather. Where all the food came from, nobody knew!

The two World Wars are still remembered in the town; there is much to remind us of them. Unfortunately the war memorial in the Strand Gardens does not bear the names of our heroes. Perhaps one effect this mention may have is to correct that omission and so give a fitting end to the story of Exmouth and its community during the war.

The new Promenade cliff steps at Orcombe, 1927.

The Flag Memorial consisting of the Flags of Nations for the Second World War.

The Battle of Britain sundial, 1940, presented to the people of the town of Exmouth by the Royal Air Force Association, in memory of all the men and women of the Royal Air Force and Allied Air Forces who gave their lives.

POST-WAR EXMOUTH

Following the cessation of the war and the period during which many families, or parts of families, were reunited – the losses had been great – Exmouth gradually began to settle down and, surprisingly, expand. The post-war reconstruction led to new shopping precincts being built in the centre of the town and new residential estates appearing on the outskirts. Thus the whole look of the town was changed, such were the results of modernisation. The loss of the Dolphin Hotel had certainly changed the centre and nothing could rectify that. A few of the pre-war buildings, some of the Georgian and Victorian houses and terraces, and one or two of the little courtyards remained, and they were given the benefits of modern comforts such as the convenience of modern sanitation, while still preserving the admirable façades of their original architectural styles.

When the initial period of reconstruction in the town centre had been completed, work began on extending estates on the verge of the old town. It was in the early years of the 1960s that building began in the area north of Pound Lane. It then continued up Bapton Estate, Pound Lane Gardens, Langstone Road, Brixington Farm (the farmhouse itself became the local pub), St John's Road (a council estate), Withycombe Park, Leone Gardens, Marpool Allotments, Cranford and Douglas Avenue. By October 1965, 2,500 new homes were nearing completion and, of that number, around 500 had been developed by the Brixington Development Company; 1967 was a record house-building year for Exmouth.

There were other changes of course; the practice of transporting cargoes in the docks from ship to railway wagon and away to their destination had gone. Road transport had taken over by this point and a new road to the docks was built to link with the road to Exeter and the motorway. The noise and disturbance created by 30- and 40-ton lorries thundering along Exmouth's roads has become a regular occurrence, much to the annoyance of local residents.

The availability of the new houses for sale or to let became known as far away as London, and several arrangements were made with councils. These agreements allowed those wishing to move or retire to the South West to be placed on a housing list, so that people could be offered housing as it became available. This scheme lasted into the early 1990s, although the system was most successfully used during the early 1970s. Hence the London accents so prevalent in our shops in Exmouth!

Exmouth floods, 1960.

E.S. Gosling

ROLL OF HONOUR, 1914–18

The First and Second World Wars are terrible milestones in Exmouth's history. Those who fell in the First World War have their names permanently recorded in the parish churches. These names are listed below.

A

William C. Abbott
A. Reginald Abell
John P.F. Adams
John B.G. Ashford

B

Frederick H. Bailey
William G. Bamsey
Reginald Barrett
Samuel Basgleoppo
William Bastard
Albert Batten
Thomas Batten
William T.A. Bazalgette
John Becker
Anthony B. Beesley
John R. Bibby
J. George Black
William H. Blackmore, Senr
William H. Blackmore, Junr
Wallace E. Bowden
Richard V. Bowerman
William H. Bowsher
J.R. Boyce
William J. Boyland
Frederick Bradford
Frederick T. Bradford
Reginald L. Bradford
William T. Breading
Edwin W. Bridle
Fred H. Bridle
Leon E. Bridle
Walter H. Brooks
John N. Brown
William H. Burrow
Edward W. Bush
Ralph G. Butcher

C

Charles P. Carder
Harold J.H. Carder
Leslie G. Carder
Stuart Carlile
Richard W. Carnell
Thomas F. Carpenter
Alfred J. Carter
Alfred W. Carter
George T. Carter
John L. Carter
William H.S. Carter
George S.D. Carver

Henry R. Clapp
Austin B. Clarke
H. Clarke
Harry T. Clarke
Bertram Coates
Andrew B. Comber
Edward Copp
Ernest J. Cornish
Christopher R. Cotgrave
Montague L.F. Cotgrave
Frank R. Crang
Harry Crang
William N. Crang
John E. Croft
William J. Crosby
Frederick D. Cusens

D

Hugh C. Darke
Raymond C. Dart
Frederick J.R. Davey
William Davey
John E. Davy
Graham Dawson
Wilfred L. Dawson
Harry Dewdney
Samuel E. Dewdney
Stanley D. Dixon
Edward Doble
Edwin Doble
Wallace Doble
R.H. Dryerre
Frederick W. Dyer

E

Walter J. Edds
Reginald W.S. Elliott
Herbert D. Ellis
Walter Q. Evans

F

Arthur J. Farrant
Ralph Field
James S. Foster

G

Isaac Gale
John Gibbons
David P. Gilliland
John L. Gilliland
Arthur H. Gooding
Harold Gooding

Archibald Goss
Percy Goss
Percy Gourd
George L.E. Gove
Archibald B. Green
Herbert W.A. Greenaway
Percy Greenaway

H

Samuel R. Hall
Samuel A. Harris
Hermon G. Hart
Tom P. Hart
Edmund A.J. Hayman
Hugh Hayman
Reginald Haywood
William Heard
Harry T. Hellier
Ernest R. Hewitt
Leslie D. Hewitt
Ralph Hewitt
William Hillman
Burnard T. Hirtzel
George W. Holman
Harry Holman
Harry L. Holman
William H. Holman
John Holmes
George Hooper
Henry J. Hooper
Daniel H. Horn
William S. Horn
Lewis H. Horne
A.G. Horsfall
Albert Hulse
Hamo L.B. Hunt

J

J.M.H. Jackson
Herbert C. Jeffrey
John W. Jenner-Clarke

K

John Kenny
Herbert Kentsbeer
Samuel Kirk
Edwin H. Knight
James W. Knight
Luther G. Knight
Bertram Knowles
Richard G. Knowling

L

Percy J. Land
George A. Langdon
Leslie L. Lavis
Cecil C. Lear
Ernest L. Le Breton
Alfred J. Letten
John C. Lewis
Frederick R. Linnell
Arthur Litton
John Litton
Jesse J. Locke
Tom Lockyer
Walter Loveridge
Frederick Lovering

M

James Maddick
Reginald J. Manley
William Mares
Edward H. Marks
Harold Marks
William J. Marks
Sidney A. Martin
William H. Martin
Frederick J. Matthews
G. Sydenham McReddie
William R.F. Miller
Walter J. Mitchell
F.G. Greir Morris
William H. Murch

N

William Newcombe
Henry G. Norman
Henry J. Northcott
Sydney J. Norton

O

Charles G. Oliver
Charles Osborn
Gordan A. Owen
George H. Oxford

P

Doris Page
Robert B. Page
Arthur Palmer
Herbert S. Palmer

Bert Pannell
Percy Pannell
Phillip H. Pannell
Reginald H. Parker
David J. Parry
W. Percival Pascoe
Lewis H. Peach
William C. Pengilley
Albert J. Perkin
Percy Perriam
Thomas E. Phillips
Frank W. Pidgeon
Henry J. Pidgeon
Ernest S.G. Pile
Reginald C. Pinniger
Arthur T. Pope
William J. Priddis
E. John Preston
William Prowse

R

Percy W.A. Reed
Albert Rendell
George A. Richards
William N. Richards
Leonard A. Rowsell

S

R.D. Sandford
Edgar M. Seager
Percy W. Searle
Edgar J. Sellek
Charles W. Shapter
Fred E. Shapter
Herbert Shapter
George Sharland
Francis J.N. Shaw
M. Marshall Shaw
Percy Shaxton
Fred W. Skinner
John W. Skinner
Louis Sleeman
Thomas Slocombe
George H. Smith
Patrick L. Smith
Stanley Smith
Julius A. Snow
Louis A. Snow
Henry B. Spencer

George Steer
Walter Stevens
Frank Stone
Albert E. Street
Arthur J. Street
Frederick E.C. Street
Samuel W.P. Street
Raymond Surridge
Revd Sidney Sweet

T

Harry Tillman
Oscar R. Titherley
Geoffrey Tome
Alfred W. Tremlett
William S. Trim
Thomas Troke
George Tucker
Sidney H.S. Tupman

V

Bertie Veysey
Lewis W. Vincent
Wallace B. Vowden

W

Bertie Walters
Thomas D. Walters
Reginald A.J. Warneford, V.C.
William H. Webber
John Weeks
Frank H. Westcott
William C. Weston
Herbert Whiddon
Bert White
Reginald C. Whiting
Thomas S. Wickham
Arthur Wills
George H. Wills
Bertram M. Wilkinson
Charles S. Willatt
Jesse Woolger
William Woolger

Y

J. Lewis Yeo
John Yeo

Reginald Warneford won his V.C. for shooting down the first zeppelin over enemy territory. A few weeks later he was killed in a flying accident in Paris.

ROLL OF HONOUR, 1939–45

Unfortunately no record of any description is available of those who lost their lives in the Second World War. An attempt is, therefore, made to create an archive in the following pages. Additional information has been added, as it may be the only way those who were scattered during the war years will have of learning of the activities, service and death of former friends.

Through the medium of the local press, requests have been made for more information, but it is highly probable that the list has many omissions. Every effort has been made to include all the information that was available at the time of publication. Any further information that comes to light at a later date will be incorporated into any future editions.

CIVILIAN DEATHS

The following civilians lost their lives in air raids on Exmouth during the period 1941–43. The asterisk denotes children under eight years of age.

Miss I.M. Batten	Miss M.P. Hancock	Miss E.L. Nickols
Mr P. Bradford	Joyce Heath *	
Mrs P.M. Brooks	Mrs I.C.E. Holme	Mrs D.M. Pannell
Mrs J. Bryant		Mrs A. Pemberthy
	Mrs G.G. Jackman	Miss A.L. Perham
Miss D.E. Coles	Patricia Jeffery *	Mrs F.B. Pidsley
Mr J.H. Clark	John Jeffery *	Mr J. Ponsford
Mrs E. Dommett	Mrs H.J. Gay Lang	Mrs L.I. Taylor
Mrs S. Down	Mrs A.R. Lockhart	Mrs L.A. Thornton
	Miss B. Lang	Mrs E.K. Tindall
Ronald Feagan *		Mrs F.I. Tothill
	Mrs E.M. Mason	Mr P.G. Turner
Miss M.W. Goodall	Miss B. Mason	
Mrs E.W. Griffiths	Norman Mason *	Mrs S.A. Walker
Maureen Griffiths *	Raymond Mason *	Miss E.R. Williams
	Edwin Mason *	Miss V. Ward
Miss E.M. Hamilton	Mr T. Maxwell	
Miss K.A. Hamilton	Miss M.J. Miller	
Mr W.E. Hancock	Mr C.H. Mortimer	

In addition to the above list ten visitors to Exmouth were killed during the raids.

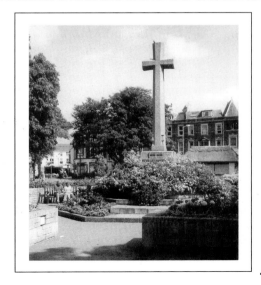

War Memorial in the gardens on The Strand.

NAME	RANK AND ARM OF SERVICE	HOW/WHERE DEATH OCCURRED	APPROXIMATE DATE
PERCY ACTON	Royal Navy	At Sea	May 1941
WILLIAM BARCLAY	Capt. Army Air Corps	Crashed – Western Europe	January 1945
DENNIS BARNES	Sgt/Bmdr, RAF	Presumed Killed	May 1944
WILLIAM GEORGE BEDWELL	Royal Engineers	Accident – N. Ireland	January 1941
RALPH BENNETT	Airborne Unit	In Action, Normandy	July 1944
J.P. BODDINGTON	Sergt, RAF	France	June 1940
KENNETH H. BONNER	F/O, RAF	Air Operations	November 1944
WILLIAM H. BOUNDY	P/O, RAF	Mulheim	June 1943
LESLIE R. BOWMER	L/Cpl, R.E.	Prison ship en route to Japan	September 1944
JOYCE F. BOWMER	A.I.D.		April 1943
E.T. BRADFORD	P/O, RAF	Accident at Sea	December 1941
WILLIAM H.T. BREADING	Ldg/Sig., RN	In Action, HMS *Lapwing*	June 1940
LESLIE W.C. BRICKNELL	Royal Artillery	While in Japanese hands	November 1942
GERALD E. BROWN	Sergt, RAF	At Sea	March 1944
CHARLES E. BURCH	C.P.O., RN	HMS *Glorious*	June 1940
PETER CABLE	Tank Corps	In Action	March 1943
E.J.L. CARPENTER	F/O, RAF	Air Operations	August 1944
CHARLES CARTER	Tank Corps	In Action, N. Africa	May 1943
FREDERICK J. CARTER	Sergt, Army	In Action, India	October 1942
STANLEY A. CARTER	Sergt, RAF	Air Operations	August 1942
GEAR E. CHAPMAN	Herefordshire Regt	Western Front	April 1945
WILLIAM CHOWN	Ldg-Stoker, RN	In Action	December 1942
J.A. CHUDLEY	Army	In Action, Italy	November 1944
CHARLES CLARE	Royal Engineers	Middle East (Tobruk)	December 1941
CYRIL COCKERTON	Infantry Regt	In Action, Burma	March 1945
LESLIE COLLINS	L.A.C., RAF	Road Accident	May 1944
DUDLEY S. COOPER	Sub/Lt RNVR	In Action	May 1943
GEORGE CORNISH	Royal Navy	In Action, HMS *Courageous*	September 1939
JOHN F.R. CRANE	F/O, RAF	Sedan, France	May 1940
E.S.C. CROSS	F/Lt, RAF	In Burma	November 1944
WILLIAM K. DANIEL	Royal Tank Regt	Middle East	July 1941
JACK DAVEY	Sergt, RAF	In Action, Duisburg	December 1942
RAYMOND DAVEY	RAF	While prisoner in Japanese hands	October 1945
LEONARD E. DAVIES	Devonshire Regt	In Action, W. Europe	August 1945
W.A.L. DAVIDSON	Sergt, RAF	Presumed killed	March 1941
WILLIAM DENNER, D.S.M.	C.P.O., RN	In Action, at Sea	June 1941
W.J. DUNSTER	Cook, RN	Presumed Killed	September 1943
SIDNEY EDWARDS	Army	Air Action, Malta	April 1942
CECIL FOWLER	Royal Engineers	Hospital	June 1940
RONALD FOWLER	Merchant Navy	At Sea, torpedoed	March 1942

Name	Rank/Service	Circumstance	Date
WILLIAM H. GARD	P/O, RAF	At Sea, torpedoed	June 1944
ALF GATTER	Devonshire Regt	In Hospital after Naval Operations	May 1944
EDDIE GILLARD	Army	In Action, Burma	June 1943
DENNIS GLOVER	RAF	Prisoner of War Camp	July 1940
JOHN GODLIMAN	Bugler, RN	In Action	July 1940
WILLIAM J. GOODING	C.P.O., RN	In Action	June 1940
ROBERT R. GRAHAM	Cmdr, RN	At Sea, HMS *Glorious*	December 1940
TONY GREENAWAY	Sergt, RAF	At Sea	June 1941
JAMES HALL	Royal Navy	Flying	December 1944
KEN HANCOCK	Chief Eng./Rm. Artificer RN	At Sea, HMS *Wolverine*	February 1944
CLIFFORD R. HARRIS	Major, RE	Presumed Killed	September 1944
FRANK R. HARTNELL	Airborne Division	In Action, Greece	March 1945
WILLIAM R. HAWKINS	RAF	In Action, W. Europe	September 1944
J. HAYMAN	P/O, RN	Japanese Hands	April 1941
W.J. HEARD	L/Cpl, RE	Air Raid, Plymouth	May 1944
J.F. HEIMSATH	Sgt/Pilot, RAF	Air Service	May 1945
TED HEWITT	P/O, RN	Middle East	February 1942
S.A. HILLMAN	F/Sgt, RAF	At Sea, torpedoed	May 1940
RICHARD HOLLOWAY	Telegraphist, RN	In Action	September 1939
C.J. HOLMAN	Elec. Artificer, RN	At Sea, HMS *Courageous*	June 1940
R.A. HOLMES	Royal Arm, Division	Presumed Killed, HMS *Glorious*	October 1944
JOHN D. (JACKIE) HOUGH	2nd Officer, MN	In Action, Holland	April 1943
PHILIP E. HUMPHRIES	Sergt, RAF	Presumed Killed	February 1945
KENNETH HUNT	F/Eng. Sgt, RAF	In Action, Middle East	September 1942
W.W. HUTCHINSON	L.A.C., RAF	Flying Accident	July 1941
GEOFFREY H. JAMES	Sergt, RAF	Flying	April 1940
DICK JARVIS	Cpl, Devonshire Regt	Flying	July 1944
JAMES F. JEFFERIES	Telegraphist, RAF	In Action, N.W. Europe	May 1941
RONALD G. JEWELL	Sgt/Pilot, RAF	Accident	March 1943
HAROLD JONES	L/Bomdr, RA	Flying Accident	June 1940
WALTER B. KEMEYS-JENKIN	Lieut, Devonshire Regt	In Action, Norway	September 1944
JOHN N.W. KERR	S/Ldr, RAF	In Action, Normandy	July 1943
O.J. LANDER	F/O, RAF	Flying Operations	September 1944
S.C. LANE	Anti-Aircraft	Flying Accident	October 1942
GORDON LANGDON	Sgt-Observer, RAF	In Action, at Sea	December 1941
HENRY J. LEWIS	Sgt, R. Artillery	Air Accident	May 1940
JOHN G. LLEWELYN	Wing Comdr, RAF	In Action, Dunkirk	May 1940
ROBERT LOMAX	P/O, RAF	Flying	July 1941
D. LOVING	Elec. Artificer, RN	In Action, Germany	December 1941
ERNEST G. LUDGATE	RSM, Devonshire Regt	In Action, HMS *Repulse*	August 1943
MARTIN H. MACPHERSON	Captain, RN	Native Service	November 1939
HARRY G. MANNING	Merchant Navy	At Sea	January 1943
LAWRENCE R. MARSHALL	P/O, RAF	In Action, at Sea	September 1941

Name	Rank/Unit	Details	Date
ROY MARSTON	F/Sgt Eng., RAF	Air Operations	March 1944
JOHN PAUL TELFORD MARTIN	Sub Lt, RNVR	Over Frankfurt	December 1942
WILLIAM H. MARTIN	RN (Submarines)	Blown up off Spain (HMS *Fidelity*)	August 1941
WILLIAM D. MINOR	P/O, RN	Presumed Killed	March 1943
HAROLD MOCK	F/O, RAF	Enemy Action	February 1945
C.A.C. MONTGOMERY	Lt Comdr, RN	Flying	December 1941
FRANCIS D. MORTON, D.F.C.	F/O, RAF	Presumed Killed, at Sea	December 1943
IVOR NORTON	Telegraphist, RN	Air Operations	September 1939
BERNARD PALFREY	Army	At Sea, HMS *Courageous*	June 1944
HERBERT PALMER	Cpl, R. Signals	In Action, Burma	February 1943
JACK PANNELL	Cpl	In Action	December 1943
WILLIAM PANNELL	P/O, RN	In Action, Central Mediterranean	May 1941
MAURICE PAVER	Royal Navy	Presumed Killed, HMS *Gloucester*	June 1942
H.P. PAYNE	Lieut Nigerian Regt, Indian Commission	In Action	May 1944
CHARLES A. PENALUNA	Cpl, RE	In Action, Burma	May 1943
NORMAN C. PERRY	Royal Navy	Hospital, Middle East	December 1941
F.C. PIESSE	Bandmaster, RMB	In Action, HMS *Repulse*	October 1943
FRANK H. PITMAN	Wireless Operator	Presumed Killed, Plymouth	January 1943
GEORGE PYNE	Devonshire Regt	At Sea	February 1944
W.H. ROBJOHNS	Sgt, RAF	Presumed Killed, Far East	February 1944
PETER H. RODWELL	F./Sgt, RAF	Operational Duties	January 1945
WILLIAM SALTER	Army	Operational Duties	November 1944
JACK SEDGEMORE	Royal Navy	In Action	November 1939
NIEL SHAPLEY	RAF	At Sea	September 1943
EDWARD J. SKINNER	P/O, RN	Air Operations	November 1939
H.J. SKINNER	Royal Artillery	At Sea, Rawalpindi	September 1944
IVOR SKINNER	Telegraphist, RN	In Action	September 1939
ROY SKINNER	Royal Navy	At Sea, HMS *Courageous*	December 1941
HARRY SMITH	Sergt, Army	Presumed Killed	August 1944
S. 'SYD' SMITH	RAF	In Action, France	August 1943
LEONARD SOPER	Royal Engineers	Japanese Prison Camp, Fukuoka	May 1942
CHARLES P. SOUTHCOTT	Sgt/Ft Eng., RAF	Enemy Action, Malta	August 1943
CECIL J. SOUTHWELL	RAF	Presumed Killed, Operations	August 1943
EUSTACE STAMP	Sub Lieut, RN	In Action, MEF	March 1943
HENRY F. STONE	Army	In Action, at Sea	October 1942
WILLIAM F.G. STRAWBRIDGE	Merchant Navy	In Action, Middle East	May 1940
DICK STREET	Army	At Sea	August 1944
F. SURRIDGE	Devonshire Regt	In Action, Normandy	December 1944
DOUGLAS E. TAYLOR	F/Lt, RAF	In Action, Mediterranean	May 1944
D.E. THOMAS	Lieut, RASC	Presumed Killed, Night Operations	September 1942
MICHAEL TICKELL	Army	Presumed Killed, at Sea	May 1941
JAMES H. TOLMAN	P/O, RAF	In Action, Kenya	December 1941
GILBERT VENNER	L/Cpl, Army	Air Operations, Sidi Barani	June 1944

FREDERICK VINCENT	P/O, RN	Burma	June 1940
GORDON R. WEBB	Major, Indian Army	Torpedoed, HMS *Ardent*	July 1944
ALBERT E. WEST	Royal Navy	Burma	September 1944
WILLIAM F. WHATMORE	Duke of Cornwall's Light Infantry	In Action	June 1945
E.H. WILLIAMS	P/O, RAF	In Action	March 1944
GEORGE WILLIS	F/Sgt, RAF	Air Operations, Germany	March 1943
STAN WILLS	Cpl, Army	France, Le Creusot Raid	October 1943
ROBERT F.J. WILTSHIRE	LAC, RAF	In Action, Italy	March 1940
HARRY B. WOOD	F/Sgt, RAF	France	May 1940
CHARLES F. WORSLEY	2nd /Lt R. Armoured Corps	Flying	July 1942
EDWARD J. WRIGHT	Lieut, RE	Flying Accident, Middle East	February 1945
ROBERT A. WRIGHT	F/Lieut, RAF	Burma	December 1941
		Air Operations	

CLUBS & SOCIETIES OF THE LATE TWENTIETH-CENTURY

Exmouth Anglo-French Society. Miss R. Whele, after one or two unsuccessful attempts in 1965, finally founded this Society for people to read and speak French and converse with one another. Meetings with lecturers were arranged and Dr Bland, Dr Perry, Prof. Nicklaus, Ms Marie and Mr Thomas each came to speak to the members. The twinning of Exmouth with Dinan in France came about because one of the members knew the Mayor of Dinan. At the time of writing, the President of the Society is still Miss R. Whele, with the Vice-President Mrs B. Bunce and a membership of over 50. Misses R. and S. Whele appear in the picture with other members.

A lifeboat crew, left to right: Giles White, Mark Sanson, Karl Stott, Greg Wreford, Tim Mock (coxswain). On the bridge: Chaplain – the late Revd Stephen Conner of St John in the Wilderness.

The naming ceremony on 9 August 1997 of the new 'D Class' boat, Spirit of the Exe.

More lifeboat men, left to right: Cecil Hocking, Dido Bradford, Jack Philips, Percy Bradford.

CLUBS & SOCIETIES OF THE LATE TWENTIETH-CENTURY

Exmouth Afternoon Women's Institute was founded in October 1987. Meetings are held monthly and attract 30 or more members. Speakers on many varied subjects are attracted. Workers on a quilt for the Marie Curie charity appear in this picture. The workers include: Anne Chapman, Joan Allen, Lilian Sealey, Jean Price, Ann Stredwick.

Exmouth Art Group at the 2001 exhibition in the Elizabeth Hall, Exmouth. The picture shows Michael Norman, the President, and Leonard Fry, the exhibition Secretary, getting ready to hang one of the pictures. The Hon. Secretary is Mrs Joan Fry.

Swifts Social Club in Exmouth Carnival.

Right: *At a meeting of the Bridge Club, the Chairman, Dr Bob Doy, is about to play.*

The Exmouth branch of the Civil Service Retirement Fellowship was formed in 1969 with over 400 members. Meetings are monthly at the Bastin Hall. This picture is of the 1996 officers, left to right: Treasurer – Peter Swift, Secretary – Lewis Crump, Chairman – the late Wally Martin.

Exmouth Town Band in the grounds of the Imperial Hotel.

CLUBS & SOCIETIES OF THE LATE TWENTIETH-CENTURY

Phear Park Bowling Club – the 1921 team, winners of the Devon County Championship. Left to right, back: J. Summers, J. Dyer, R. Cowerd, Colonel R. Handcock (President), J. Rattenbury, A. Hanson, E. Blight, H. Buttle; front: R.W.C. Axon, O. Hart, C. Aylesbury, R.C. Cooper (Hon. Secretary), S. Hutton (Captain), H. Taylor (Vice Captain), J. Nicholson, C. Webber. The grandson of R.C. Cooper (Hon. Sec.) is a playing member of the club at the time of writing.

Withycombe Rugby Club was founded in c.1921 and has become a very successful side, with three or four of its players being chosen to play for Devon County. In 1999 it was runner-up in the Cornwall and Devon League and winner of the Devon Junior Cup. The picture shows the 1999 team. The officials are: President – the late Ted Elliot (centre), Chairman – Mr M. Richards, Treasurer – Mrs Barley. The Captain was Nigel Symins and the coach Trevor Harris. It is interesting to note that one of the players at the time of writing is Geoff Wilmot, the grandson of founder member Raleigh Wilmot.   The well-known groundsman is Peter Farley.

CLUBS & SOCIETIES OF THE LATE TWENTIETH-CENTURY

Exmouth Town A.F.C. 1950–1 team. Devon Senior Cup winners and East Devon Cup winners. Left to right, back: I. Taylor, W. Totball, G. Lear, P. Drew, L. Goss, H. Penu; front: G. Marsham, J. Angus (Captain), W. Coombe, A. Callender, E. Sparrow.

Exmouth Amatuer Boxing Club, 1950–1. Left to right: George Hillman (Trainer), Terry Nicholls, Mike Norrish, Les Vowden (Trainer), Ian Mackay, Brian Pollard, Peter Bourne, Roy Priddis (Manager). Photo taken at the Drill Hall (Leisure Centre Gymnasium).

Withycombe Cricket Club. The team in a recent year consisted of, left to right, back: G. Ferris, Chris Hookway, Peter Burch, Roy Fairchild, D. Reynolds; front: Peter Muir Southall, Jim Gittings, Geoffrey Axon. The picture was donated by Mrs Prideaux.

Exmouth Secondary Modern School football team, 1948–9. They finished second in the Exeter and District Schools League and runners-up in the Cup final. Left to right, back: R.P.T. Master – John Yeo, Ken Hill, Derek West, Mike Norrish, ?, John Derryman, John England; front: Bill Gill, John Coles, Terry Heather, Jackie Dorran, J. Hawkins.

Exmouth Town A.F.C. 1982–3. Devon and Exeter League Champions. Included in photo: Tom Hayman, Sian Rees, Ted Baker, Alf Lavis, Arthur Sanderscroft, Lawrie Hockings, Jack Elworthy, Fred Davy, Ed Tobyn, Archie Smith, Bert Phillips, Archie Wright, Jack Phillips, M. Hugo, Ivor Norton (Captain), Fred Perry.

CLUBS & SOCIETIES OF THE LATE TWENTIETH-CENTURY

E.S. Gosling

Exmouth Floral Queen, c.1958.

The Exmouth Family History Club, founded in 1984 following an evening class on family history. It has proved very popular with all members tracing their family trees. This is a picture of members enjoying a barbecue. Left to right: O. Moss, Harry Pascoe, Jean Chase, Tom and Jean Haynes, Margaret Hopper, Elizabeth Maycock, Jenepher Allen.

Brixington Ladies Getaway Club, 25 years celebrations 1974–1999. Members present left to right: Mrs Cynthia Foster, Mrs Shelagh Mogridge, Mrs Carol Wilson, Mrs Avril Dunn, Mrs Shirley Ruffell, Miss Moyra Pemberton, Mrs Joyce Buller, Mrs Jill Crowther, Mrs Pam Dolby, Mrs Margaret Newman.

In 1976 the Drama Group appeared on Westward Television in the programme 'Women of the Week'. Left to right: Ivy Bond, Pat Slade, Jean Grant, Jean Barnes, Pat Gill.

Flowers being judged at Exmouth Garden Club 2001 Show. On the far right is Frank Norton, Exmouth's Gardener-in-Chief.

Above left: Kate Hadley, the retiring Chairman of the Exmouth Historical and Archaeological Society in 2002, after more than five years in office. Above right: Bob Lankaster, the succeeding Chairman in 2002, formerly the Society's Treasurer.

The Exmouth Society

Having now arrived at the end of this book about Exmouth, it may be appropriate to remind Exmothians that their interests have been cared for during the last quarter of a century by the Exmouth Society. The Exmouth Society was founded in 1976 with the objective of providing the citizens of Exmouth with a Civic Society dedicated to maintaining and enhancing the quality of the town's environment. It is a registered charity affiliated to the Civic Trust, which is the parent body to all local societies. The Society concerns itself with planning issues, not only within the prescribed area of benefit but also where wider issues may affect the local area, and is also involved with County, regional and national issues. It is dedicated to the conservation of the town's historic environment and natural habitats. As its millennium project, the Society has been responsible for erecting information plaques on around 25 buildings of historic interest, a project which is ongoing.

The Society is consultee to the Devon County, District and Town Councils in their proposals for local legislation and other matters where the views of local residents can make a contribution. The group were involved in the production of the 'Where is Exmouth Going?' document in the early 1990s, which won first prize in the Royal Town Planning Institute competition. In addition, the Society was instrumental in the establishment of the Exmouth Museum, both physically and financially.

Members benefit from regular lectures devoted to environmental and historic issues, as well as walks and outings. Mr Ian Cann has been the Society's Secretary since its inception, with another founder member, Edna Barlow, as its first President. The first Chairman, Walter Steedman, was succeeded by Tony Jones, who in turn handed on to the Chairman at the time of writing, Peter Higgins.

Peter Higgins

APPENDICES

APPENDIX (A)

SOME OF THE SHIPS BASED AT EXMOUTH
IN THE MEDIEVAL PERIOD

1303   *St Marie; Le Sauvage.*

1326   *La Patrie; La Nicholas; La Margarete; La Mighel.*
        La Rodecogge (Master John de Auncrey and crew of 26).
        La Saint Maricogge (Master Walter Edmond & crew of 33).

1328   *La Ridecogge* and *La Notre Dame* were captured by French pirates.

1343   *La Godyer.*

1360   *Peter* (100 tons). The ship *Le George* could not discharge at Topsham as the entrance was too narrow.

1363   *La Trinitee* (Master Walter Prous).

1393   *Nicholas.*

1395   *La Margarete.*

1397   *La James.*

1413   *Le Marie.*

1430   *La Trinitee* (Master W.M. Kyde).

APPENDIX (B)

SEE PAGE 147

APPENDIX (C)

SHIPS BUILT BY MESSRS WALTERS
& WISHART (1830–1922)

1830   *Exmouth* (139 tons).
1832   *Betsey* (a schooner of 76 tons). Lost at Waterford 1868.

1837   *Britannia* (90 tons). Lengthened by 10 feet at Exmouth but Topsham built. Broken up in 1878.
1839   *Exmouth* (a schooner of 134 tons). The second of her name. Lost in the Channel 1865.
1841   *Maria* (95 tons). Broken up in 1888.
1842   *William & Charles* (120 tons). Lost by collision off the Humber in 1872.
1846   *Ada* (99 tons). Lost in 1853.
1846   *Stranger* (38 tons). Lengthened by 18 feet. Lost in North Sea 1847.
1855   *Matford.* Originally Topsham built – lengthened by 20 feet. Lost at sea in 1879.
1856   A new boat laid down 200–300 tons register and 96 feet long.
1858   *Carmel* (126 tons).
1859   *Hebe of the Exe* (169 tons). Wrecked off Brazil 1865.
1860   *Sunbeam* (a schooner of 99 tons). Sold to Ireland 1873.
1861   *Topsy* (a 36 ton Ketch). Lost in 1869.
1863   *Cygnet* (25 tons).
1866   *John Walters* (161 tons). Broken up in 1932.

APPENDIX (D)

SHIPS BUILT BY JOHN HAYMAN

1793   *Catherine* (a sloop of 17 tons).
1793   *Ranger* (a sloop of 56 tons).
1794   *Blessing* (a sloop of 18 tons).
1795   *Adventure* (a brig of 79 tons).
1797   *Friendship* (a brig of 49 tons).
1798   *Happy Return* (a sloop of 13 tons).

APPENDIX (E)

SHIPS BUILT BY JAMES HOOK

1845   *Zedora* (31 tons).
1846   *Surprise* (38 tons).
1852   *Lily of the Exe* (a sloop of 26 tons).
1858   *Laura* (a yawl of 22 tons).
1862   *Black Pioneer* (a sloop of 37 tons).

APPENDIX (B) A Few Ships of Exmouth That Went to Newfoundland

Sailing Date	Name	Tonnage	Master	Owner	Remarks
9 March 1571	Genett	40	John Abbot	John Perriam	Both of these ships sailed for La Rochelle as well.
12 March 1571	Bartholomew	50	John Polkny	Will Wynton	
29 August 1583	Marie Thomas	30	Will Wychalls of Dawlish		
3 Sept. 1583	Whitt Beare	40	Andreas Rule of Lympstone	The Master	On 1 October she was cleared for St Lucas under the same master with a cargo belonging to John Morris, Thos. Spicer and John Sampforde of Exeter.
4 Sept. 1583	Savior	40	Thomas Bolter	The Master	On 26 October she was cleared for La Rochelle under John Styl of Kenton with goods of Thomas Gibbons of Taunton and Richard Knight of Silverton.
5 October 1584	Lion	30	Richard Crosse	George Rawleigh	
26 August 1586	Primrose	25	Thomas Porke		
26 Sept. 1588	Bartholomew	90	Robert Langford		
26 August 1589	Primrose	25	Thomas Porke	Master & Ors.	
28 August 1589	Gifte	50	William Witchells		
	Lyon	40	Richard Crosse	George Rawleye	On 13 December 1588 the *Lyon* under Robert Winton cleared for La Rochelle.
12 Sept. 1589	Primrose	30	John Drewe	Henry Wade	On 29 October 1588 the *Primrose* cleared for Bordeaux under John Swete.
6 October 1592	Raigne Bowe	50	John Bane Filde	Henry Wade	
	Revenge	80	John Underhill		
31 October 1592	Good Tidings	40	Robert Langford	John Tusse of Exeter	
24 August 1593	Dieu Grace	26	George Peron		
31 August 1593	William & John	30	John Drake		
12 Sept. 1593	Mayflower	50	John Whitborne	Master & Ors.	
24 August 1594	Dieu Grace	26	George Peron		
31 August 1594	William & John	30	John Drake		
12 Sept. 1594	Grace	25	John Drew		
12 Sept. 1594	Mayflower	50	John Whitborne		
10 Sept. 1600	Heart's Desire	30	George Peron	Master & Ors.	
17 Sept. 1600	Mayflower	50	William Underhill		
19 Sept. 1600	Swiftshewer	40	Thomas Russell		
19 Sept. 1600	Dieu Grace	30	Christopher Langford	Master & Ors.	

NB. Between these dates the ships from neighbouring ports were: Topsham 15; Teignmouth 10; Kenton 6; Dawlish 2; Exeter 1; Sidmouth 1.

APPENDIX (F)
SHIPS BY UNKNOWN BUILDERS

1812   *Sidmouth* (a sloop of 24 tons).
1840   *Brothers* (a ketch of 16 tons).

APPENDIX (G)
SHIPS BUILT BY R. & T. REDWAY (1864–69)

1864   *Exonian* (a barque of 371 tons). The Exmouth Band played at its launching. Sold to Spain in 1870.
1865   *Amazon* (1,100 tons).
1866   *Belle of the Exe* (a brig of 315 tons). Built for Graham & Co. of Newport. Wrecked at Cuba in 1867.
1867   *Belle of the Exe* (2) (a barquentine of 233 tons).
1867   *Amazon* (2) (a barque of 604 tons). Lost at Singapore in 1871.
1868   *Isca* (a brig of 239 tons). Broken up in 1891.
1869   *Memento* (321 tons). Lost at Cape of Good Hope 1876. One of the last of the large sailing vessels to be built on the Exe.

REDWAY SHIPS, DATES UNKNOWN

Argus; Jane Archibald; Rajah of Sarawak; Francis Millar; Earl of Derby; William IV; Cyprus; Rochester; Duchess of Sutherland; Victory; Iron Gem; Isabella; Laura; Magna Bona; Camperdown; North Star; Anne; Mary; John Norman; Dauntless; Dagmar; Tarsa; Victoria; Garland; Lion; Foam; Alcyone; Tamarac; Mary Ann; Elphin; Rio; Jeanette.

APPENDIX (H)
SHIPS BUILT BY THOMAS REDWAY (1869–80)

1869   *Coquette* (142 tons). Built for W. Thomas & Partners of Exeter and sold to the French in 1877.
1875   *Exonian* (a ketch of 75 tons).
        Rippling Wave (a ketch of 67 tons).
        Both were used as trawlers on the east coast.
1876   *Belle of the Exe* (a barquentine of 234 tons). The third of this name, 120 feet long. Described as a most beautiful ship, she collected the mail from New York on one occasion and beat the regular Mail Steamer to Liverpool. She was meant for the Newfoundland trade by H.J. Stabb & Co. but went missing in 1908.
1878   *Cyprus* (a schooner of 66 tons). Lost off West Africa in 1884.

APPENDIX (I)
EXMOUTH SHIP OWNERS AND THEIR SHIPS

ADAMS, JOHN (1853–68)
Paul	46 tons
Alpha	95 tons
Beacon	113 tons
North Star	242 tons
Scottish Maid	101 tons
Rachel	90 tons

ALGAR, JAMES AND JOHN (1859–81)
Rambler	160 tons
Venus	132 tons
Edward Vittery	119 tons

AXON, JAMES AND WILLIAM CHARLES (1867–?)
Adelaide	197 tons

BASTIN, ROBERT AND JAMES (?–1875)
Mary Jane	135 tons
Perseus	133 tons

BEAVIS, ROBERT, WILLIAM AND EDWARD (?–1869)
Balfour	69 tons
Regina	133 tons
Astrea	183 tons
Eliza Jane	64 tons
Hirondelle	78 tons
Anna Maria	168 tons
Greyhound	159 tons
Pearl	121 tons
Barnard Castle	145 tons
Magyar	215 tons
Boyne	93 tons
Mary Ann	129 tons

BEAR, ANDREW
Fame	122 tons
Jenny Jenkins	189 tons
Magyar	215 tons

(*Magyar* was wrecked in 1861 and owner drowned.)

BELL, JACOB
Unity	38 tons
Hopewell	33 tons
Malta	97 tons
William	32 tons
Betsey	76 tons
Jane	94 tons
Camilla	217 tons

BELMANO, DAVID & JOHN (1802–54)
Owners Delight	13 tons
Orange Branch	54 tons
New Jane	74 tons

BANMORE, THOMAS

Scythian	110 tons
Lord Raglan	370 tons
Matilda	22 tons

BICKFORD, NICHOLAS

Argus	150 tons
William	198 tons
Empire	193 tons
Exonian	360 tons
Adelaide	197 tons

BRICKNELL, SAMUEL & WEBBER, CHARLES

Rachell	37 tons
Judy	140 tons
Cambria	121 tons
Hydrus	115 tons

CARTER, ALFRED A.

Earl of Derby	200 tons

COPP, JAMES, JOSEPH, WILLIAM, LORENZO & ALBERT WITH JOSEPH HOPPING & WILLIAM WALLER

Brothers	19 tons
Elizabeth Ann	26 tons
Albion	84 tons
Neptune	79 tons
Samuel	112 tons
Gem	154 tons
Peamore	139 tons
Rover	139 tons
Emma	179 tons
Lively	37 tons
Devonshire Lass	183 tons
Alma	138 tons

COTTON, GEORGE POLEY (?–1873)

Spring	29 tons
Freedom	32 tons
Lively	37 tons
Louisa	45 tons

CREED, JOHN HINTON

Feronia	71 tons
Mary Ann	55 tons
Astrea	57 tons

DOVE, JOHN & DIXON, THOMAS

Cambria	121 tons
Caroline Daly	121 tons

DYER, WILLIAM

Levant Star	127 tons
Mary Ann	129 tons
Ruth	199 tons

ELLETT, GEORGE

Jenny Jenkins	189 tons
Britannia	99 tons
Cousins	31 tons
Autumna	140 tons
John Walters	161 tons

ELSON, THOMAS & ROBERT

Sally	69 tons
Friendship	59 tons
Choice	118 tons
Donegal	125 tons
Hersey	168 tons

FERRIS, ALEXANDER

Nora	143 tons
Adelaide	197 tons

GIBBENS, WILLIAM

Rover	139 tons
Spec	109 tons

GRIGG, JAMES

Donegal	125 tons
Europa	142 tons

HARRIS, EDWARD & JOHN

Rachel	28 tons
Atlanta	90 tons
Spec	109 tons
Rover	139 tons
Donegal	123 tons
Lalla Rookin	106 tons
Lord Raglan	370 tons
Mary Ann	129 tons
Arta Xerxes	187 tons
Rachel	90 tons
Mary Ann	149 tons
Dauntless	130 tons

HAYMAN, JOSEPH, JOHN, HENRY, GEORGE & RICHARD

Prosper	35 tons
Two Brothers	36 tons
Brothers	19 tons
Neptune	79 tons
Samuel	112 tons
Gem	134 tons
Peamore	139 tons
Rover	139 tons
Cambria	121 tons

HAYNE, GEORGE

Levant Star	127 tons

HEARN, WILLIAM (?–1881)

Cygnet	25 tons
Ann & Jane	30 tons

HEYWOOD, GEORGE

Brownfield	97 tons

HOOPER, ROBERT, MICHAEL, RICHARD, WILLIAM & HENRY

King George	21 tons
Majestic	49 tons
Robert & Ann	58 tons
Elizabeth	147 tons
Joseph Hopping	

HORE, JAMES, GEORGE, & JANE, WILLIAM & MARY TURNER HORE

Alert	68 tons
Perseverance	76 tons
Mary Jane	129 tons
Sarah	89 tons
Scythian	110 tons
Alice	61 tons
Lord Raglan	370 tons
Susan	313 tons
Caroline Daly	121 tons
British Empire	491 tons

LEE, JOHN

Autumna	140 tons
Mary	196 tons

LETTON, RICHARD, WILLIAM & JOHN

Elizabeth	28 tons
Mary	21 tons
Dart	81 tons
Friends	84 tons

LIFFITON, JOHN (?–1852)

Exmouth	134 tons
Maria	95 tons
Favourite	206 tons

LUKES, THOMAS & THOMAS (JUNR)

Thomas & Nancy	22 tons
Ann & Susan	44 tons
Two Brothers	35 tons
Argo	53 tons
Pultenay	50 tons
Whitby	66 tons
Cambria	121 tons

MACER, JOHN CLODE

Regina	133 tons
Astrea	183 tons
Barnard Castle	145 tons

MAYPEE, CHARLES (MOVED TO LONDON 1867)

Samuel Cunard	206 tons

Anne	168 tons
Volyo	149 tons
Dominica	204 tons
Nina	211 tons
Perseus	133 tons

MEARS, WILLIAM & WILLIAM GEORGE, JOHN CLODE & WILLIAM STRETCHLY

Owners Goodwill	32 tons
William & Sarah	46 tons
William	114 tons
Donegal	115 tons
Edina	155 tons
Elizabeth	160 tons
Magyar	215 tons
Atalanta	113 tons
Ocean Sprite	204 tons
Telegraph	181 tons

MITCHELL, WILLIAM & JENKINS, JAMES (?–186?)

Atalanta	90 tons
Sisters	77 tons
Jessy	136 tons
Barnard Castle	145 tons

MUDFORD, WILLIAM

Good Intent	44 tons

NICKS, JAMES DANE

Maria	95 tons
Favourite	206 tons

NOLLOTH, JOSEPH

Maria	95 tons
Southampton	218 tons
Favourite	206 tons

NORMAN, HENRY, ROBERT HENRY, & SALTER, RICHARD

Grocer	81 tons
Experiment	95 tons
Pandema	197 tons
Polly Hopkins	241 tons
Wilhelmina	187 tons
Elizabeth Brown	234 tons

NORRIE, JOSEPH

Julia ?	149 tons

PARKER, ARTHUR, JOHN, THOMAS, WILLIAM & CHARLES

Hannah & Susan	31 tons
Jane	65 tons
John	97 tons
Mary	83 tons
Britannia	99 tons
Plenty	86 tons
Reward	151 tons
Two Brothers	21 tons

Speculator	88 tons
Vansittart	98 tons
Elizabeth	147 tons
Astrea	57 tons
Exmouth	134 tons
Maria	95 tons
Southampton	218 tons
Favourite	206 tons
Ada	99 tons
Albion	84 tons
Helmsley	99 tons
Celerity	107 tons
Reform	90 tons
Caroline Daly	121 tons
John Brown	134 tons

PARSONS, WILLIAM (?–1871)

Brownfield	97 tons

PERRIAM, JOHN, MICHAEL, RICHARD, JOHN WANHILL, HENRY & RICHARD OF EXMOUTH, TOPSHAM & EXETER

Two Brothers	15 tons
Sally	69 tons
John & Jane	39 tons
Devon	84 tons
King George	21 tons
Brownfield	97 tons
Perseus	133 tons

PERRY, HENRY

Volga	106 tons
Agnes Jermyn	95 tons

PHILLIPS, CHARLES

Whitby	66 tons
Pultenay	50 tons

PINCOMBE JOHN & JOHN (JUNR)

Blessing	18 tons
Welcome	20 tons

PLIMSOLL, JOHN

Diadem	141 tons
Charles	149 tons

POTTER, RICHARD

Freedom	124 tons
Enterprise	118 tons
Native	85 tons
Hope	110 tons
Demetrius	129 tons

PURLE, SAMUEL

Mary	195 tons
Queen of the Exe	243 tons

PYLE, JOHN

Volga	106 tons

PYNE, JOHN, GEORGE, RICHARD & HENRY JOHN

Welcome	20 tons
Two Sisters	18 tons
Stranger	32 tons
Jenny Jenkins	189 tons
Matilda	22 tons

REEVES, HORATIO NELSON

Maria	95 tons

SALTER, CHARLES & EDWARD

Britannia	99 tons

SCOBLE, GEORGE CALLARD

Rapid	131 tons
St Vincent	100 tons

SHEPPARD, WILLIAM

Trinity	132 tons
Unity	136 tons
Conrad	?
Eleanor	157 tons
John Brown	276 tons
Naparima	343 tons
Volga	106 tons

SKINNER, EDWARD

Earl of Derby	200 tons

SNOW, SAMUEL OSMENT

Cygnet	25 tons
Ann & Jane	30 tons

SOLOMON, JOSIAH DAVIS

Alma	138 tons

STRETCHLY, WILLIAM (SEE MEARS)

TOBY, JOHN

Enterprise	162 tons
Samuel Cunard	206 tons
Anne	168 tons
Volvo	149 tons
Dominica	204 tons

TOWNING, JOHN LETTER

Dora	143 tons
Two Brothers	12 tons
Demetrius	141 tons

TREATT, RICHARD, RICHARD COURT, ANDREW & JOHN BURFORD

Richard & Jane	37 tons
Active	52 tons
Sarah Anna	62 tons
Flower	56 tons
Dispatch	88 tons
Magnet	82 tons

Reward	151 tons
Cambria	121 tons
Judy	140 tons
Sisters	101 tons
Eliza	136 tons
Fancy	154 tons
Lillydale	180 tons

TRIBBLE, GEORGE
Devonshire Lass	133 tons

TRUSCOTT, RICHARD BATE
Alletha	227 tons

TUPMAN, JOHN, GEORGE, CHARLES, HENRY & SAMUEL
Catherine	17 tons
Feronica	66 tons
Nestor	184 tons
Donegal	125 tons

WEEKS, NICHOLAS, MARY HIS WIFE & (?–1873) EXECUTRIX
Rapid	131 tons
Gipsey	97 tons
Clipper	115 tons
Alma	138 tons

WICKING, JOHN JAMES
Margaret	101 tons

WICKS, JAMES
Exmouth	134 tons *

WALTERS, JOHN & WISHART, JAMES
William & Charles	120 tons *
Trinity	132 tons
Stranger	38 tons
Sarah	89 tons
Mary	16 tons
Venus	104 tons
Concordia	273 tons
Queen of the Exe	243 tons
Matford	100 tons
Hebe of the Exe	169 tons *
Sunbeam	99 tons*
Topsy	36 tons *
Europa	187 tons
John Walters	161 tons *
Louisa	45 tons

WIDDICOMBE, WILLIAM
Sarah	89 tons
Concordia	273 tons

WILLS, THOMAS MARTIN & WILLIAM
Equity	125 tons
Perimede	215 tons

WITHALL, RICHARD
Prosper	35 tons
Richard & Jane	37 tons
Charlotte & Esther	63 tons

YORE, PETER
Edward Vittery	119 tons

NOTES

1) The ships marked with * were built in Exmouth.

2) The names of many ships are repeated under different owners indicating that they changed hands.

APPENDIX (J)
SHIPS TRADING OUT OF EXMOUTH AND THEIR PORTS OF ORIGIN

TOPSHAM
Judy	1846	
Peamore	1839	(L)
Britannia	1822	
Cousins	1857	
Majestic	1821	
Robert & Ann	1820	(L)
Alert	1813	
Perseverence	1818	(L)
Alice	1834	
Sarah Anna	1815	
Flower	1819	
Magnet	1826	
Sisters	1837	(L)
Venus	1849	
Matford	1819	
Two Sisters	1827	(L)
Mary	1798	
Friends	1815	(L)
William & Sarah	1830	
Grocer	1822	
Experiment	1826	(L)
Mary	1816	
Plenty	1805	(L)
Two Brothers	1831	
Vansittart	1834	
Devon	1823	
Queen of the Exe	1852	

SALCOMBE
Freedom	1833	
Argo	1805	(L)
Atalanta	1818	(L)

GLOUCESTER
Autumna	1866	(L)

NB: (L) = Ship locally owned in Exmouth

	FOWEY				**POOLE**	
Brownfield	1828	(L)		*Trinity*	1828	
	DURHAM				**C. KERRY**	
Reward	1831			*Agnes Jermyn*	1842	(L)
	PWLHELLI				**BRISTOL**	
Ann & Jane	1835			*Dauntless*	1844	(L)
				Susan	1826	(L)
	BARMOUTH			*Favourite*	1845	
Levant Star	1819	(L)				
					APPLEDORE	
	PRIZES			*Devonshire Lass*	1940	
Gally	1804	(L)				
Prosper	1815	(L)			**GUERNSEY**	
Two Brothers	1807			*Spring*	1841	
Thomas & Nancy	1802	(L)		*Sisters*	1837	(L)
	BIDEFORD				**PETERHEAD**	
Earl of Derby	1851	(L)		*Eliza*	1828	
	SALTASH				**ARBROATH**	
Elizabeth Ann	1837			*Margaret*	1830	(L)
	BOSTON				**LEITH**	
Albion	1826			*Astrea*	1830	
Reform	1831	(L)				
					SHALDON	
	PEMBROKE			*Stranger*	1832	(L)
Emma	1833					
Lalla Rookh	1845	(L)			**SOUTHAMPTON**	
				Southampton	1829	(L)
	MONTROSE					
Hersey	1834				**BARNSTAPLE**	
				Speculator	1820	
	JERSEY					
Atalanta	1837	(L)			**SELBY**	
Mary	1858			*Helmsley*	1788	(L)
Diadem	1840	(L)				
					CHEPSTOW	
	EX ROYAL NAVY			*Elizabeth*	1788	(L)
Good Intent	1816	(L)				
					FOREIGN	
	LYME REGIS			*Dominica*	1858	(L)
Sarah	1819			*Julia*	1861	(L)
Welcome	1824			*Volga*	1853	
				Hope	1858	
	LITTLEHAMPTON			*Concordia*	1851	(L)
Anne	1837					
Nina	1849	(L)			**PRINCE EDWARD ISLAND**	
Charlotte & Esther	1778			*Arta Xerxes*	1859	(L)
				Paul	1850	(L)
	YARMOUTH			*North Star*	1853	(L)
Jessy	1842	(L)		*Venus*	1854	(L)
				Mary Jane	1850	
	RYE			*Perseus*	1860	(L)
Alma	1854	(L)		*Regina*	1839	(L)
				Greyhound	1847	(L)
Ann & Susan	1806	(L)		*Pearl*	1849	
Owners Goodwill	1823			*Jenny Jenkins*	1858	(L)
Hannah & Susan	1793					

Argus	1852	(L)
William	1850	(L)
Empire	1852	(L)
Hydrus	1845	
Rover	1848	(L)
Dora	1851	(L)
Spec	1840	
Europa	1861	
Equity	1849	(L)
Perimede	1854	
Feronia	1815	
Caroline Daly	1855	(L)
Edina	1850	(L)
Pandema	1856	(L)
Polly Hopkins	1857	(L)
Charles	1840	(L)
Demetrius	1841	(L)
Mary	1848	(L)
Unity	1833	
Clipper	1850	
Enterprise	1846	(L)
Fancy	1849	(L)
Lillydale	1855	(L)
Alletha	1872	
Nestor	1841	

NOVA SCOTIA

Alpha	1848	(L)
Rambler	1857	(L)
Europa	1853	(L)
Samuel Cunard	1839	(L)
William	1838	
Donegal	1846	(L)

NEW BRUNSWICK

Adelaide	1857	
Anna Maria	1848	(L)
Donegal	1837	
Wilhelmina	1861	

QUEBEC

Magyar	1852	(L)
Gem	1844	(L)
Choice	1824	
Naparima	1828	

SUNDERLAND

Rachel	1826	(L)
Astrea	1826	(L)
Barnard Castle	1838	
Jane	1827	
Camilla	1840	
Scythian	1847	(L)
Cambria	1825	(L)
Mary Ann	1847	(L)
Ruth	1862	(L)
British Empire	1848	(L)
Elizabeth	1847	(L)
Ocean Sprite	1854	

John Brown	1847	
Eleanor	1848	

LYMPSTONE

William	1811	
Neptune	1808	(L)
Friendship	1803	
Two Brothers	1794	

TORQUAY

Beacon	1840	(L)

BRIDPORT

Fame	1824	(L)
Samuel	1828	(L)
Pultenay	1804	

CARDIGAN

Enterprise	1822	(L)

BANFF

Boyne	1836	

POOLE

Trinity	1828	

COWES

Owners Delight	1766	(L)
Lively	1859	
Louisa	1856	
King George	1800	

TYNE

John Brown	1838	

CARDIFF

Eliza Jane	1842	
Celerity	1835	(L)

BRIXHAM

Malta	1806	
Orange Branch	1826	(L)
Matilda	1802	(L)
Elisabeth	1785	
Dart	1803	(L)

TEIGNMOUTH

Hopewell	1807	
Volvo	1839	(L)
Rapid	1825	(L)

DARTMOUTH

Edward Vittery	1860	(L)
Rachel	1817	(L)
Freedom	1830	(L)
Dispatch	1820	

PERTH

Scottish Maid	1850	(L)
Elizabeth Brown	1854	(L)

	NEWFOUNDLAND		
Native	1833	(L)	

	SWANSEA	
Unity	1792	

	PLYMOUTH		
Balfour	1826		
Hirondelle	1836	(L)	
New Jane	1827	(L)	
Cygnet	1892	(L)	
Whidby	1814	(L)	

	ILFRACOMBE	
St Vincent	1826	

	MIDDLESBROUGH		
Mary Ann	1840	(L)	
Telegraph	1847		
Gipsey	1847		

	FINLAND		
Lord Raglan	1852	(L)	

TOTALS

FROM CANADA & THE USA: 53

Prince Edward Island	36
New Brunswick	4
Newfoundland	1
Nova Scotia	6
Quebec	4
Boston	2

CHANNEL ISLES: 5

Jersey	3
Guernsey	2

CORNWALL: 2

Saltash	1
Fowey	1

PORTS ON THE EXE: 31

Lympstone	4
Topsham	27

WALES: 9

Cardigan	1
Cardiff	2
Barmouth	1
Pembroke	2
Chepstow	1
Pwlhelli	1
Swansea	1

NORTHERN ENGLAND: 20

Durham	1
Selby	1
Peterhead	1
Sunderland	13
Tyne	1
Middlesbrough	3

OTHER DEVON PORTS: 26

Torquay	1
Teignmouth	3
Plymouth	5
Dartmouth	4
Ilfracombe	1
Brixham	5
Bideford	1
Appledore	1
Salcombe	3
Shaldon	1
Barnstaple	1

SCOTLAND: 7

Banff	1
Arboath	1
Leith	1
Montrose	1
Garmouth	1
Perth	2

SOUTHERN ENGLAND: 20

Lyme Regis	2
Rye	1
Yarmouth	1
Cowes	4
Littlehampton	3
Southampton	1
Gloucester	1
Poole	1
Bristol	3
Bridport	3

EXMOUTH BUILT: 13 ships

FOREIGN PORTS: 7

PRIZES: 12

APPENDIX (K)
SHIPPING CHARGES 1824–27

Coal	10s. per ton.	Hides	4s. per ton.	China Clay	12s. per ton.
Flour	8s.6d. per ton.	Salt	14s. per ton.	Rock salt	6s. per ton.
Common salt	10s. per ton.				
Fruit	(from Spain & Portugal) £5.5s.0d. per ton plus a gratuity of £10.10s.0d.				

APPENDIX (L)
FERRY TOLLS IN 1838

Passenger	2d.	Two-wheeled carriages	1s.0d.
Horse	4d.	Four- wheeled carriages	1s.6d.

If drawn by more than one horse – 3s.0d. All tolls were doubled after sunset.

The Ropewalk at the Point, as it was when the shipbuilding yards there were at their zenith. The rear wall can be seen to this day. When the area around the Dock was the hub of a prosperous shipbuilding centre, the Ropewalk was a quarter of a mile in length, extending from Point Cottage to the river opposite Starcross.

SUBSCRIBERS

David Adams, Exmouth, Devon
Alastair Adams, Pebworth, Warwickshire
Ceri Adams, London
Nicholas Adams, North Vancouver, Canada
Margaret Adams, Exmouth, Devon
Age Concern, Exmouth
Jenepher Allen, Lympstone, Devon
Frank Allitt, Exmouth, Devon
John and Anita Anderson
L.J. Ashford, Exmouth, Devon
Dorothy E. Ayres
Hazel Baker, Exmouth, Devon
Mr T.D. Baker, Exmouth, Devon
Tracey Baker, Exmouth, Devon
Hillman Bamsey, Exmouth, Devon
Kath Bamsey, Littleham, Exmouth, Devon
Vivienne Barnham, Exmouth, Devon
Steve and Mary Bartholomew, Exmouth, Devon
Trevor Bartlett MBE, Exmouth, Devon
Ruby Beech (née Greenaway), Exmouth, Devon
W.J. and M.A. Beed, Exmouth, Devon
Mike Bennett, Exmouth, Devon
Miss Kathleen M. Betts
Paul W. Bidmead, Exmouth, Devon
W. and M. Bloser, Langerwehe, Germany
Sue Bond, Exmouth, Devon
Mr John Pitman Bowden, Exmouth, Devon
Mr and Mrs I.P. Bradford, Exeter, Devon
Nicholas S. Bradford, Exmouth, Devon
Kathleen M. Bryant, Exmouth, Devon
Fred and Edwin (Nibs) Burch, Exmouth, Devon
Charles Burch, Exeter, Devon
Tina M. Burke, Exmouth, Devon
Ena M. Burridge, Exmouth, Devon
K.J. Burrow, Bucks Cross, Devon
Tony and Ann Carter, Bristol
Garry and Dawn Carter, Exmouth, Devon
Victor F. Castle, Exmouth, Devon
T.W. Chandler, Exmouth, Devon
Michael and Jacqueline Chapman and Ann
    Challis, Exmouth, Devon
Mrs Jean Chase
Charlie and Jayne Cherry, Exmouth, Devon
Dennis S.G. Chudley, Exmouth, Devon
Mrs P.G. Clare
Michael and Valerie Clarke
Dr Peter Clements

J.A. Coad, Exmouth, Devon
Teresa Margaret Collins, Exmouth, Devon
Mr and Mrs F.W. Coombs, Exmouth, Devon
Mr and Mrs R.J. Cope, Exmouth, Devon
Mr and Mrs T.W. Cordin
Mr Kenneth J. Courtney
Brian James Cross, Exmouth, Devon
Mike Cudd, Exmouth, Devon
J. and P.M. Danzelman, Exmouth, Devon
Mr and Mrs F.J. Davies, Exmouth, Devon
Daniela Deighton, Exmouth, Devon
Jen Derbyshire, Exmouth, Devon
Peter T. Dixon, Exmouth, Devon
Paul and Angela Douglas, Lympstone, Devon
J. and E. Duggan, Willenhall, West Midlands
Mervyn J. Dymond, Exmouth, Devon
Eagle Investments Ltd, Exmouth, Devon
Wilf Easterbrook, Exmouth, Devon
Arthur and Carolle Easton, Lympstone, Devon
Timothy J. Edwards, Exmouth, Devon
Donna Ellis, Exmouth, Devon – 1964
Anne Ellis, Exmouth, Devon – 1964
B.K. and A.J. Elsegood, Exmouth, Devon
Jill M. Elson, Exmouth, Devon
David E. England, Exmouth, Devon
Exmouth Community College
Exmouth Family History Club
The Exmouth Society
The Fairclough family, Exmouth, Devon
Gloria Farrant, Exmouth, Devon
Frances M. Fellows, Pelsall, West Midlands
Dr Greg Finch, Hexham, Northumberland
Enid I. Floyd, Exmouth, Devon
Betty Forshaw, Exmouth, Devon
Mary Foss, Exmouth, Devon
Mr Paul D. Fowler, Exmouth, Devon
Margaret Fox
Mrs Freeman, Exmouth, Devon
John E. French, Exmouth, Devon
Mrs Peggy M. Furmston, Exmouth, Devon
Dr Norman Garwood
Tricia and Michael Gerrish, Exmouth, Devon
Mr and Mrs N.R. Gibbs, Exmouth, Devon
F. Tregarthen Gibson, The Town Crier of Exmouth
Molly and Graham Giles, Exmouth, Devon
Carol Ann Gill, Exmouth, Devon
Ron Gleghorn, Exmouth, Devon

Adrian Gliddon, Exmouth, Devon
John and Julie Goodfellow, Exmouth, Devon
Tom and Judy Gorfin, Exmouth, Devon
Dr Robert Grant, Steyning, Sussex
Revd and Mrs R.B. Grant, Exmouth, Devon
Peter Greenaway, Exmouth, Devon
Miss M. Griffin
Penny Gripper, Ferryside, CARMS
Norma Hall (née Pickets), Slough
Mrs June Hallett, Lympstone, Devon
David Halson, Exmouth, Devon
Barbara Hammond, Exmouth, Devon
Kay Patricia Hammond, Broadstairs, Kent
Mrs Kath Harding, Exmouth, Devon
Cllr May L. Hardy (EDDC), Exmouth, Devon
Christine and Norman Harvey
John and Christine Hatchard, Exmouth, Devon
Allen J. Havill, Exmouth, Devon
Keith Hawes, Exmouth, Devon
John T. Hawkins, Exmouth, Devon
David and Louise Hay
W. Joan Haynes
Andrew and Irene Hearn, The Point, Exmouth, Devon
Hilary and Peter Higgins, Exmouth, Devon
Steven R. Hocking, Exmouth, Devon
Kevin W. Hockings, Exmouth, Devon
Mrs V. Holloway, Exmouth, Devon
Kathleen Hookway, Exmouth, Devon
D.S. and C.M. Hopper, Exmouth, Devon
Kenneth W. Horn, Exmouth, Devon
Anthony W. Howe, Exmouth, Devon
Roberta Howkins, Exmouth, Devon
Christopher Humphries, Launceston, Cornwall
David Huntley, Exmouth, Devon
Dulcie L. Hyde, Exmouth, Devon
Anthony J. Iles, Exmouth, Devon
John C. Iles, Exmouth, Devon
Freda Jackson
Miss Pamela M. Jackson, Exmouth, Devon
Tony Jackson, Exmouth, Devon
David F. Jefford, Exmouth, Devon
Joy D. Jelfs, Exmouth, Devon
Dr and Mrs Roy Johnson, Exmouth, Devon
Philip R. Jones, Exmouth, Devon
H.C. Jones
Conrad and Nicola Jones, Exmouth, Devon
Patricia L. Jones (née Humphries), Exmouth, Devon
J.E. and C.J. Jones and family, Exmouth, Devon
Mr and Mrs J.B. Jowitt, Exmouth, Devon
Philip Keddie, Exmouth, Devon
Robert S. Knowling, Exmouth, Devon
Jean Lake, Exmouth, Devon
Mr and Mrs L. Lake
Bob and Veronica Lankester, Budleigh Salterton, Devon
Lt Cdr and Mrs D.M. Laskey, Exmouth, Devon
Don and Mary Latham, Exmouth, Devon
Mr Edward F.W. Lavis, Exmouth, Devon
David Chown Lee, Exmouth, Devon

Russell M. Lee, Exmouth, Devon
Mrs Sylvia Pearl LeFevre, Yeovil, Somerset
Diane J. Leworthy, Exmouth, Devon
Mr and Mrs D.H. Ley, Exmouth, Devon
Mrs P.N. Ley, Exmouth, Devon
Miss Dorothy G. Lloyd, Exmouth, Devon
Nigel I. Lockyer
The Lott family, Exmouth, Devon
Ann and Bob Louis, Exmouth, Devon
J. Alan Lowe, Exmouth, Devon
David Lowe, Hindhead, Surrey
Jenny Luesby, Aveyron, France
Trevor Luesby, Redgates, Exmouth, Devon
Christopher Macassey, Exmouth, Devon
Ray and Jeanne Mallett, Exmouth, Devon
Howard and Nicola Mallett, Exmouth, Devon
Dick Manning, Exmouth, Devon
Paul G. Manning, Exmouth, Devon
M. and M. Marriott, Exmouth, Devon
Irene K. Martin, Exmouth, Devon
David W. Mayne, Exmouth, Devon
Margaret McDougall, Exmouth, Devon
G.R. and A.L. McGee, Exmouth, Devon
Shannon McMahon, Exmouth, Devon
P.S. McMillan, Exmouth, Devonshire
Miss E.A.A. Meaden, Exmouth, Devon
The Medlock family, Exmouth, Devon
Pauline Menhenitt, Exmouth, Devon
Margaret Mitchell, Exmouth, Devon
Robert and Joy Moass, Exmouth, Devon
Neil and Cathy Moass, Bridport, Dorset
Tony and Lesley Moore, Exmouth, Devon
Michael J. Moore, Strand, Exmouth, Devon
Florence M. Morgan
Sybil and Ivor Morris, Exmouth, Devon
Geoff and Denise Morris, Exmouth, Devon
Pat Moss, Exmouth, Devon
John W. Murch, Dawlish, Devon
David E. Murch, Exmouth, Devon
Anne R. Nicholson, Exmouth, Devon
Mr David Nicholson, Wells, Somerset
Mr Stephen Nicholson, Bedford
Mr Peter Nicholson, Exmouth, Devon
Crystal E. Nicholson (née Perriam)
Michael J. Norrish, Exmouth, Devon
Richard W. Olive, Exmouth, Devon
Christopher J. Parkinson, Exmouth, Devon
Miss Vera J. Pascoe
David and Frances Pearce, Exmouth, Devon
Christopher Charles Penaluna, Exmouth, Devon
Joan Perratt, Exmouth, Devon
G.D. Perriam, Exmouth, Devon
Mrs Gill Phillips, Exmouth, Devon
E.S.T. Pickett, Exmouth, Devon
Trevor J. Pitman
Malcolm Pomeroy, Exmouth, Devon
Mirian D.M. Pratt, Exmouth, Devon
J. and R.M. Price, Exmouth, Devon
Dr Pauline A. Primrose, Dundry, Bristol

Theo Redway, Victoria, Vancouver Island
Robin Reffell, Exmouth, Devon
Kenneth Rendall, Dorchester, Dorset
Arthur Rice, Exmouth, Devon
Carole M. Rice, Exmouth, Devon
Dennis M. Rich, Exmouth, Devon
Mrs Doreen A.H. Richards, Exmouth, Devon
Marlene Richards, Exmouth, Devon
Janet E. Robson, Exmouth, Devon
Mary P. and Andrew P. Rowsell, Exmouth, Devon
Karl D. Rowsell, Exmouth, Devon
Derek and Freda Rowsell and family
Margaret Russell
Mark C. Sadler, Exmouth, Devon
Brian Sansom, Exmouth, Devon
Sandie Satterly, Exmouth, Devon
Janet T. Sawyer, Exmouth, Devon
Laura Scott, Exmouth, Devon
Mr John W.N. Sedgemore, Exmouth, Devon
Christine Sedgemore, Exmouth, Devon
Barry and Margaret Setter (née Thorn), Exmouth, Devon
Andy Simpson, Exmouth, Devon
Mick Simpson, Exmouth, Devon
Leslie Roy Skinner, Exmouth, Devon
Joan H. Skyner, Exmouth, Devon
Aubrey L.J.J. Sleeman, Exmouth, Devon
Diana M. Slocombe, Exmouth, Devon
Basil Smale, Exmouth, Devon
Terry Smeath, Exmouth, Devon
Gerald Smith, Exmouth, Devon
Lee K. Soloman, Exmouth, Devon
Maurice Southwell, Withycombe, Exmouth, Devon
Peter M. Southwell
Jan A.F. Southwell, Potters Bar, Hertfordshire
Robin S.M. Southwell OBE, Cobham, Surrey
Richard and Eileen Sowter, Bristol
Kristopher P. Statham, Exmouth, Devon
W.P. and K.R. Stenlake, Exmouth, Devon
Mr R.J.F. Stephens, Exmouth, Devon
Robert Stevenson
Tony and Steph Story, Exmouth, Devon
Raymond and Christine Street, Exmouth, Devon
Robert and Amy Street, Exmouth, Devon
Adrian P. Street, Exmouth, Devon
Jacqueline Street (née Thorn), Luppitt, Devon
Dr Clive Stubbings, Exmouth, Devon
P.G. Swift, Exmouth, Devon
Leonard R. Sylvester
Nigel R. Tant, Exmouth, Devon
M.G. Taylor, Wellington, New Zealand
Jeffrey, Robert and Clive Taylor
Brenda Taylor c.c., Exmouth, Devon
John and Sheila Thorn, Exmouth, Devon
Derry Titterton, Exmouth, Devon
Dickson and Miriam Tolman
G.P. and J.C. Tolman-May, Exmouth, Devon
Pearl Turner, Exmouth, Devon
Christine Twells, Exmouth, Devon

Michael J. Upton, Exmouth, Devon
James and Pam Vardy (née Davey), Exmouth, Devon
Mr M. A. Vass, Harrow, Middlesex
Mr C.W. Vass, Exmouth, Devon
P.M. Vicknair, Exmouth, Devon
Bryan Vinnicombe, Exmouth, Devon
George K. Voysey, Exmouth, Devon
Eric G. Voysey, Topsham, Devon
Elaine Wade, Exmouth, Devon – 1964
John Wakefield, Littleham, Exmouth, Devon
Mr and Mrs G.M. Wallen
John F.W. Walling, Newton Abbot, Devon
Pat Walters, Heanton Punchardon, North Devon
Mr and Mrs M. Ward
Ron, Jean and David Webster, Exmouth, Devon
Christine M. Weller, Exmouth, Devon
Peter West, Littleham, Exmouth, Devon
Carol Westacott, Exmouth, Devon
Janet A.E. Williams, Exmouth, Devon
Joy Williams, Exmouth, Devon
Brian Williams
Michael 'Buster' Williams
Ken and Vera Willoughby
Heddus R.A. Wills, Exmouth, Devon
Frederick D. Wilson, Exmouth, Devon
Mr John L. Wood, Exmouth, Devon
Woodbury Local History Society
Josephine A. Woodgate (née Bovey), Exmouth, Devon
Brian T. Worts, Exmouth, Devon
Kayleigh and Emma Wright, Exmouth, Devon
Judith A. Wright, Wilmington, Kent

Garth Gibson, Exmouth's town crier.

Titles from the Series

The Book of Addiscombe • Various
The Book of Addiscombe, Vol. II • Various
The Book of Bampton • Caroline Seward
The Book of Barnstaple • Avril Stone
Book of Bickington • Stuart Hands
Blandford Forum: A Millennium Portrait • Various
The Book of Bridestowe • R. Cann
The Book of Brixham • Frank Pearce
The Book of Buckland Monachorum & Yelverton • Hemery
The Book of Carshalton • Stella Wilks
The Parish Book of Cerne Abbas • Vale & Vale
The Book of Chagford • Ian Rice
The Book of Chittlehamholt with
Warkleigh & Satterleigh • Richard Lethbridge
The Book of Chittlehampton • Various
The Book of Colney Heath • Bryan Lilley
The Book of Constantine • Moore & Trethowan
The Book of Cornwood & Lutton • Various
The Book of Creech St Michael • June Small
The Book of Cullompton • Various
The Book of Dawlish • Frank Pearce
The Book of Dulverton, Brushford,
Bury & Exebridge • Various
The Book of Dunster • Hilary Binding
The Ellacombe Book • Sydney R. Langmead
The Book of Exmouth • W.H. Pascoe
The Book of Grampound with Creed • Bane & Oliver
The Book of Hayling Island & Langstone • Rogers
The Book of Helston • Jenkin with Carter
The Book of Hemyock • Clist & Dracott
The Book of Hethersett • Various
The Book of High Bickington • Avril Stone
The Book of Ilsington • Dick Wills
The Book of Lamerton • Ann Cole & Friends
Lanner, A Cornish Mining Parish • Scharron Schwartz &
Roger Parker
The Book of Leigh & Bransford • Various
The Book of Litcham with Lexham & Mileham • Various
The Book of Loddiswell • Various
The Book of Lulworth • Rodney Legg
The Book of Lustleigh • Joe Crowdy
The Book of Manaton • Various
The Book of Markyate • Richard Hogg
The Book of Mawnan • Various
The Book of Meavy • Pauline Hemery
The Book of Minehead with Alcombe • Binding & Stevens
The Book of Morchard Bishop • Jeff Kingaby
The Book of Newdigate • John Callcut
The Book of Northlew with Ashbury • Various
The Book of North Newton • Robins & Robins
The Book of North Tawton • Various
The Book of Okehampton • Radford & Radford
The Book of Paignton • Frank Pearce
The Book of Penge, Anerley & Crystal Palace • Various
The Book of Peter Tavy with Cudlipptown• Various
The Book of Pimperne • Jean Coull
The Book of Plymtree • Tony Eames
The Book of Porlock • Denis Corner
Postbridge – The Heart of Dartmoor • Reg Bellamy
The Book of Priddy • Various
The Book of Rattery • Various
The Book of Silverton • Various

The Book of South Molton • Various
The Book of South Stoke • Various
South Tawton & South Zeal with Sticklepath • Radfords
The Book of Sparkwell with Hemerdon & Lee Mill • Pam James
The Book of Staverton • Pete Lavis
The Book of Stithians • Various
The Book of Studland • Rodney Legg
The Book of Swanage • Rodney Legg
The Book of Torbay • Frank Pearce
Uncle Tom Cobley & All: Widecombe-in-the-Moor • Stephen
Woods
The Book of Watchet • Compiled by David Banks
The Book of West Huntspill • Various
Widecombe-in-the-Moor • Stephen Woods
The Book of Williton • Michael Williams
Woodbury: The Twentieth Century Revisited • Roger Stokes
The Book of Woolmer Green • Various

Forthcoming

The Book of Bakewell • Various
The Book of Barnstaple, Vol. II • Avril Stone
The Book of Brampford • Various
The Book of Breage & Gurmoe • Stephen Polglase
The Book of the Bedwyns • Various
The Book of Bideford • Peter Christie
The Book of Bridport • Rodney Legg
The Book of Buckfastleigh • Sandra Coleman
The Book of Carharrack • Various
The Book of Castleton • Geoff Hill
The Book of Edale • Gordon Miller
The Book of Kingskerswell • Various
The Book of Lostwithiel • Barbara Frasier
The Book of Lydford • Barbara Weeks
The Book of Lyme Regis • Rodney Legg
The Book of Nether Stowey • Various
The Book of Nynehead • Various
The Book of Princetown • Dr Gardner-Thorpe
The Book of St Day • Various
The Book of Sampford Courtenay
with Honeychurch • Stephanie Pouya
The Book of Sculthorpe • Garry Windeler
The Book of Sherborne • Rodney Legg
The Book of Southbourne • Rodney Legg
The Book of Tavistock • Gerry Woodcock
The Book of Thorley • Various
The Book of Tiverton • Mike Sampson
The Book of West Lavington • Various
The Book of Witheridge • Various
The Book of Withycombe • Chris Boyles

For details of any of the above titles or if you are
interested in writing your own history, please contact:
Commissioning Editor Community Histories, Halsgrove
House, Lower Moor Way, Tiverton Business Park,
Tiverton, Devon EX16 6SS, England;
email: naomic@halsgrove.com

In order to include as many historic photographs as
possible in this volume, a printed index is not included.
However, the Community History Series is indexed by
Genuki. For further information and indexes to
volumes in the series, please visit:
http://www.cs.ncl.uk/genuki/DEV/indexingproject.html